Portuguese

A ROUGH GUIDE
PHRASEBOOK

Compiled
by Lexus

Credits

Compiled by Lexus with Norma de Oliveira Tait

Lexus Series Editor:	Sally Davies
Rough Guides Phrasebook Editor:	Jonathan Buckley
Rough Guides Series Editor:	Mark Ellingham

This first edition published in 1996 by Rough Guides Ltd, 1 Mercer Street,
London WC2H 9QJ.

Distributed by the Penguin Group.

Penguin Books Ltd, 27 Wrights Lane, London W8 5TZ
Penguin Books USA Inc., 375 Hudson Street, New York 10014, USA
Penguin Books Australia Ltd, 487 Maroondah Highway, PO Box 257,
    Ringwood, Victoria 3134, Australia
Penguin Books Canada Ltd, Alcorn Avenue, Toronto, Ontario, Canada
    M4V 1E4
Penguin Book (NZ) Ltd, 182–190 Wairau Road, Auckland 10, New Zealand

Typeset in Rough Serif and Rough Sans to an original design by Henry Iles.
Printed by Cox & Wyman Ltd, Reading.

© Lexus Ltd 1996
272pp.

British Library Cataloguing in Publication Data
A catalogue for this book is available from the British Library.

ISBN 1-85828-175-X

CONTENTS

INTRODUCTION

The Rough Guide Portuguese phrasebook is a highly practical introduction to the contemporary language. Laid out in clear A-Z style, it uses key-word referencing to lead you straight to the words and phrases you want – so if you need to book a room, just look up 'room'. The Rough Guide gets straight to the point in every situation, in bars and shops, on trains and buses, and in hotels and banks.

The main part of the Rough Guide is a double dictionary: English-Portuguese then Portuguese-English. Before that, there's a section called **The Basics**, which sets out the fundamental rules of the language, with plenty of practical examples. You'll also find here other essentials like numbers, dates, telling the time and basic phrases.

Forming the heart of the guide, the **English-Portuguese** section gives easy-to-use transliterations of the Portuguese words wherever pronunciation might be a problem, and to get you involved quickly in two-way communication, the Rough Guide includes dialogues featuring typical responses on key topics – such as renting a car and asking directions. Feature boxes fill you in on cultural pitfalls as well as the simple mechanics of how to make a phone call, what to do in an emergency, where to change money, and more. Throughout this section, cross-references enable you to pinpoint key facts and phrases, while asterisked words indicate where further information can be found in The Basics.

In the **Portuguese-English** dictionary, we've given not just the phrases you're likely to hear (starting with a selection of slang and colloquialisms), but also all the signs, labels, instructions and other basic words you might come across in print or in public places.

Finally the Rough Guide rounds off with an extensive **Menu Reader**. Consisting of food and drink sections (each starting with a list of essential terms), it's indispensable whether you're eating out, stopping for a quick drink, or browsing through a local food market.

boa viagem!
have a good trip!

The Basics

PRONUNCIATION

In this phrasebook, the Portuguese has been written in a system of imitated pronunciation so that it can be read as though it were English, bearing in mind the notes on pronunciation given below:

a	as in h**a**t
ay	as in m**ay**
eh	as in g**e**t
g	as in **g**oat
i	as in **i**t
ī	as the 'i' sound in m**i**ght
J	as the 's' sound in plea**s**ure
o	as in n**o**t
oh	like the exclamation **oh**
oo	as in b**oo**t
ow	as in n**ow**

In words such as **não** [nowng] and **bem** [bayng], the final 'g' in the pronunciation signifies a nasal sound and should barely be sounded.

Letters given in bold type indicate the part of the word to be stressed.

ABBREVIATIONS

adj	adjective
f	feminine
fam	familiar
m	masculine
pl	plural
pol	polite
sing	singular

NOUNS

All nouns in Portuguese have one of two genders: masculine or feminine. Generally speaking, those ending in -o are masculine:

o sapato
oo sap**a**too
the shoe

Nouns ending in -or are masculine. To make the corresponding feminine, add -a:

o professor	**a professora**
oo proofes**ohr**	a proofes**ohra**
the (male) teacher	the (female) teacher

Nouns ending in -a, -ade or -ão are usually feminine (although there are exceptions):

a cama	**a cidade**
a k**a**ma	a sid**ad**
the bed	the city

a pensão
a payns**ow**ng
the boarding house

A small number of nouns ending in -a and -e (usually professions) can be either masculine or feminine:

o/a guia	**o/a intérprete**
oo/a g**ee**-a	oo/a int**eh**rprit
the tourist guide	the interpreter

Plural Nouns

The plurals of nouns are formed according to the rules below.

For nouns ending in a vowel, add -s:

a empregada	**as empregadas**
a aympreg**a**da	az aympreg**a**dash
the waitress	the waitresses

To obtain the plural of nouns ending in -ão, remove the -ão and add -ões:

a pensão
a payns**ow**ng
the guesthouse

as pensões
ash payns**oy**ngsh
the guesthouses

To obtain the plural of nouns ending in -l, remove the -l and add -is:

o hotel	**os hotéis**
oo oht**ehl**	ooz oht**eh**-ish
the hotel	the hotels

To obtain the plural of nouns ending in -m, remove the -m and add -ns:

o homem	**os homens**
oo **oh**mayng	ooz **oh**mayngsh
the man	the men

For nouns ending in other consonants, the plural is formed by adding -es:

o condutor
oo kondoot**ohr**
the driver

os condutores
oosh kondoot**oh**rish
the drivers

uma mulher
ooma mool-y**eh**r
a woman

umas mulheres
oomash mool-y**eh**rish
some women

ARTICLES

The words for articles in Portuguese depend on the number (singular or plural) and gender of the noun.

The Definite Article

The definite article (the) is as follows:

	singular	plural
masculine	o	os
	oo	oosh
feminine	a	as
	a	ash

o livro   os livros
oo **lee**vroo   ooJ **lee**vroosh
the book   the books

a piscina
a pishs**ee**na
the swimming pool

as piscinas
ash pishs**ee**nash
the swimming pools

When the definite article is used in combination with **a** (to), **de** (of), **em** (in, on) or **por** (by), it changes as follows:

	o	a	os	as
a +	ao	à	aos	às
	ow	a	owsh	ash
de +	do	da	dos	das
	doo	da	doosh	dash
em +	no	na	nos	nas
	noo	na	noosh	nash
por +	pelo	pela	pelos	pelas
	p**i**loo	p**i**la	p**i**loosh	p**i**lash

vamos ao museo   perto do hotel
v**a**mooz ow moos**ay**-oo p**eh**rtoo doo oht**eh**l
let's go to the museum   near the hotel

The Indefinite Article

The indefinite article (a, an, some) also changes according to the gender and number of the accompanying noun:

	singular	plural
masculine	um	uns
	oong	oonsh
feminine	uma	umas
	ooma	**oo**mash

um selo	uns selos
oong s**ay**loo	oonsh s**ay**loosh
a stamp	some stamps

uma rapariga	umas raparigas
ooma	**oo**mash
rapar**ee**ga	rapar**ee**gash
a girl	some girls

When the indefinite article is used in combination with em (in, on) it changes as follows:

masculine
em + um = num
noong

feminine
em + uma = numa
n**oo**ma

gostava de ir numa viagem ao Brasil
goosht**a**va deer n**oo**ma v-ya**Ja**yng ow braz**ee**l
I'd like to go on a trip to Brazil

ADJECTIVES AND ADVERBS

Adjectives must agree in gender and number with the noun they refer to. In the English-Portuguese section of this book, all adjectives are given in the masculine singular. Unlike English, Portuguese adjectives usually follow the noun.

The feminine singular of the adjective is formed by changing the masculine endings as follows:

masculine	feminine
-o	-a
-or	-ora
-ês	-esa

um cozinheiro estupendo
oong koozeen-y**ay**roo shtoop**ay**ndo
a wonderful cook

uma cozinheira estupenda
ooma koozeen-y**ay**ra shtoop**ay**nda
a wonderful cook

um senhor encantador
oong sin-y**ohr** aynkantad**ohr**
a nice man

uma senhora encantadora
ooma sin-y**o**ra aynkantad**o**ra
a nice woman

um rapaz inglês
oong rapaz inglaysh
an English boy

uma rapariga inglesa
ooma rapareega inglayza
an English girl

For other types of adjective, the feminine form is the same as the masculine:

um homem agradável
oong ohmayng agradavil
a nice man

uma mulher agradável
ooma mool-yehr agradavil
a nice woman

Note that the adjective mau (bad) is irregular: the feminine is má.

The plurals of adjectives are formed in the same way as the plurals of nouns, by adding an -s, an -es or changing -l to -is:

o preço alto
oo praysoo altoo
the high price

os preços altos
oosh praysooz altoosh
the high prices

uma taxa alta
ooma tasha alta
a high rate

as taxas altas
ash tashaz altash
the high rates

um homem agradável
oong ohmayng agradavil
a nice man

uns homens agradáveis
oonz ohmayngz agradavay-ish
some nice men

When the adjective ends in -ês, the ê is replaced by e in the plural:

um rapaz inglês
oong rapaz inglaysh
an English boy

uns rapazes ingleses
oonsh rapaziz inglayzish
some English boys

Comparatives

The comparative is formed by placing mais (more) or menos (less) in front of the adjective or adverb and que (than) after it:

bonito	mais bonito
booneetoo	mīJ booneetoo
beautiful	more beautiful
quente	menos quente
kaynt	maynoosh kaynt
hot	less hot

este hotel é mais/menos caro que o outro
aysht ohtehl eh mīsh/ maynoosh karoo ki oo ohtroo
this hotel is more/less expensive than the other one

tem um quarto mais barato?

t**ay**ng oong kw**a**rtoo mīʃ bar**a**too

do you have a cheaper room?

pode falar mais devagar, por favor?

pod fal**a**r mīʃ divag**a**r poor fav**oh**r

could you speak more slowly please?

Superlatives

Superlatives are formed by placing one of the following before the adjective: o/a mais or os/as mais (depending on the noun's gender and number):

qual é o mais divertido?

kwal**eh** oo mīʃ divirt**ee**doo

which is the most entertaining?

o dia mais quente

oo d**ee**-a mīsh kaynt

the hottest day

o carro mais rápido

oo k**a**rroo mīsh r**a**pidoo

the fastest car

The following adjectives have irregular comparatives and superlatives:

bom	good	melhor	better	o melhor	the best
bong		mil-y**o**r		oo mil-y**o**r	
grande	big	maior	bigger	o maior	the biggest
grand		mī-**o**r		oo mī-**o**r	
mau	bad	pior	worse	o pior	the worst
mow		p-yor		oo p-yor	
pequeno	small	menor	smaller	o menor	the smallest
pik**ay**noo		min**o**r		oo min**o**r	

Note that mais pequeno 'smaller' is also used.

As ... as ... is translated as follows:

Lisboa está tão bonita como sempre!

liʒb**oh**-a shta towng boon**ee**ta k**oh**moo saympr

Lisbon is as beautiful as ever!

The superlative form ending in -íssimo indicates that something is 'very/extremely ...' without actually comparing it to something else:

lindo	lindíssimo
l**ee**ndoo	lind**ee**simoo
beautiful	very beautiful

Adverbs

There are two ways to form an adverb. If the adjective ends in **-o**, take the feminine and add **-mente** to form the corresponding adverb:

exacto	exactamente
iz**a**too	izatam**ay**nt
accurate	accurately

If the adjective ends in any other letter, add **-mente** to the basic masculine form:

feliz
fil**ee**sh
happy

felizmente
filiJm**ay**nt
happily

Possessive Adjectives

Possessive adjectives, like other Portuguese adjectives, agree with the noun in gender and number:

	singular masculine	feminine	plural masculine	feminine
my	o meu	a minha	os meus	as minhas
	oo m**ay**-oo	a m**ee**n-ya	ooJ m**ay**-oosh	aJ m**ee**n-yash
your (sing, fam)	o teu	a tua	os teus	as tuas
	oo t**ay**-oo	a t**oo**-a	oosh t**ay**-oosh	ash t**oo**-ash
his/her/its, your, their	o seu	a sua	os seus	as suas
	oo s**ay**-oo	a s**oo**-a	oosh s**ay**-oosh	ash s**oo**-ash
our	o nosso	a nossa	os nossos	as nossas
	oo n**o**soo	a n**o**sa	ooJ n**o**soosh	aJ n**o**sash

A more formal way of translating 'your' is:

	singular	plural
masculine	**do senhor**	**dos senhores**
	doo sin-y**oh**r	doosh sin-y**oh**rish
feminine	**da senhora**	**das senhoras**
	da sin-y**o**ra	dash sin-y**o**rash

See pages 11-12 for when to use this.

a tua casa	as suas pastilhas
a t**oo**-a k**a**za	ash s**oo**-ash pasht**ee**l-yash
your house	his/her/your/their tablets

a sua mala	os nossos amigos
a soo-a mala	oJ nosooz ameegoosh
his/her/your/their suitcase	our friends

If when using o seu, o sua etc, it is unclear whether you mean
'his', 'her', 'your' or 'their', you can use the following after the
noun instead:

dele	[dayl]	his
dela	[dehla]	her
deles	[daylish]	their (m)
delas	[dehlash]	their (f)
de vocês	[di vosaysh]	your (pl)

o dinheiro dela	o dinheiro dele	o dinheiro de vocês
oo deen-yayroo dehla	oo deen-yayroo dayl	oo deen-yayroo di vosaysh
her money	his money	your money

POSSESSIVE PRONOUNS

To translate 'mine', 'yours', 'theirs' etc, use one of the
following forms. Like possessive adjectives, possessive
pronouns must agree in gender and number with the object or
objects referred to:

	singular		plural	
	masculine	feminine	masculine	feminine
mine	meu	minha	meus	minhas
	may-oo	meen-ya	may-oosh	meen-yash
yours (sing, fam)	teu	tua	teus	tuas
	tay-oo	too-a	tay-oosh	too-ash
his/hers,	seu	sua	seus	suas
yours,theirs	say-oo	soo-a	say-oosh	soo-ash
ours	nosso	nossa	nossos	nossas
	nosoo	nosa	nosoosh	nosash

A more formal way of translating 'yours' is:

	singular	plural
masculine	**do senhor** doo sin-**yohr**	**dos senhores** doosh sin-**yoh**rish
feminine	**da senhora** da sin-**yo**ra	**das senhoras** dash sin-**yo**rash

See the section on subject pronouns for when to use this.

Generally, possessive pronouns are used with the definite article.

esta é a sua chave e esta é a minha
ehshteh a **soo**-a sh**a**vee **eh**shteh a m**ee**n-ya
this is your key and this is mine

este carro não é o seu
aysht k**a**rroo nowng eh oo s**ay**-oo
this car is not yours

If when using **seu**, **sua** etc, it is unclear whether you mean 'his', 'hers', 'yours' or 'theirs', you can use the following after the noun instead:

dele	[dayl]	his
dela	[d**a**hla]	hers
deles	[d**a**ylish]	theirs (m)
delas	[d**a**hla]	theirs (f)
de vocês	[di vos**ay**sh]	yours (pl)

não é dele, é dos amigos dele
nowng eh dayl eh dooz am**ee**gooJ dayl
it's not his, it's his friends'

PERSONAL PRONOUNS

Subject Pronouns

eu	[**ay**-oo]	I
tu	[too]	you (sing, fam)
ele	[ayl]	he, it
ela	[**eh**la]	she, it
você	[vos**ay**]	you (sing, pol)
nós	[nosh]	we
eles	[aylsh]	they (m)
elas	[**eh**lash]	they (f)
vocês	[vos**ay**sh]	you (pl)

Tu is used when speaking to one person and is the familiar form generally used when speaking to family, close friends and children.

Você and vocês are more formal and are used to address people you don't know well. They take the third person forms of verbs: você takes the same form as 'he/she/it'; vocês takes the same form as 'they'.

There is another way of saying 'you', which is used to address complete strangers or in formal situations. These forms all take the third person of the verb, i.e. the same as 'he/she/it' for the singular and 'they' for the plural:

	singular	plural
masculine	**o senhor**	**os senhores**
	oo sin-y**oh**r	oosh sin-y**oh**rish
feminine	**a senhora**	**as senhoras**
	a sin-y**o**ra	ash sin-y**o**rash

(Note that Senhor also means 'Mr' and Senhora means 'Mrs'.)

a senhora é a mãe da Rita?
a sin-y**o**ra eh a m**ay**ng da r**ee**ta
are you Rita's mother?

In Portuguese the subject pronoun is usually omitted:

não sabem   está cansado
nowng s**a**bayng sht**a** kans**a**doo
they don't   he/she is
  know   tired

Although it may be retained for emphasis or to avoid confusion:

sou eu!   somos nós!
soh **ay**-oo s**oh**mooj nosh
it's me!   it's us!

eu pago as sandes e você paga as cervejas
ay-oo p**a**gwash sandsh ee vos**ay** p**a**gash sirv**ay**jash
I'll pay for the sandwiches and you pay for the beers

ele é inglês e ela é americana
ayl**eh** ingl**ay**z ee **eh**leh amirik**a**na
he's English and she's American

Object Pronouns

object pronoun added to verb			object pronoun used with prepositions		
me	[mi]	me	mim	[meeng]	me
te	[ti]	you (sing, fam)	ti	[tee]	you (sing, fam)
o	[oo]	him, it, you (sing, pol)	ele	[ayl]	he, it
a	[a]	her, it, you (sing, pol)	ela	[**eh**la]	she, it
você	[vos**ay**]	you (sing, pol)	você/si	[vos**ay**/see]	you (sing, pol)
nos	[noosh]	us	nós	[nosh]	we
os	[oosh]	them (m), you (mpl)	eles	[**ay**lsh]	them (m)
as	[ash]	them (f), you (fpl)	elas	[**eh**lash]	them (f)
vocês	[vos**ay**sh]	you (pl)	vocês	[vos**ay**sh]	you (pl)

The object pronouns (as listed in the left-hand column of the table on page 12) generally follow the verb:

pode ajudar-me?
pod aJood**a**rmi
can you help me?

comprei-as
kompr**ay**-ash
I bought them

But note the word order in the following:

não o vi
nowng oo vee
I didn't see him

The object pronouns (as listed in the right-hand column of the table on page 12) are used after prepositions:

para você
p**a**ra vos**ay**
for you

com ele
kong ayl
with him

sem ela
sayng **eh**la
without her

depois de você
dip**oh**-ish di vos**ay**
after you

isso é para mim
eesoo eh p**a**ra meeng
that's for me

isso é para ti/si
eesoo eh p**a**ra tee/see
that's for you

After the preposition **com** (with), **mim**, **ti** and **si** change as follows:

comigo	**contigo**	**consigo**
koom**ee**goo	kont**ee**goo	kons**ee**goo
with me	with you	with you

If you are using an indirect object pronoun to mean 'to me', 'to you' etc (although 'to' might not always be said in English), you generally use the following:

me	[mi]	to me
te	[ti]	to you (sing, fam)
lhe	[l-yi]	to him, to her, to you (sing, pol)
o/a	[oo/a]	to It
nos	[noosh]	to us
lhes	[l-yish]	to them, to you (pl)

comprei-lhe flores
kompr**ay**l-yi fl**oh**rish
I bought flowers for him/her

pedi-lhe um favor
pid**ee**l-yi oong fav**oh**r
I asked him/her a favour

importa-se de lhe pedir que ...?
imp**o**rtasi di l-yi pid**ee**r ki
could you ask him/her to ...?

Reflexive Pronouns

These are used with reflexive verbs like **lavar-se** 'to wash (oneself)', i.e. where the subject and the object of the verb are one and the same person:

me	[mi]	myself
te	[ti]	yourself (fam)
se	[si]	himself, herself, itself, yourself (pol), themselves, yourselves, oneself
nos	[noosh]	ourselves

apresentar-se to introduce oneself
apresento-me: chamo-me Richard
apris**ay**ntoomi: sha**moo**mi Richard
may I introduce myself? my name's Richard

divertir-se to enjoy oneself
divertimo-nos muito na festa
divirt**ee**moonooɹ m**wee**engtoo na **feh**shta
we enjoyed ourselves a lot at the party

DEMONSTRATIVES

The English demonstrative adjective 'this' is translated by **este**. 'That' is translated either by **esse** or **aquele**. **Esse** refers to something nearby. **Aquele** refers to something further away.

Like other adjectives, demonstrative adjectives agree with the noun they qualify in gender and number but they are positioned in front of the noun. Their forms are:

masculine singular			feminine singular		
este	esse	aquele	esta	essa	aquela
aysht	ays	ak**ay**l	**eh**shta	**eh**sa	ak**eh**la

masculine plural			feminine plural		
estes	esses	aqueles	estas	essas	aquelas
ayshtish	**ay**sish	ak**ay**lish	**eh**shtash	**eh**sash	ak**eh**lash

este restaurante	**esse camareiro**	**aquela praia**
aysht rishtowr**a**nt	ays kamar**ay**roo	ak**eh**la prī-a
this restaurant	that waiter	that beach (in the distance)

GRAMMAR

The demonstrative pronouns 'this one', 'that one', 'those', 'these' etc are the same as demonstrative adjectives in Portuguese:

> queria estes/esses/aqueles
> kir**ee**-a **ay**shtish/**ay**sish/ak**ay**lish
> I'd like these/those/those (over there)

However, a neuter form also exists which is used when no specific noun is being referred to:

isto	isso	aquilo
eeshtoo	**ee**soo	ak**ee**loo
this	that	that (over there)

isso não é justo	o que é isto?
eeso nowng eh J**oo**stoo	oo ki eh **ee**shtoo
that's not fair	what is this?

VERBS

The basic form of the verb given in the **English-Portuguese** and **Portuguese-English** sections is the infinitive (e.g. to drive, to go etc). There are three verb types in Portuguese which can be recognized by their infinitive endings. -ar, -er, -ir. For example:

amar	[am**ar**]	to love
comer	[koom**ayr**]	to eat
partir	[part**eer**]	to leave

Present Tense

The present tense corresponds to 'I leave' in English. To form the present tense for the three main types of verb in Portuguese, remove the -ar, -er or -ir and add the following endings:

amar to love

am-o	[**a**moo]	I love
am-as	[**a**mash]	you love (sing, fam)
am-a	[**a**ma]	he loves, she loves, you love (sing, pol)
am-amos	[am**a**moosh]	we love
am-am	[**a**mowng]	they love, you love (pl)

comer to eat

com-o	[**koh**moo]	I eat
com-es	[**koh**mish]	you eat (sing, fam)
com-e	[**koh**mi]	he eats, she eats, you eat (sing, pol)
com-emos	[kom**ay**moosh]	we eat
com-em	[**koh**mayng]	they eat, you eat (pl)

partir to leave

part-o	[**pa**rtoo]	I leave
part-es	[partsh]	you leave (sing, fam)
part-e	[part]	he leaves, she leaves, it leaves, you leave (sing, pol)
part-imos	[part**ee**moosh]	we leave
part-em	[**pa**rtayng]	they leave, you leave (pl)

Some common verbs are irregular:

dar to give

dou	[doh]	I give
dás	[dash]	you give (sing, fam)
dá	[da]	he gives, she gives, it gives, you give (sing, pol)
damos	[**da**moosh]	we give
dão	[downg]	they give, you give (pl)

ir to go

vou	[voh]	I go
vais	[vīsh]	you go (sing, fam)
vai	[vī]	he goes, she goes, it goes, you go (sing, pol)
vamos	[**va**moosh]	we go
vão	[vowng]	they go, you go (pl)

pôr to put

ponho	[**poh**n-yoo]	I put
pões	[poyngsh]	you put (sing, fam)
põe	[poyng]	he puts, she puts, it puts, you put (sing, pol)
pomos	[**poh**moosh]	we put
põem	[**poh**-ayng]	they put, you put (pl)

ter	to have	
tenho	[**tay**n-yoo]	I have
tens	[tayngsh]	you have (sing, fam)
tem	[tayng]	he has, she has, it has, you have (sing, pol)
temos	[**tay**moosh]	we have
têm	[t**ay**-ayng]	they have, you have (pl)

vir	to come	
venho	[**vay**n-yoo]	I come
vens	[vayngsh]	you come (sing, fam)
vem	[vayng]	he comes, she comes, it comes, you come (sing, pol)
vimos	[**vee**moosh]	we come
vêm	[v**ay**-ayng]	they come, you come (pl)

The first person singular (the 'I' form) of the following verbs is irregular:

dizer	to say	digo	[**dee**goo]
fazer	to do, to make	faço	[**fa**soo]
saber	to know	sei	[say]
sair	to go out	saio	[s**ī**-oo]
poder	to be able	posso	[**po**soo]

See page 23 for the present tense of the verbs **ser** and **estar**.

Past Tense:

Preterite Tense

The preterite is the tense most commonly used to express a completed action that has taken place in the past. To form the preterite tense for the three main types of verb in Portuguese, remove the -ar, -er or -ir and add the following endings:

am-ei	[am**ay**]	I loved
am-aste	[am**a**sht]	you loved (sing, fam)
am-ou	[am**oh**]	he loved, she loved, you loved (sing, pol)
am-ámos	[am**a**moosh]	we loved
am-aram	[am**a**rowng]	they loved, you loved (pl)

com-i	[komee]	I ate
com-este	[komaysht]	you ate (sing, fam)
com-eu	[komay-oo]	he ate, she ate, it ate, you ate (sing, pol)
com-emos	[komaymoosh]	we ate
com-eram	[komayrowng]	they ate, you ate (pl)

part-i	[partee]	I left
part-iste	[parteesht]	you left (sing, fam)
part-iu	[partee-oo]	he left, she left, it left, you left (sing, pol)
part-imos	[parteemoosh]	we left
part-iram	[parteerowng]	they left, you left (pl)

The following verbs are irregular in the preterite:

dizer to say

disse	[dees]	I said
disseste	[disehsht]	you said (sing, fam)
disse	[dees]	he said, she said, you said (sing, pol)
dissemos	[disaymoosh]	we said
disseram	[disehrowng]	they said, you said (pl)

fazer to do

fiz	[feesh]	I did
fizeste	[fizehsht]	you did (sing, fam)
fez	[faysh]	he did, she did, it did, you did (sing, pol)
fizemos	[fizaymoosh]	we did
fizeram	[fizehrowng]	they did, you did (pl)

ter to have

tive	[teev]	I had
tiveste	[tivehsht]	you had (sing, fam)
teve	[tayv]	he had, she had, it had, you had (sing, pol)
tivemos	[tivaymoosh]	we had
tiveram	[tivehrowng]	they had, you had (pl)

vir to come

vim	[veeng]	I came
vieste	[v-yehsht]	you (sing, fam)
veio	[vay-oo]	he came, she came, it came, you came (sing, pol)
viemos	[v-yaymoosh]	we came
vieram	[v-yehrowng]	they came, you came (pl)

The verbs **ser** (to be) and **ir** (to go) are irregular and have the same form in the preterite:

fui	[fwee]	I was; I went
foste	[fohsht]	you were (sing, fam); you went (sing, fam)
foi	[**foh**-i]	he/she/it was, you were (sing, pol); he/she/it went, you went (sing, pol)
fomos	[**foh**moosh]	we were; we went
foram	[**foh**rowng]	they were, you were (pl, pol); they went, you went (pl)

quem te disse isso?	conhecemos o seu pai ontem
kayng ti dees **ee**soo	kon-yes**ay**mooz oo s**ay**-oo pī **oh**ntayng
who told you that?	we met your father yesterday

comprámos um carro no ano passado
kompr**a**mooz oong k**a**rroo noo **a**noo pas**a**doo
we bought a car last year

See page 23 for the preterite tense of the verbs **ser** and **estar**.

Imperfect Tense

This tense is used to express what was going on regularly over an indefinite period of time and is often translated by 'used to + verb'. It is formed as follows:

amar to love

am-ava	[am**a**va]	I used to love
am-avas	[am**a**vash]	you used to love (sing, fam)
am-ava	[am**a**va]	he/she used to love, you used to love (sing, pol)
am-ávamos	[am**a**vamoosh]	we used to love
am-avam	[am**a**vowng]	they used to love, you used to love (pl)

comer to eat

com-ia	[kom**ee**-a]	I used to eat, I was eating etc
com-ias	[kom**ee**-ash]	you used to eat (sing, fam)
com-ia	[kom**ee**-a]	he/she/it used to eat, used to eat (sing, pol)
com-íamos	[kom**ee**-amoosh]	we used to eat
com-iam	[kom**ee**-owng]	they used to eat, you used to eat (pl)

partir to leave

part-ia	[part**ee**-a]	I used to leave, I was leaving etc
part-ias	[part**ee**-ash]	you used to leave (sing, fam)
part-ia	[part**ee**-a]	he/she/it used to leave, you used to leave (sing, pol)
part-íamos	[part**ee**-amoosh]	we used to leave
part-iam	[part**ee**-owng]	they used to leave, you used to leave (pl)

todas as quartas-feiras saíamos para dar um passeio
t**oh**dazash kw**a**rtash f**ay**rash sa-**ee**-amoosh p**a**ra dar oong pass**ay**-oo
every Wednesday we used to go for a walk, every Wednesday
  we went for a walk

sempre chegávamos cedo ao emprego
saympr shig**a**vamoosh s**ay**dwow aympr**ay**goo
we always arrived early at work

One useful irregular verb in the imperfect tense is:

ter to have

tinha	[t**ee**n-ya]	I used to have
tinhas	[t**ee**n-yash]	you used to have (sing, fam)
tinha	[t**ee**n-ya]	he/she/it used to have, you used to have (sing, pol)
tínhamos	[t**ee**n-yamoosh]	we used to have
tinham	[t**ee**n-yowng]	they used to have, you used to have (pl)

See page 23 for the imperfect tense of the verbs ser and estar.

Future Tense

To form the future tense in Portuguese (I will do, you will do
etc), add the following endings to the infinitive. The same
endings are used whether verbs end in -ar, -er or -ir:

amar to love

amar-ei	[amar**ay**]	I will love
amar-ás	[amar**a**sh]	you will love
amar-á	[amar**a**]	he will love, she will love, you will love
amar-emos	[amar**ay**moosh]	we will love
amar-eis	[amar**ay**-ish]	you will love
amar-ão	[amar**ow**ng]	they will love, you will love (pl)

voltarei mais tarde
voltar**ay** mīsh tard
I'll come back later

The immediate future can
also be translated by ir +
infinitive:

vamos comprar uma garrafa
de vinho tinto
va**moosh** kompr**ar** **oo**ma
garr**a**fa di v**ee**n-yoo t**ee**ntoo
we're going to buy a bottle
of red wine

irei buscá-lo
ir**ay** booshk**a**loo
I'll fetch him, I'll go and
fetch him

In Portuguese, as in English,
the future can sometimes be
expressed by the present
tense:

o seu avião parte à uma
oo s**ay**-oo av-y**ow**ng p**a**rta
ooma
your plane takes off at one
o'clock

However, Portuguese often
uses the present tense where
the future would be used in
English:

dou-lhe oitocentos escudos
d**oh**l-yi oh-itos**ay**ntooz
shk**oo**doosh
I'll give you eight hundred
escudos

The following verbs are irregular in the future tense:

dizer to say

dir-ei	[dir**ay**]	I will say
dir-ás	[dir**a**sh]	you will say (sing, fam)
dir-á	[dir**a**]	he will say, she will say, you will say (sing, pol)
dir-emos	[dir**ay**moosh]	we will say
dir-ão	[dir**ow**ng]	they will say, you will say (pl)

fazer to do

far-ei	[far**ay**]	I will do
far-ás	[far**a**sh]	you will do (sing, fam)
far-á	[far**a**]	he will do, she will do, it will do, you will do (sing, pol)
far-emos	[far**ay**moosh]	we will do
far-ão	[far**ow**ng]	they will do, you will do (pl)

See page 24 for the future tense of the verbs ser and estar.

GRAMMAR

Use of the Past Participle

There are two auxiliary verbs in Portuguese: ter (more commonly used) and haver. These two combine with the past participle to make a compound form of the past tense.

To form the past participle, remove the infinitive endings and add the endings -ado or -ido as indicated below:

infinitive	past participle
amar	am-ado [am**a**doo]
comer	com-ido [kom**ee**doo]
partir	part-ido [part**ee**doo]

ela já tinha comprado o bilhete
ehla Ja t**ee**n-ya kompr**a**doo oo bil-y**ay**t
she had already bought the ticket

Some further examples using the past participle:

este livro foi comprado em Lisboa
aysht l**ee**vroo f**oh**-i kompr**a**doo ayng liJb**oh**-a
this book was bought in Lisbon

temos comido bem
t**ay**moosh kom**ee**doo bayng
we've been eating well

ela deve ter partido ontem
ehla dehv tayr part**ee**doo **oh**ntayng
she should have left yesterday

Some verbs have irregular past participles:

fazer to do, to make	feito	[**fay**too]
abrir to open	aberto	[ab**eh**rtoo]
dizer to say	dito	[d**ee**too]
pôr to put	posto	[**poh**shtoo]
ver to see	visto	[v**ee**shtoo]
vir to come	vindo	[v**ee**ndoo]
satisfazer to satisfy	satisfeito	[satishf**ay**too]

The Verb 'To Be'

There are two verbs 'to be' in Portuguese: ser and estar. They are conjugated as follows:

Present Tense

ser

sou	[soh]	I am
és	[ehsh]	you are (sing, fam)
é	[eh]	he is, she is, it is, you are (sing, pol)
somos	[**soh**moosh]	we are
são	[sowng]	they are, you are (pl)

estar

estou	[shtoh]	I am
estás	[shtash]	you are (sing, fam)
está	[shta]	he is, she is, it is, you are (sing, pol)
estamos	[sht**a**moosh]	we are
estão	[shtowng]	they are, you are (pl)

Preterite Tense (I was etc)

ser		estar	
fui	[fwee]	estive	[shteev]
foste	[fohsht]	estiveste	[shtiv**eh**sht]
foi	[**foh**-i]	esteve	[shtayv]
fomos	[**foh**moosh]	estivemos	[shtiv**ay**moosh]
foram	[**foh**rowng]	estiveram	[shtiv**eh**rowng]

Imperfect Tense (I used to be etc)

ser		estar	
era	[**eh**ra]	estava	[sht**a**va]
eras	[**eh**rash]	estavas	[sht**a**vash]
era	[**eh**ra]	estava	[sht**a**va]
éramos	[**eh**ramoosh]	estávamos	[sht**a**vamoosh]
eram	[**eh**rowng]	estavam	[sht**a**vowng]

Future Tense (I will be etc)

ser		estar	
serei	[sir**ay**]	estarei	[shtar**ay**]
serás	[sir**a**sh]	estarás	[shtar**a**sh]
será	[sir**a**]	estará	[shtar**a**]
seremos	[sir**ay**moosh]	estaremos	[shtar**ay**moosh]
serão	[sir**ow**ng]	estarão	[shtar**ow**ng]

Ser

Ser indicates an inherent quality, a permanent state or characteristic, i.e. something which is unlikely to change:

> a neve é branca
> a n**eh**v eh br**a**nka
> snow is white

Ser is also used with occupations, nationalities, the time and to indicate possession:

> somos escoceses
> s**oh**moosh shkoos**ay**zish
> we are Scottish

> minha mãe é professora
> m**ee**n-ya mayng eh proofes**oh**ra
> my mum is a teacher

> este é o nosso carro
> **ay**shteh oo n**o**soo k**a**rroo
> this is our car

> são cinco da tarde
> sowng s**ee**nkoo da tard
> it's five o'clock in the afternoon

Estar

Estar, on the other hand, is used to describe the temporary or passing qualities of something or someone:

> estou zangado contigo
> shtoh zang**a**doo kont**ee**goo
> I'm angry with you

> estou cansado
> shtoh kans**a**doo
> I'm tired

> este café está frio
> aysht kaf**eh** shta fr**ee**-oo
> this coffee is cold

Notice the difference between the following two phrases:

> Isabel é muito bonita
> Izab**eh**l eh m**wee**ngtoo bon**ee**ta
> Isabel is very pretty

> Isabel está muito bonita (hoje)
> Izab**eh**l shta m**wee**ngtoo bon**ee**ta (ohJ)
> Isabel looks pretty (today)

Negatives

To express a negative in Portuguese, to say 'I don't want', 'it's not here' etc, place the word **não** in front of the verb:

percebo
pirs**ay**boo
I understand

n**ão** percebo
nowng pirs**ay**boo
I don't understand

gosto deste gelado
g**o**shtoo daysht Jil**a**doo
I like this ice cream

n**ão** gosto deste gelado
nowng g**o**shtoo daysht Jil**a**doo
I don't like this ice cream

aluguel-o aqui
aloog**ay**-oo ak**ee**
I rented it here

n**ão** o aluguei aqui
nowng oo aloog**ay** ak**ee**
I didn't rent it here

v**ão** cantar
vowng kant**a**r
they're going to sing

n**ão** v**ão** cantar
nowng vowng kant**a**r
they're not going to sing

Unlike English, Portuguese makes use of double negatives with words like

'nothing/anything' or 'nobody/anybody':

n**ão** h**á** ningu**é**m aqui
nowng a ning**ay**ng ak**ee**
there's nobody here

n**ão** compr**á**mos nada
nowng kompr**a**moosh n**a**da
we didn't buy anything

n**ão** sabemos nada dela
nowng sab**ay**moosh n**a**da d**eh**la
we don't know anything about her

To say 'there's no ...', 'I've no ...' etc, make the accompanying verb negative:

n**ão** h**á** vinho
nowng a v**ee**n-yoo
there's no wine

n**ão** tenho f**ó**sforos
nowng t**ay**n-yoo f**o**shfooroosh
I've no matches

To say 'not him', 'not her' etc, just use the personal pronoun followed by **não**:

n**ó**s, n**ão**
noJ nowng
not us

ela, n**ão**
ehla nowng
not her

eu, n**ão**
ay-oo nowng
not me

Imperative

The imperative form of the verb is used to give commands. To form the imperative, remove the -ar, -er or -ir from the infinitive and add these endings:

tu	você	vocês

amar to love
| ama | am-e | am-em |
| **a**ma | **a**mi | **a**mayng |

comer to eat
| come | com-a | com-am |
| kohm | **koh**ma | **koh**mowng |

partir to leave
| parte | part-a | part-am |
| part | **pa**rta | **pa**rtowng |

coma devagar
kohma diva**ga**r
eat slowly

When you are telling someone not to do something, use the forms above and place não in front of the verb:

não me interrompa, por favor
nowng mintir**roh**mpa poor fav**oh**r
don't interrupt me, please

não beba álcool!
nowng **bay**ba **a**lko-ol
don't drink alcohol!

não venha esta noite
nowng **vay**n-ya **eh**shta n**oh**-it
don't come tonight

por favor, não fale tão rápido (to one person)
poor fav**oh**r nowng **fa**li towng **ra**pidoo
please, don't speak so fast

por favor, não falem tão rápido (to several people)
poor fav**oh**r nowng **fa**layng towng **ra**pidoo
please, don't speak so fast

Pronouns are added to the end of the imperative form:

acorde-me às oito, por favor
a**kor**dimi az**oh**-itoo poor fav**oh**r
wake me up at eight o'clock, please

ajude-me, por favor
a**Joo**dimi poor fav**oh**r
help me please

However, when the imperative is negative, pronouns are placed in front of it:

não as deixe aqui
nowng aJ daysh ak**ee**
don't leave them here

QUESTIONS

Often the word order remains the same in a question, but the intonation changes, the voice rising at the end of the question:

queres dançar?
kehrish dans**a**r
do you want to dance?

fica longe?
feeka lohnJ
is it far?

DATES

Use the numbers on page 28
to express the date.

um de Setembro [oong di
sit**ay**mbroo] the first of
September
dois de Dezembro [d**oh**-iJ di
diz**ay**mbroo] the second of
December
vinte-e-um de Janeiro [veenti-
oong di Jan**ay**roo] the twenty
first of January

DAYS

Monday segunda-feira
[sig**oo**nda f**ay**ra]
Tuesday terça-feira [t**ay**rsa
f**ay**ra]
Wednesday quarta-feira [kw**a**rta
f**ay**ra]
Thursday quinta-feira [k**ee**nta
f**ay**ra]
Friday sexta-feira [s**ay**shta
f**ay**ra]
Saturday sábado [s**a**badoo]
Sunday domingo [doom**ee**ngoo]

MONTHS

January Janeiro [Jan**ay**roo]
February Fevereiro [fivr**ay**roo]
March Março [m**a**rsoo]
April Abril [abre**el**]
May Maio [m**ī**-oo]
June Junho [J**oo**n-yoo]

July Julho [J**oo**l-yoo]
August Agosto [ag**oh**shtoo]
September Setembro
[sit**ay**mbroo]
October Outubro [oht**oo**broo]
November Novembro
[noov**ay**mbroo]
December Dezembro
[diz**ay**mbroo]

TIME

what time is it? que horas são?
[k-y**o**rash sowng]
one o'clock uma hora [**oo**ma
ora]
two o'clock duas horas [d**oo**-az
orash]
it's one o'clock é uma hora [eh
ooma **o**ra]
it's two o'clock são duas horas
[sowng doo-az**o**rash]
it's three o'clock são três horas
[trayz**o**rash]
five past one uma e cinco
[**oo**mi s**ee**nkoo]
ten past two duas e dez
[d**oo**-azi dehsh]
quarter past one uma e um
quarto [**oo**mi-oong kw**a**rtoo]
quarter past two duas e um
quarto [d**oo**-azi-oong]
half past ten dez e meia [dehz ee
m**ay**-a]
twenty to ten dez menos vinte
[dehJ m**ay**nooJ veent]
quarter to ten dez menos um
quarto [dehJ m**ay**nooz oong
kw**a**rtoo]
at eight o'clock às oito horas

[azoh-itoo orash]

at half past four às quatro e meia [ash kwatroo ee may-a]

2 a.m. duas da manhã [doo-aɹ da man-yang]

2 p.m. duas da tarde [tard]

6 a.m. seis da manhã [saysh da man-yang]

6 p.m. seis da tarde [tard]

noon meio-dia [may-oo dee-a]

midnight meia-noite [may-a noh-it]

an hour uma hora [ooma ora]

a minute um minuto [oong minootoo]

two minutes dois minutos [doh-iɹ minootoosh]

a second um segundo [oong sigoondoo]

a quarter of an hour um quarto de hora [kwatroo dora]

half an hour meia hora [may-a ora]

three quarters of an hour três quartos de hora [traysh kwartoosh dora]

NUMBERS

0	zero	[zehroo]
1	um	[oong]
2	dois	[doh-ish]
3	três	[traysh]
4	quatro	[kwatroo]
5	cinco	[seenkoo]
6	seis	[saysh]
7	sete	[seht]
8	oito	[oh-itoo]
9	nove	[nov]
10	dez	[dehsh]

11	onze	[ohnz]
12	doze	[dohz]
13	treze	[trayz]
14	catorze	[katohrz]
15	quinze	[keenz]
16	dezasseis	[dizasaysh]
17	dezassete	[dizaseht]
18	dezoito	[dizoh-itoo]
19	dezanove	[dizanov]
20	vinte	[veent]
21	vinte e um	[veenti-oong]
22	vinte e dois	[veenti doh-ish]
23	vinte e três	[veenti traysh]
30	trinta	[treenta]
31	trinta e um	[treentī-oong]
32	trinta e dois	[treentī doh-ish]
40	quarenta	[kwaraynta]
50	cinquenta	[sinkwaynta]
60	sessenta	[sesaynta]
70	setenta	[setaynta]
80	oitenta	[oh-itaynta]
90	noventa	[noovaynta]
100	cem	[sayng]
101	cento e um	[sayntwee oong]
120	cento e vinte	[veent]
200	duzentos [doozayntoosh], duzentas [doozayntash]
300	trezentos [trizayntoosh], trezentas [trizayntash]
400	quatrocentos [kwatrosayntoosh], quatrocentas [kwatrosayntash]
500	quinhentos [keen-yayntoosh], quinhentas [keen-yayntash]

600	seiscentos [sayshs**ay**ntoosh], seiscentas [sayshs**ay**ntash]
700	setecentos [setes**ay**ntoosh], setecentas [setes**ay**ntash]
800	oitocentos [oh-itoos**ay**ntoosh], oitocentas [oh-itoos**ay**ntash]
900	novecentos [noves**ay**ntoosh], novecentas [noves**ay**ntash]
1,000	mil [meel]
2,000	dois mil [**doh**-ish]
5,000	cinco mil [**see**nkoo]
10,000	dez mil [dehsh]
1,000,000	um milhão [mil-**yow**ng]

um is used with masculine nouns:

> um carro
> oong **ka**rroo
> one car

uma is used with feminine nouns:

> uma bicicleta
> **oo**ma bisikl**eh**ta
> one bike

With multiples of a hundred, the -as ending is used with feminine nouns:

trezentos homens
triz**ay**ntooz **oh**mayngsh
300 men

quinhentas mulheres
keen-y**ay**ntaJ mool-y**eh**rish
500 women

Ordinals

1st	primeiro [prim**ay**roo]
2nd	segundo [sig**oo**ndoo]
3rd	terceiro [tirs**ay**roo]
4th	quarto [k**wa**rtoo]
5th	quinto [k**ee**ntoo]
6th	sexto [s**ay**shtoo]
7th	sétimo [s**eh**timoo]
8th	oitavo [oh-it**a**voo]
9th	nono [n**oh**noo]
10th	décimo [d**eh**simoo]

BASIC PHRASES

yes
sim
seeng

no
não
nowng

OK
está bem
shta bayng

hello/hi
olá

good morning
bom dia
bong dee-a

good evening/good night
boa noite
boh-a noh-it

see you!
até logo!
ateh logoo

goodbye
adeus
aday-oosh

please
se faz favor, por favor
si fash favohr, poor

yes please
sim, por favor
seeng

thanks, thank you
(said by man/woman) obrigado/
obrigada
obrigadoo

no thanks, no thank you
não obrigado/obrigada
nowng

thank you very much
muito obrigado/obrigada
mweengtoo

don't mention it
não tem de quê
nowng tayng di kay

not at all
de nada
di nada

how do you do?
muito prazer
mweengtoo prazayr

how are you?
como está?
kohmoo shta

fine, thanks
(said by man/woman) bem,
obrigado/obrigada
bayng obrigadoo

pleased to meet you
(said to man/woman) muito prazer
em conhecê-lo/conhecê-la
m**wee**ngtoo praz**ay**r ayng kon-
yis**ay**loo

excuse me
(to get past) com licença
kong lis**ay**nsa
(to get attention) se faz favor
si fash fav**oh**r
(to say sorry) desculpe
dishk**oo**lp

(I'm) sorry
tenho muita pena
t**ay**n-yoo mw**ee**ngta p**ay**na

sorry?/pardon (me)?
(didn't understand) como?
k**oh**moo

what did you say?
o que disse?
oo ki dees

I see/I understand
percebo
pirs**ay**boo

I don't understand
não percebo
nowng

do you speak English?
fala inglês?
ingl**ay**sh

I don't speak Portuguese
não falo português
nowng f**a**loo poortoog**ay**sh

can you speak more slowly?
pode falar mais devagar?
pod fal**a**r mīJ divag**a**r

could you repeat that?
podia repetir?
pood**ee**-a ripit**ee**r

can you write it down?
pode escrever isso?
pod shkriv**ay**r **ee**soo

I'd like ...
queria ...
kir**ee**-a

can I have ...?
pode dar-me ...?
pod d**a**rmi

do you have ...?
tem ...?
tayng

how much is it?
quanto é?
kwantw**eh**

cheers!
saúde!
sa-**oo**d

it is ...
é ...; está ...
eh; shta

where is ...?
onde é ...?; onde está ...?
ohnd**eh**; ohnd shta

is it far?
é longe?
eh lohnJ

CONVERSION TABLES

1 centimetre = 0.39 inches	1 inch = 2.54 cm

1 metre = 39.37 inches = 1.09 yards

1 foot = 30.48 cm

1 yard = 0.91 m

1 kilometre = 0.62 miles = 5/8 mile

1 mile = 1.61 km

km	1	2	3	4	5	10	20	30	40	50	100
miles	0.6	.1.2	1.9	2.5	3.1	6.2	12.4	18.6	24.8	31.0	62.1

miles	1	2	3	4	5	10	20	30	40	50	100
km	1.6	3.2	4.8	6.4	8.0	16.1	32.2	48.3	64.4	80.5	161

1 gram = 0.035 ounces

1 kilo = 1000 g = 2.2 pounds

g	100	250	500
oz	3.5	8.75	17.5

1 oz = 28.35 g

1 lb = 0.45 kg

kg	0.5	1	2	3	4	5	6	7	8	9	10
lb	1.1	2.2	4.4	6.6	8.8	11.0	13.2	15.4	17.6	19.8	22.0

kg	20	30	40	50	60	70	80	90	100
lb	44	66	88	110	132	154	176	198	220

lb	0.5	1	2	3	4	5	6	7	8	9	10	20
kg	0.2	0.5	0.9	1.4	1.8	2.3	2.7	3.2	3.6	4.1	4.5	9.0

1 litre = 1.75 UK pints / 2.13 US pints

1 UK pint = 0.57 l	1 UK gallon = 4.55 l
1 US pint = 0.47 l	1 US gallon = 3.79 l

centigrade / Celsius

$C = (F - 32) \times 5/9$

C	-5	0	5	10	15	18	20	25	30	36.8	38
F	23	32	41	50	59	65	68	77	86	98.4	100.4

Fahrenheit

$F = (C \times 9/5) + 32$

F	23	32	40	50	60	65	70	80	85	98.4	101
C	-5	0	4	10	16	18	21	27	29	36.8	38.3

English-Portuguese

A

a, an* um, uma [oong, **oo**ma]
about: about 20 mais ou
  menos vinte [mīz oh
  m**ay**noosh veent]
  it's about 5 o'clock por v**o**lta
  das cinco [poor – s**ee**nkoo]
  a film about Portugal um filme
  sobre Portugal [oong feelm
  sohbr poortoog**a**l]
above acima [as**ee**ma]
abroad no estrangeiro [noo
  shtranj**ay**roo]
absolutely! (I agree) com
  certeza! [kong sirt**ay**za]
absorbent cotton o algodão em
  r**a**ma [ayng]
accelerator o acelerador
  [asilirad**oh**r]
accept aceitar [asayt**ar**]
accident o acidente [aseed**ay**nt]
  there's been an accident
  houve um acidente [ohv oong]
accommodation o alojamento
  [alooJam**ay**ntoo]
  see room and hotel
accurate exacto [ez**a**too]
ache a dor [dohr]
  my back aches tenho dor nas
  costas [t**ay**n-yoo – nash
  k**o**shtash]
across: across the road do
  outro lado da rua [doo **oh**troo
  l**a**doo da r**oo**-a]
adapter o adaptador
  [adaptad**oh**r]
address a morada [moor**a**da]
  what's your address? qual é a

sua morada? [kwal eh a s**oo**-a]

Most addresses in Portugal con-
sist of a street name and
number followed by a storey
number, for example Rua de
Alfonso Henriques 34-3°. This
means that you need to go up to
the third floor of no. 34 (US,
fourth floor). An 'esq' or 'E'
(standing for **esquerda**) after a
floor number means you should
go to the left; 'dir' or 'D' (for
direita) indicates the apartment
or office you're looking for is on
the right.

For example:
Sr. Dr. Manuel Santos de
  Oliveira
Av. da Liberdade, 48, 2° Esq.
1100 - Lisboa
Portugal

address book o livro de
  moradas [l**ee**vroo di
  moor**a**dash], o livro de
  endereços [ayndir**ay**soosh]
admission charge a entrada
  [ayntr**a**da]
adult (man/woman) o adulto
  [ad**oo**ltoo], a ad**u**lta
advance: in advance adiantado
  [ad-yant**a**doo]
aeroplane o avião [av-y**ow**ng]
Africa a **Á**frica
African (adj) africano [afrik**a**noo]
after depois [dip**oh**-ish]
  after you você primeiro

[vos**ay** prim**ay**roo]
after lunch depois do almoço
[dwalm**oh**soo]
afternoon a tarde [tard]
in the afternoon à tarde
this afternoon esta tarde
[**eh**shta]
aftershave o aftershave
aftersun cream a loção para
depois do sol [loos**ow**ng –
dip**oh**-ish doo]
afterwards depois
again outra vez [**oh**tra vaysh]
against contra
age a idade [eed**ad**]
ago: a week ago há uma
semana [a **oo**ma sim**a**na]
an hour ago há uma hora
[**o**ra]
agree: I agree concordo
[konk**o**rdoo]
AIDS a SIDA [s**ee**da]
air o ar
by air de avião [dav-y**ow**ng]
air-conditioning o ar
condicionado [kondis-
yoon**a**doo]
airmail: by airmail por via aérea
[poor v**ee**-a-**eh**r-ya]
airmail envelope o envelope de
avião [aynvil**o**p dav-y**ow**ng]
airport o aeroporto
[a-ayroop**oh**rtoo]
to the airport, please para o
aeroporto, se faz favor
[paroo – si fash fav**oh**r]
airport bus o autocarro do
aeroporto [owtook**a**rroo doo]
aisle seat o lugar de corredor

[loog**a**r di koorrid**oh**r]
alarm clock o despertador
[dishpirtad**oh**r]
alcohol o álcool [**a**lko-ol]
alcoholic alcoólico [alko-**o**likoo]
all: all the boys todos os
meninos [t**oh**dooz ooJ
min**ee**noosh]
all the girls todas as meninas
[t**oh**daz aJ min**ee**nash]
all of it todo [t**oh**doo]
all of them todos [t**oh**doosh]
that's all, thanks (said by man/
woman) é tudo, obrigado/
obrigada [eh t**oo**doo
obriga**doo**]
allergic: I'm allergic to ... (said by
man/woman) sou alérgico/
alérgica a ... [soh al**eh**rJikoo]
allowed: is it allowed? é
permitido? [eh pirmit**ee**do]
all right está bem [shta bayng]
I'm all right estou bem [shtoh]
are you all right? estás bem?
[shtash]
almond a amêndoa
[am**ay**ndoo-a]
almost quase [kwaz]
alone só [saw]
alphabet o alfabeto [alfab**e**too]

a	a	j	Jota	s	ehs
b	bay	k	kapa	t	tay
c	say	l	el	u	oo
d	day	m	em	v	vay
e	eh	n	en	w	vay d**oo**ploo
f	ehf	o	o	x	sheesh
g	Jay	p	pay	y	**ee**psilon
h	aga	q	kay	z	zay
i	ee	r	err		

already já [Ja]
also também [tambayng]
although embora [aymbora]
altogether totalmente
[tootalmaynt]
always sempre [saympr]
am*: I am sou [soh]; estou
[shtoh]
a.m.: at seven a.m. às sete da
manhã [ash – man-yang]
amazing (surprising) espantoso
[shpantohzoo]
(very good) estupendo
[shtoopayndoo]
ambulance a ambulância
[amboolans-ya]
call an ambulance! chame
uma ambulância! [sham
ooma]

For all emergency services dial
115.

America a América
American americano
[amirikanoo]
I'm American (man/woman) sou
americano/americana
among entre [ayngtr]
amount a quantia [kwantee-ya]
amp: a 13-amp fuse um fusível
de treze amperes [oong
foozeevel di – ampehrish]
and e [ee]
angry zangado
animal o animal
ankle o tornozelo
[toornoozayloo]
anniversary (wedding) o

aniversário (de casamento)
[anivirsar-yoo (di
kazamayntoo)]
annoy: this man's annoying me
este homem está a
aborrecer-me [aysht ohmayng
shta aboorrisayrmi]
annoying aborrecido
[aboorriseedoo], importuno
[importoonoo]
another outro [ohtroo]
can we have another room?
pode dar-nos outro quarto?
[pod dar-nooz – kwartoo]
another beer, please outra
cerveja, por favor [sirvayJa
poor favohr]
antibiotics os antibióticos
[antib-yotikoosh]
antifreeze o anticongelante
[–konJilant]
antihistamines os anti-
histamínicos
[–ishtameenikoosh]
antique: is it an antique? é uma
antiguidade? [eh ooma
antigweedad]
antique shop a casa de
antiguidades [kaza
dantigweedadsh]
antiseptic o anti-séptico
any: have you got any bread/
tomatoes? tem pão/tomates?
[tayng]
do you have any? tem?
sorry, I don't have any
desculpe não tenho
[dishkoolp nowng tayn-yoo]
anybody* alguém [algayng]

does anybody speak English?
alguém fala inglês?
[inglaysh]
there wasn't anybody there
não estava lá ninguém
[nowng shtava la ningayng]
anything* qualquer coisa
[kwalkehr koh-iza]

anything else? mais alguma
coisa? [mīz algooma koh-iza]
nothing else, thanks (said by man/
woman) mais nada, obrigado/
obrigada [obrigadoo]

would you like anything to drink?
gostaria de beber alguma coisa?
[goostaree-a di bibayr]
I don't want anything, thanks (said
by man/woman) não quero nada,
obrigado/obrigada [nowng
kehroo]

apart from além de [alayng di]
apartment o apartamento
[apartamayntoo]
apartment block o bloco de
apartamentos [blokoo
dapartamayntoosh]
aperitif o aperitivo [apiriteevoo]
apology as desculpas
[diskoolpash]
appendicitis a apendicite
[apendi-seet]
appetizer a entrada [ayntrada]
apple a maçã [masang]
appointment a marcação
[markasowng]

good morning, how can I help you?
bom dia, que deseja? [bong dee-a
ki disayJa]
I'd like to make an appointment
queria fazer uma marcação
[kiree-a fazayr]
what time would you like? que
hora prefere? [k-yora prefehri]
three o'clock três horas [trayz
orash]
I'm afraid that's not possible, is four
o'clock all right? infelizmente, não
é possível, quatro horas está
bem? [infiliJmayngt nowng eh
pooseevil kwatroo orash shta bayng]
yes, that will be fine sim, está bem
[seeng]
the name was ...? o nome é ...?
[oo nohm]

apricot o damasco [damashkoo]
April Abril [abreel]
Arab (adj) árabe [arabi]
are*: we are somos [sohmoosh];
estamos [shtamoosh]
you are (você) é [(vosay-)eh];
(você) está [shta]
they are são [sowng]; estão
[shtowng]
area a região [riJ-yowng]
area code o código
arm o braço [brasoo]
arrange: will you arrange it for
us? pode organizar isto para
nós? [podi – eeshtoo – nosh]
arrival a chegada [shigada]
arrive chegar
when do we arrive? a que

horas chegamos? [k-**yo**rash
shi**ga**moosh]

has my fax arrived yet? meu
fax já chegou? [m**ay**-oo – Ja
shig**oh**]

we arrived today chegámos
hoje [shi**ga**moosh ohJ]

art a arte [art]

art gallery a galeria de arte
[gali**ree**-a dart]

artist (man/woman) o/a artista
[art**ee**shta]

as: as big as tão grande
quanto [towng gr**a**nd kw**a**ntoo]

as soon as possible logo que
possível [**lo**goo ki poos**ee**vil]

ashtray o cinzeiro [sinz**ay**roo]

ask perguntar [pirgoont**a**r],
pedir [pid**ee**r]

I didn't ask for this não pedi
isto [nowng pid**ee ee**shtoo]

could you ask him to ...?
importa-se de lhe pedir
que ...? [imp**o**rtasi di l-yi – ki]

asleep: she's asleep ela está a
dormir [**eh**la shta a doorm**ee**r]

aspirin a aspirina [ashpir**ee**na]

asthma a asma [**a**Jma]

astonishing espantoso
[shpant**oh**zoo]

at: at the hotel no hotel [noo]

at the station na estação
[nashtas**ow**ng]

at six o'clock às seis horas
[ash sayz **o**rash]

at Américo's na casa do
Américo [dwam**eh**rikoo]

athletics o atletismo
[atlet**ee**Jmoo]

Atlantic Ocean o Oceano
Atlântico [ohs-y**a**noo
atl**a**ntikoo]

attractive atraente [atra-**ay**nt]

aubergine a beringela
[bireenJ**eh**la]

August Agosto [ag**oh**shtoo]

aunt a tia [t**ee**-a]

Australia a Austrália
[owshtr**a**l-ya]

Australian (adj) australiano
[owshtral-y**a**noo]

I'm Australian (man/woman) sou
australiano/australiana [soh]

automatic automático
[owtoom**a**tikoo]

automatic teller o caixa
automático [kīsha
owtoom**a**tikoo]

autumn o Outono [oht**oh**noo]

in the autumn no Outono
[noo]

avenue a avenida [avin**ee**da]

average (not good) mais ou
menos [mīz oh m**ay**noosh]

on average em média [ayng
m**eh**d-ya]

awake: is he awake? ele já
·acordou? [ayl Ja akoord**oh**]

away: go away! vá-se embora!
[v**a**si aymb**o**ra]

is it far away? fica longe?
[**fee**ka lohnJ]

awful horrível [ohr**ree**vil]

axle o eixo [**ay**shoo]

B

baby o bebé [beb**eh**]
baby food a comida de bebé
  [koom**ee**da di]
baby's bottle o biberão
  [bibir**ow**ng]
baby-sitter a baby-sitter
back (of body) as costas
  [k**o**shtash]
  (back part) a parte posterior
  [part pooshteri**ohr**]
  at the back atrás [atr**a**sh]
  can I have my money back?
  posso reaver o meu
  dinheiro? [p**o**soo r-yav**a**yr oo
  m**ay**-oo deen-y**ay**roo]
  to come/go back volt**a**r
backache a dor nas costas
  [dohr nash k**o**shtash]
bacon o b**a**con
bad mau [mow], (f) má
  a bad headache uma dor de
  cabeça forte [**oo**ma dohr di
  kab**ay**sa fort]
badly mal
bag o saco [s**a**koo]
  (handbag) a m**a**la de mão [di
  mowng]
  (suitcase) a mala
baggage a bagagem [b**a**ga Jayng]
baggage check o depósito de
  bagagem [dip**o**zitoo di baga-
  Jayng]
baggage claim a reclamação de
  bagagens [riklamas**ow**ng di
  baga-Jayngsh]
bakery a padaria [padar**ee**-a]
balcony a varanda

a room with a balcony um
quarto com varanda [oong
kw**a**rtoo kong]
bald careca [kar**eh**ka]
ball a b**o**la
  (small) a bolinha [bol**ee**n-ya]
ballet o ballet
ballpoint pen a caneta
  esferográfica [shfiroo-
  gr**a**fika]
banana a banana
band (musical) a b**a**nda
bandage a ligadura [ligad**oo**ra]
Bandaid® o adesivo
  [adez**ee**voo]
bank (money) o banco [b**a**nkoo]

All banks now charge a hefty
commission on changing travellers' cheques; there are much
lower commissions on foreign
currency exchanges at **caixas**
(savings banks or building
societies) though this of course
means carrying around large
amounts of foreign cash.
You'll find a bank in all but the
smallest towns. Standard opening hours are Monday to Friday
from 8.30 a.m. to 3 p.m. In
Lisbon and some of the Algarve
resorts they may also open in the
evening to change money, while
some banks have installed
automatic exchange machines
for various currencies and
denominations.
see **cheque**

bank account a conta bancária
[bankar-ya]

bar o bar

> In most bars in Portugal, you do
> not have to pay when ordering:
> you wait until just before you
> leave. In a few places, you pay
> first at the cash desk then show
> your receipt (a senha) at the
> bar when ordering. Sometimes
> you may see the sign pré-
> pagamento when you have to
> pay in advance.
> Larger cities and coastal resorts
> have cosmopolitan and sophis-
> ticated clubs and bars, although
> in rural areas local bars remain
> very much a male domain.
> Women travelling alone may
> find that they'll attract un-
> wanted attention in such bars.

a bar of chocolate uma
tablete de chocolate [tableht
di shookoolat]

barber's o barbeiro [barbayroo]

basket o cesto [sayshtoo]
(in shop) o cesto de compras
[di kohmprash]

bath o banho [ban-yoo]
can I have a bath? posso
tomar banho? [posoo toomar]

bathroom a casa de banho
[kaza di]
with a private bathroom com
casa de banho [kong]

bath towel a toalha de banho
[twal-ya]

bathtub a banheira [ban-yayra]

battery a pilha [peel-ya]
(for car) a bateria [batiree-a]

bay a baía [ba-ee-a]

be* ser [sayr]; estar [shtar]

beach a praia [prī-a]
on the beach na praia

> The Portuguese tend to stick to
> a rather rigid swimming season,
> from early June until mid-
> September. Therefore you could
> have the beach to yourself on a
> baking hot day in May, while on
> an overcast weekend in August
> the beach will be packed.
> Open-air pools tend to close in
> September, regardless of the
> weather.
> Beware of the heavy undertow
> on many of Portugal's Atlantic
> beaches and don't swim if you
> see a red or yellow flag.

beach mat o colchão de praia
[kolshowng di prī-a]

beach umbrella o chapéu de sol
[shapeh-oo]

beans os feijões [faiJoyngsh]
French beans os feijões-
verdes [–vayrdsh]
broad beans as favas [favash]

beard a barba

beautiful bonito [booneetoo]

because porque [poorkay]
because of ... por causa do ...
[poor kowza doo]

bed a cama
I'm going to bed now vou

para a cama agora [voh]
bed and breakfast cama e
  pequeno almoço [ee pikaynoo
  almohsoo]
  see hotel
bedroom o quarto [kwartoo]
beef a carne de vaca [karn di]
beer a cerveja [sirvayJa]
  two beers, please duas
  cervejas, por favor [doo-ash
  sirvayJash poor favohr]

> The most common Portuguese
> beer is **Sagres**, but there are a
> fair number of local varieties.
> Probably the best Portuguese
> beer is the blue-labelled **Super
> Bock**, which is rivalled only by
> **Sagres Europa**. For something
> unusual (and not recommended
> on a hot afternoon) try the
> green-labelled **Sagres . Preta**,
> which is a dark beer, resembling
> British brown ale.
> When drinking draft beer, order
> **uma imperial** if you want a
> regular glass; **uma caneca** will
> get you a half-litre. And when
> buying bottles, don't forget to
> take your empties back: they can
> represent as much as a third of
> the price.
> Beer is sold in a **cervejaria**
> (literally: beer house), where
> you can go at all hours for a
> beer and a snack, and is also
> widely available in cafés and
> restaurants.

before antes [antsh]
begin começar [koomesar]
  when does it begin? quando é
  que começa? [kwandoo eh ki
  koomehsa]
beginner (man/woman) o/a
  principiante [prinsip-yant]
beginning: at the beginning no
  início [noo inees-yoo]
behind atrás [atrash]
  behind me atrás de mim [di
  meeng]
beige bege
Belgian (adj) belga
Belgium a Bélgica [behlJika]
believe acreditar
below abaixo [abishoo]
belt o cinto [seentoo]
bend (in road) a curva [koorva]
berth (on ship) o beliche
  [bileesh]
beside: beside the ... junto
  da ... [Joontoo]
best o melhor [mil-yor]
better melhor
  are you feeling better? está
  melhor? [shta]
between entre [ayntr]
beyond para além de
  [paralayng di]
bicycle a bicicleta [bisiklehta]
big grande [grand]
  too big grande demais
  [dimish]
  it's not big enough não é
  suficientemente grande
  [nowng eh soofis-yayntimaynt]
bike a bicicleta [bisiklehta]
  (motorbike) a motocicleta

[mootoosikl**eh**ta]
bikini o bik**i**ni
bill a c**o**nta
(US) a n**o**ta
could I have the bill, please?
pode-me dar a conta, por
favor? [p**o**d-mi – poor fav**oh**r]
bin o caix**o**te de l**i**xo [k**ī**sh**o**t di
l**ee**shoo]
bin liners os s**a**cos de l**i**xo
[s**a**koosh]
bird o p**á**ssaro [p**a**saroo]
birthday o d**i**a de anos [d**ee**-a
d**a**noosh]
happy birthday! feliz
aniversário! [fil**ee**z
anivirs**a**r-yoo]
biscuit a bol**a**cha [bool**a**sha]
bit: a little bit um p**o**uco [oong
p**oh**koo]
a big bit um ped**a**ço gr**a**nde
[pid**a**soo grand]
a bit of ... uma fat**i**a de ...
[**oo**ma fat**ee**-a di]
a bit expensive um p**o**uco
c**a**ro [p**oh**koo k**a**roo]
bite (by insect) a pic**a**da [pik**a**da]
(by dog) a morded**u**ra
[moorded**oo**ra]
bitter (taste etc) am**a**rgo
[am**a**rgoo]
black preto [pr**a**ytoo]
blanket o cobert**o**r [koobirt**oh**r]
bleach (for toilet) a lix**í**via
[lish**ee**v-ya]
bless you! santinho! [sant**een**-
yoo]
blind cego [s**eh**goo]
blinds as persi**a**nas [pirs-

y**a**nash]
blister a b**o**lha [b**o**l-ya]
blocked (road) cort**a**do
[koort**a**doo]
(pipe, sink) entup**i**do
[ayntoop**ee**doo]
blond (adj) l**o**uro [l**oh**roo]
blood o s**a**ngue [sang]
high blood pressure a tens**ã**o
arteri**a**l **a**lta [tayns**ow**ng
artir-y**a**l]
blouse a bl**u**sa [bl**oo**za]
blow-dry sec**a**r com secad**o**r
[kong sikad**oh**r]
I'd like a cut and blow-dry
queri**a** cort**a**r e faz**e**r
brushing [kir**ee**-a – ee faz**ay**r]
blue az**u**l [az**oo**l]
blue eyes os **o**lhos az**u**is
[**o**l-yoosh az**oo**-ish]
blusher o bl**u**sher
boarding house a pens**ã**o
[payns**ow**ng]
boarding pass o cart**ã**o de
emb**a**rque [kart**ow**ng
daymb**a**rk]
boat o b**a**rco [b**a**rkoo]
(for passengers) o ferry-boat
body o c**o**rpo [k**oh**rpoo]
boiled egg o **o**vo coz**i**do [**oh**voo
kooz**ee**doo]
boiler a cald**e**ira [kald**ay**ra]
bone o **o**sso [**oh**soo]
(in fish) a esp**i**nha [shp**ee**n-ya]
bonnet (of car) o cap**o**t
[kap**oh**]
book o l**i**vro [l**ee**vroo]
(verb) reserv**a**r [rizirv**a**r]
can I book a seat? posso

reservar um lugar? [po̱soo –
oong loogar]

•••••• DIALOGUE ••••••

I'd like to book a table for two
queria reservar uma mesa para
dois [kiree-a – ooma mayza para
doh-ish]
what time would you like it booked
for? para que horas? [k-yorash]
half past seven sete e meia [seh-
tee-may-a]
that's fine está bem [shta bayng]
and your name? e o seu nome?
[yoo say-oo nohm]

bookshop a livraria [livraree-a]
bookstore a livraria [livraree-a]
boot (footwear) a bota
 (of car) o porta-bagagens
 [porta-bagaJayngsh]
border (of country) a fronteira
 [frontayra]
bored: I'm bored (said by man/
 woman) estou chateado/
 chateada [shtoh shat-yadoo]
boring maçador [masadohr]
born: I was born in Manchester
 nasci em Manchester [nash-
 see ayng]
 I was born in 1960 nasci em
 mil novecentos e sessenta
borrow pedir emprestado
 [pideer aymprishtadoo]
 may I borrow ...? posso
 pedir ... emprestado? [po̱soo]
both ambos [amboosh]
bother: sorry to bother you
 desculpe incomodá-lo
 [dishkoolp eenkoo-moodaloo]

bottle a garrafa
 a bottle of house red uma
 garrafa de vinho da casa
 tinto [ooma – di veen-yoo da
 kaza teentoo]
bottle-opener o abre-garrafas
 [abrigarrafash]
bottom (of person) o traseiro
 [trazayroo]
 at the bottom of ... (hill) no
 sopé do ... [noo soopeh doo]
box a caixa [kisha]
box office a bilheteira [bil-
 yitayra]
boy o rapaz [rapash]
boyfriend o namorado
 [namooradoo]
bra o soutien [soot-yang]
bracelet a pulseira [poolsayra]
brake o travão [travowng]
brandy o brandy
Brazil Brasil [brazeel]
Brazilian (adj) brasileiro
 [brazilayroo]
bread o pão [powng]
 white bread o pão branco
 [brankoo]
 brown bread o pão escuro
 [shkooroo]
 wholemeal bread o pão
 integral [eentigral]
break partir
 I've broken the ... quebrei
 o/a ... [kibray oo]
 I think I've broken my wrist
 acho que parti o pulso
 [ashoo ki – oo poolsoo]
break down avariar
 I've broken down meu carro

avariou [may-oo karroo
avari-**oh**]
breakdown (mechanical) a avaria
[avar**ee**-a]

If you break down you can get
assistance from the **Automóvel
Clube de Portugal**, which has
reciprocal arrangements with
foreign automobile clubs. If
you're involved in a road accident, use the nearest roadside
orange-coloured SOS telephone
– press the button and wait for
an answer.

---

breakdown service o pronto-
socorro [pr**oh**ntoo
sook**oh**rroo]
breakfast o pequeno almoço
[pik**ay**noo alm**oh**soo]
break-in: I've had a break-in
minha casa foi roubada
[m**ee**n-ya k**a**za f**oh**-i rohb**a**da]
breast o peito [p**ay**too]
breathe respirar [rishpir**ar**]
breeze a brisa [br**ee**za]
bridge (over river) a ponte [pohnt]
brief breve [brehv]
briefcase a pasta [p**a**shta]
bright (light etc) brilhante [bril-
y**a**nt]
   bright red vermelho vivo
   [v**ee**voo]
brilliant (idea, person) brilhante
[bril-y**a**nt]
bring trazer [traz**ay**r]
   I'll bring it back later trago isto
   de volta mais tarde [tr**a**goo

eeshtoo di – mīsh tard]
Britain a Grã-Bretanha [grang
britan-ya]
British britânico [brit**a**nikoo]
brochure o folheto [fool-y**ay**too]
broken partido [part**ee**doo]
bronchitis bronquite [bronk**ee**t]
brooch o alfinete [alfin**ay**t]
broom a vassoura [vas**oh**ra]
brother o irmão [eerm**ow**ng]
brother-in-law o cunhado [koon-
y**a**doo]
brown castanho [kasht**a**n-yoo]
bruise a contusão
   [kontooz**ow**ng]
brush (for hair, cleaning) a escova
[shk**o**va]
   (artist's) o pincel [peens**eh**l]
bucket o balde [bowld]
buffet car a carruagem
restaurante [karrw**a**-Jayng
rishtowr**a**nt]
buggy (for child) a cadeirinha de
bebé [kadayr**ee**n-ya di beb**eh**]
building o edifício [idif**ee**s-yoo]
bulb (light bulb) a lâmpada
bullfight a tourada [tohr**a**da]
bullfighter o toureiro
[tohr**ay**roo]

---

bullfighting
The Portuguese pride themselves on having a more humane
attitude to bullfighting than
their Spanish neighbours. In
Portugal it is common to see
matadors fighting on horseback,
and the emphasis is more on
                              →

ENGLISH ❖ PORTUGUESE | Bu

skilled horsemanship than on macho daring. However, though the matadors do not kill the bulls in the ring in front of the audience, those animals deemed too weak to fight another day are killed immediately afterwards.

bullring a praça de touros [pra**sa** di to**hr**oosh]
bull-running as garraiadas [garrī-**a**dash]
bumper o pára-choques [para-sho**k**sh]
bunk o beliche [bil**ee**sh]
bureau de change o câmbio [k**a**mb-yoo]
see **bank**
burglary o roubo [ro**h**boo]
burn a queimadura [kaymad**oo**ra]
(verb) queim**ar**
burnt: this is burnt isto está queimado [**ee**shtoo shta kaym**a**doo]
burst: a burst pipe um cano rebentado [oong k**a**noo ribaynt**a**doo]
bus o autocarro [owtook**a**rroo]
what number bus is it to ...? qual é o número do autocarro para ...? [kwal-**eh** oo no**o**miroo doo]
when is the next bus to ...? a que horas é o próximo autocarro para ...? [k-y**o**raz eh oo pr**o**simoo]

what time is the last bus? a que horas é o último autocarro? [**oo**ltimoo]

Buses shadow many of the main train routes as well as linking most of the country's smaller towns and villages. It's almost always quicker to go by bus though you'll pay slightly more than for the equivalent train ride. Comfortable express buses operate on longer routes, for which you'll usually have to reserve tickets in advance – certainly for the Lisbon-Algarve routes in summer.

The local bus station is the place to pick up timetables and reserve seats on long-distance journeys, and local tourist offices can usually help with bus information. It's as well to be aware that bus services are considerably less frequent – occasionally non-existent – at weekends, especially on rural routes; while at other times, you'll find that departures can be extremely early in the morning. This is because bus services are often designed to fit around school and market hours.

see **ticket**

•••••• DIALOGUE ••••••

does this bus go to ...? este autocarro vai para ...? [aysht – vī]

no, you need a number ... não,
tem que apanhar o número ...
[nowng tayng k-yapang-yar oo
noomiroo]

business o negócios [nigos-
yoosh]

bus station a estação dos
autocarros [shtasowng dooz
owtookarroosh]

bus stop a paragem do
autocarro [paraJayng doo
owtookarroo]

bust o peito [paytoo]

busy (restaurant etc) frequentado
[frikwayntadoo]
  I'm busy tomorrow (said by man/
  woman) estou ocupado/
  ocupada amanhã [shtoh
  okoopadoo – aman-yang]

but mas [mash]

butcher's o talho [tal yoo]

butter a manteiga [mantayga]

button o botão [bootowng]

buy comprar
  where can I buy ...? onde
  posso comprar ...? [ohnd
  posoo]

by*: by bus de autocarro
  [dowtookarroo]
  by car de carro [di karroo]
  written by ... escrito por ...
  [shkreetoo poor]
  by the window à janela
  by the sea à beira-mar
  by Thursday na quinta-feira

bye adeus [aday-oosh]

C

cabbage a couve [kohv]

cabin (on ship) o camarote
  [kamarot]

cable car o teleférico
  [telefehrikoo]

café o café [kafeh]
  see **bar**

cagoule o impermeável de
nylon [impirmia-vil di]

cake o bolo [bohloo]

cake shop a pastelaria [pashtila-
ree-a]

call chamar [shamar]
  (to phone) telefonar
  [telefoonar]
  what's it called? como se
  chama isto? [kohmoo si
  shama eeshtoo]
  he/she is called ... ele/ela
  chama-se ... [ayl/ehla
  shamasi]
  please call the doctor por
  favor, chame o médico [poor
  favohr sham-yoo mehdikoo]
  **please give me a call at 7.30
  a.m. tomorrow** chame-me,
  por favor, às ... horas
  amanhã [shami-mi – ash ...
  orash aman-yang]
  please ask him to call me por
  favor, peça a ele que me
  telefone [pesa-a ayl ki-mi
  telefohn]

call back: I'll call back later volto
mais tarde [voltoo mĩsh tard]
  (phone back) volto a telefonar
  mais tarde [voltwa telefoonar]

call round: I'll call round
tomorrow vou aí amanhã [voh
a-**ee** aman-y**a**ng]

camcorder a c**â**mara de vídeo
[di v**ee**d-yoo]

camera a m**á**quina fotogr**á**fica
[m**a**kina footoogr**a**fika]

camera shop a loja de artigos
fotogr**á**ficos [l**o**Ja dart**ee**goosh
fotogr**a**fikoosh]

camp acamp**ar**
can we camp here? podemos
acampar aqui? [pood**ay**moosh
– ak**ee**]

camping gas o g**á**s para
campismo [g**a**sh par
kamp**ee**Jmoo]

campsite o parque de
campismo [park di
kamp**ee**Jmoo]

Portugal has over a hundred au-
thorized campsites, most of
them small, low-key and attrac-
tively located. Charges are per
person and per tent, with
showers and parking extra; even
so, they are very reasonably
priced. You can get a fairly
complete list of campsites from
any Portuguese tourist office, or
a detailed booklet called **Roteiro
Campista** (with prices, exact
locations, facilities, etc) from
Portuguese bookshops.
You'll need an international
camping carnet to stay on most
sites in Portugal. It serves as
→

useful identification and covers
you for third party insurance
when camping.
Camping outside official
grounds is legal, but has certain
restrictions. You're not allowed
to camp in urban zones, in
zones where the water sources
are protected, or less than 1km
from campsites, beaches or
other places frequented by the
public.
However, the Algarve is an
exception: this is the only
region where camping rough is
banned.

can a l**a**ta
a can of beer uma lata de
cerveja [di sirv**ay**Ja]

can*: can you ...? pode
voc**ê** ...? [pod vos**ay**]
can I have ...? posso ter ...?
[p**o**soo tayr]
I can't ... n**ã**o posso ... [nowng]

Canada o Canad**á**

Canadian canadiano [kanad-
y**a**noo]
I'm Canadian (man/woman) sou
canadiano/canadi**a**na [soh]

canal o can**al**

cancel cancelar [kansil**a**r]

candle a v**e**la

candies os rebuçados
[riboos**a**doosh]

canoe a canoa [kan**oh**-a]

canoeing a canoagem [kanwa-
J**ay**ng]

can-opener o abre-latas
[abrilatash]

cap (hat) o boné [booneh]
(of bottle) a tampa

car o carro [karroo]
by car de carro

caravan a roulotte [roolot]

caravan site o parque de
campismo [park di
kampeeJmoo]

carburettor o carburador
[karbooradohr]

card (birthday etc) o cartão
[kartowng]
here's my (business) card aqui
está o meu cartão (de
visitas) [akee shta oo may-oo
kartowng (di vizeetash)]

cardigan o casaco de malha
[kazakoo di mal-ya]

cardphone o telefone de cartão
[telefohn di kartowng]

careful cuidadoso
[kwidadohzoo]
be careful! cuidado!
[kwidadoo]

caretaker (man/woman) o/a
guarda [gwarda]

car ferry o ferry-boat

car hire o aluguer de
automóveis [aloogehr
dowtoomovaysh]
see rent

carnival o carnaval

car park o parque de
estacionamento [park di sh
tas-yonamayntoo]

carpet a carpete [karpeht]

carriage (of train) a carruagem

[karrwa-Jayng]

carrier bag o saco plástico
[sakoo plashtikoo]

carrot a cenoura [sinohra]

carry levar [livar]

carry-cot o porta-bebés [porta-
bebehsh]

carton o pacote [pakot]

carwash a lavagem automática
[lavaJayng owtoomatika]

case (suitcase) a mala [mala]

cash o dinheiro [deen-yayroo]
(verb) descontar
[dishkongtar]
will you cash this for me?
pode descontar isto para
mim? [pod – eeshtoo – meeng]
see bank

cash desk a caixa [kīsha]

cash dispenser o caixa
automático [owtoomatikoo]

cassette a cassete

cassette recorder o gravador de
cassetes [gravadohr di]

castle o castelo [kashtehloo]

casualty department o serviço
de urgências [sirveesoo
doorJayns-yash]

cat o gato [gatoo]

catch pegar, apanhar [apan-
yar]
where do we catch the bus
to ...? onde podemos
apanhar o autocarro
para ...? [ohnd poodaymooz
apan-yar oo owtookarroo]

cathedral a catedral [katidral]

Catholic (adj) católico
[katolikoo]

cauliflower a couve-flor [kohv-flor]

cave a caverna

ceiling o tecto [tehtoo]

celery o alho francês [al-yoo fransaysh]

cellar (for wine) a cave [kav]

cellular phone o telefone celular [telefohn siloolar]

cemetery o cemitério [simitehr-yoo]

centigrade* centígrado [senteegradoo]

centimetre* o centímetro [senteemitroo]

central central [sen-tral]

central heating o aquecimento central [akesimayntoo]

centre o centro [sayntroo]
how do we get to the city centre? como é que vamos para o centro da cidade? [kohmoo eh ki vamoosh – oo sayntroo da sidad]

cereal os cereais [siri-īsh]

certainly certamente [sirtamaynt]
certainly not certamente que não [ki nowng]

chair a cadeira [kadayra]

champagne o champanhe [shampan-yi]

change (money) o troco [trohkoo]
(verb: money) trocar [trookar]
can I change this for ...? posso trocar isto por ...? [posoo – eeshtoo]
I don't have any change não

tenho troco [nowng tayn-yoo]
can you give me change for a 10 escudos note? pode trocar-me uma nota de dez escudos? [pod trookarmi ooma – di dez-shkoodoosh]

•••••• DIALOGUE ••••••

do we have to change (trains)? temos de mudar? [taymoosh di moodar]
yes, change at Coimbra/no, it's a direct train sim, troque em Coimbra/não, é um comboio directo [seeng tro-keeng kweembra/nowng eh oong komboh-yo direhtoo]

changed: to get changed mudar de roupa [moodar di rohpa]

chapel a capela [kapehla]

charge o preço [praysoo]
(verb) custar [kooshtar]

charge card o cartão de débito total [kartowng di dehbeetoo tootal]
see credit card

cheap barato [baratoo]
do you have anything cheaper? tem alguma coisa mais barata? [tayng algooma koh-iza mīsh]

check (US) o cheque [shehk]
(US: bill) a conta
see bill

check verificar
could you check the ..., please? pode verificar o ..., se faz favor? [pod – oo ... si fash favohr]

checkbook o livro de cheques
[**lee**vroo di shehksh]
check card o cartão de
garantia [kart**ow**ng di
garant**ee**-a]
check-in o ch**e**ck-in
check in fazer o check in
[faz**ay**r oo]
where do we have to check in?
onde temos que fazer o
check in? [**oh**nd t**ay**mooshk]
cheek (on face) a bochecha
[boosh**ay**sha]
cheerio! adeuzinho! [aday-
ooz**ee**n-yoo]
cheers! (toast) saúde! [sa-**oo**d]
cheese o queijo [k**ay**Joo]
chemist's a farmácia [farm**a**s-ya]
see **pharmacy**
cheque o cheque [shehk]
do you take cheques? aceitam
cheques? [as**ay**towng shehksh]

Travellers' cheques are accepted by all Portuguese banks
and by exchange bureaux
(**câmbios**) at airports and
major train stations. However,
commission rates can be
extremely high, so you might
prefer to use a credit card at
a cashpoint machine/ATM,
which incurs a small charge.
Alternatively, most British
banks can issue current account
holders with a Eurocheque card
and cheque book, with which
you can pay for things in some →

shops and get cash from the
majority of Portuguese banks;
you'll pay a few pounds service
charge a year but usually no
commission on transactions.

cheque book o livro de
cheques [**lee**vroo di shehksh]
cheque card o cartão de
garantia [kart**ow**ng di
garant**ee**-a]
cherry a cereja [sir**ay**Ja]
chess o xadrez [shadr**ay**sh]
chest o peito [p**ay**too]
chewing gum a pastilha
elástica [pasht**ee**l-ya il**a**shtika]
chicken o frango [frangoo]
chickenpox a varicela
[varis**eh**la]
child a criança [kry-**a**nsa]
children as crianças
[kry-**a**nsash]

Portugal is child-friendly and
families should find it as easy a
place to roam as any other
country. Cheap hotels and
pensões will only rarely charge
extra for children in their
parents' room, and restaurants
routinely offer small portions
and extra plates. Museums and
most sights don't usually charge
for small children.

child minder a **a**ma
children's pool a piscina
infantil [pish-s**ee**na infant**ee**l]

children's portion a dose para
crianças [doz – kry-**a**nsash]

chin o queixo [k**a**yshoo]

china a porcelana [poorsil**a**na]

Chinese (adj) chinês [shin**a**ysh]

chips as batatas fritas [bat**a**tash
fr**ee**tash]

chocolate o chocolate
[shookool**a**t]

  milk chocolate o chocolate
  com leite [kong layt]

  plain chocolate o chocolate
  puro [p**oo**roo]

  a hot chocolate um chocolate
  quente [oong – kaynt]

choose escolher [shkool-y**a**yr]

Christian name o nome próprio
[nohm pr**o**pr-yoo]

Christmas o Nat**a**l

  Christmas Eve a Véspera de
  Natal [v**eh**shpira di]

  merry Christmas! feliz Natal!
  [fil**ee**J]

church a igreja [igr**a**yJa]

cider a cidra [s**ee**dra]

cigar o charuto [shar**oo**too]

cigarette o cigarro [sig**a**rroo]

Portuguese public transport has
a no smoking policy. However,
mainly on the buses, you'll find
that some passengers don't obey
this rule – it is up to the driver
to enforce it.

cigarette lighter o isqueiro
[ishk**a**yroo]

cinema o cinema [sin**a**yma]

Going to the movies in Portugal
is extremely cheap, and films
are often shown with the
original (usually English-
language) soundtrack with
Portuguese subtitles. Listings
can be found in the local newspaper or on boards placed in the
central square of every small
town.

circle o círculo [s**ee**rkooloo]
(in theatre) a plateia [plat**a**y-a]

city a cidade [sid**a**d]

city centre o centro da cidade
[s**a**yntroo]

clean (adj) limpo [l**ee**mpoo]

  can you clean this for me?
  pode limpar isto para mim?
  [pod leemp**a**r **ee**shtoo –
  meeng]

cleaning solution (for contact
lenses) a solução de limpeza
[sooloos**ow**ng di leemp**a**yza]

cleansing lotion o creme de
limpeza [kraym di]

clear claro [kl**a**roo]

clever inteligente [intiliJ**a**ynt]

cliff o rochedo [roosh**a**ydoo]

climb escalar [shkal**a**r]

cling film a película aderente
[pil**ee**koola adir**a**ynt]

clinic a clínica [kl**ee**nika]

cloakroom o vestiário [visht-
y**a**r-yoo]

clock o relógio [ril**o**J-yoo]

close (verb) fechar [fish**a**r]

• • • • • DIALOGUE • • • • •

what time do you close? a que
horas fecham? [k-yorash
fayshowng]

we close at 8 p.m. on weekdays
and 6 p.m. on Saturdays fechamos
às oito da noite durante a
semana e às seis da tarde aos
sábados [fisha-mooz az-oh-itoo da
noh-it dooranta simana yash saysh
da tard owsh sabadoosh]

do you close for lunch? fecham
para almoço? [almohsoo]

yes, between 1 and 3.30 p.m. sim,
entre a uma e as três e meia da
tarde [seeng ayntri-a-ooma ee-ash
traysh ee may-a da tard]

closed fechado [fishadoo]
cloth (fabric) o tecido [tiseedoo]
  (for cleaning etc) pano [panoo]
clothes a roupa [rohpa]

---

clothing
Some of the more remote inland
regions of Portugal are still very
conservative in outlook, with
Catholicism and the family as
the bedrocks of society. Whilst
shorts are perfectly acceptable
in cities and beach resorts, more
modest attire is required when
visiting a church or religious
site. Nude sunbathing is illegal
except for in a few designated
areas and going topless is rare,
other than in the Algarve.

---

clothes line o estendal

[shtendal]
clothes peg a mola de roupa
  [di rohpa]
cloud a nuvem [noovayng]
cloudy enevoado [inivwadoo]
clutch a embraiagem [aymbrï-
  aJayng]
coach (bus) o autocarro
  [owtookarroo]
  (on train) a carruagem
  [karrwa-Jayng]
coach station a estação dos
  autocarros [shtasowng dooz
  owtookarroosh]
coach trip a excursão
  [shkoorsowng]
coast a costa [koshta]
  on the coast na costa
coat (long coat) o sobretudo
  [soobritoodoo]
  (jacket) o casaco [kazakoo]
coathanger a cruzeta
  [kroozayta]
cockroach a barata
cocoa o cacau [kakow]
coconut o coco [kohkoo]
cod o bacalhau fresco [bakal-
  yow frayshkoo]
  dried cod o bacalhau
code (for phoning) o indicativo
  [indikateevoo]
  what's the (dialling) code for
  Oporto? qual é o indicativo
  do Porto? [kwal eh oo – doo
  pohrtoo]
coffee o café [kafeh]
  two coffees, please dois
  cafés, por favor [doh-ish
  kafehsh poor favohr]

Useful terms are:

uma bica/um café small black, espresso-type coffee

um garoto/um pingo small coffee with milk

um galão large coffee with milk, often very weak, served in a tall glass

café descafeinado decaffeinated coffee

For white coffee that tastes of coffee rather than diluted warm milk, ask for **um café duplo com um pouco de leite** [oong kaf**eh** d**oo**ploo kong oong p**oh**koo di layt].

coin a moeda [mw**eh**da]

Coke® a coca-c**o**la

cold frio [fr**ee**-oo]

  I'm cold tenho frio [t**ay**n-yoo]

  I have a cold estou constipado [shtoh konshtip**a**doo]

collapse: he's collapsed ele desmaiou [ayl diJm**ee**-oh]

collar o colarinho [koolar**een**-yoo]

collect buscar [boosh**kar**]

  I've come to collect ... vim buscar ... [veeng boosh**kar**]

collect call a chamada paga no destinatário [sham**a**da p**a**ga noo dishtinat**ar**-yoo]

college o colégio [kool**ehJ**-yoo]

colour a cor [kohr]

  do you have this in other colours? tem isto de outras

cores? [tayng **ee**shto-di **oh**trash k**oh**rish]

colour film o filme colorido [feelm kooloor**ee**doo]

comb o pente [paynt]

come* vir [veer]

•••••• **DIALOGUE** ••••••

  where do you come from? donde é? [dohnd**eh**]

  I come from Edinburgh sou de Edimburgo [soh dedeenb**oo**rgoo]

come back volt**ar**

  I'll come back tomorrow volto amanhã [v**o**ltoo aman-y**a**ng]

come in entrar [aynt**rar**]

comfortable confortável [konfoort**a**vil]

compact disc o CD [say day]

company (business) a companhia [kompan-y**ee**-a]

compartment (on train) o compartimento [kompartim**ay**ntoo]

compass a bússola [b**oo**soola]

complain reclamar [riklam**ar**]

complaint a reclamação [riklamas**ow**ng]

  I have a complaint tenho uma reclamação [t**ay**n-yoo]

completely completamente [komplitam**ay**nt]

computer o computador [kompootad**ohr**]

concert o concerto [kons**ay**rtoo]

concussion o traumatismo [trowmat**ee**Jmoo]

conditioner (for hair) o creme amaciador [kraym amas-yad**ohr**] condom o preservativo [prizirvat**ee**voo]

conference a conferência [konfir**ayn**s-ya]

confirm confirmar [konfir**mar**]

congratulations! parabéns! [parab**ayn**gsh]

connecting flight o voo de ligação [v**oh**-oo di ligas**ow**ng]

connection a ligação

conscious consciente [konsh-sy**ayn**t]

constipation a prisão de ventre [priz**ow**ng di vayntr]

consulate o consulado [konsool**a**doo]

contact contactar

contact lenses as lentes de contacto [layntsh di kont**a**too]

contraceptive o contraceptivo [kontrasipt**ee**voo]

convenient conveniente [konvin-y**ay**nt]
  that's not convenient não é conveniente [nowng eh]

cook cozinhar [kozeen-y**ar**]
  not cooked mal cozido [kooz**ee**doo]

cooker o fogão [foog**ow**ng]

cookie a bolacha [bool**a**sha]

cooking utensils os utensílios de cozinha [ootaynse**el**-yoosh di kooz**ee**n-ya]

cool fresco [fr**ay**shkoo]

cork a rolha [r**oh**l-ya]
  (material) a cortiça [koorte**e**sa]

corkscrew o saca-rolhas [saka-r**oh**l-yash]

corner o canto [k**an**too]
  in the corner no canto [noo]

cornflakes os cornflakes

correct (right) certo [s**eh**rtoo]

corridor o corredor [koorrid**ohr**]

cosmetics os cosméticos [kooJm**eh**tikoosh]

cost custar [koosht**ar**]
  how much does it cost? quanto custa? [kwantoo k**oo**shta]

cot a cama de bebé [k**a**ma di beb**eh**]

cotton a algodão [algood**ow**ng]

cotton wool o algodão em rama [ayng]

couch (sofa) o sofá [soof**a**]

couchette o beliche [bil**ee**sh]

cough a tosse [tos]

cough medicine o xarope [shar**op**]

could: could you ...? podia ...? [pood**ee**-a]
  could I have ...? queria ...? [kir**ee**-a]
  I couldn't ... não seria capaz de ... [nowng sir**ee**-a kapaJ di]

country (nation) o país [pa-**ee**sh]
  (countryside) o campo [k**a**mpoo]

countryside o campo

couple (two people) o casal [kaz**al**]
  a couple of ... um par de ... [oong par di]

courgette a courgette

courier (man/woman) o/a guia [g**ee**-a]

course (main course etc) o prato [pr**a**too]

of course é claro [eh klaroo]
of course not claro que não [ki nowng]
cousin (male/female) o primo [preemoo], a prima
cow a vaca
crab o caranguejo [karang-gayJoo]
cracker a bolacha de água e sal [boolasha dagwa ee]
craft shop a loja de artesanato [loJa dartizanatoo]
crash a colisão [kolisowng]
  I've had a crash tive uma colisão [teev ooma]
crazy doido [doh-idoo]
cream as natas [natash]
  (lotion) o creme [kraym]
  (colour) creme
creche a creche
credit card o cartão de crédito [kartowng di krehdeetoo]
  do you take credit cards? aceitam cartões de crédito? [asaytowng kartoyngsh]

Visa, American Express and Mastercard are the most useful credit cards in Portugal, though many smaller places and even some upmarket hotels do not accept them. In the banks of large towns, however, there are increasing numbers of cashpoint machines/ATMs for credit card cash advances (don't forget your PIN number). They charge interest on the with-→

drawal from day one, plus a currency conversion fee, as do the banks which give cash advances on the cards over the counter.

•••••• DIALOGUE ••••••

can I pay by credit card? posso pagar com cartão de crédito? [posoo – kong]
which card do you want to use? que cartão deseja utilizar? [ki kartowng disayJa ootilizar]
Access/Visa
yes, sir sim, senhor [seeng sin-yor]
what's the number? qual é o número? [kwaleh oo noomiroo]
and the expiry date? e a data de validade? [ya data di validad]

crisps as batatas fritas [batatash freetash]
crockery a loiça [loh-isa]
crossing (by sea) a travessia [travisee-a]
crossroads o cruzamento [kroozamayntoo]
crowd a multidão [mooltidowng]
crowded apinhado [apeen-yadoo]
crown (on tooth) a ponte [pohnt]
cruise o cruzeiro [kroozayroo]
crutches as muletas [moolaytash]
cry chorar [shoorar]
cucumber o pepino [pipeenoo]
cup a chávena [shavena]
  a cup of ..., please uma

chávena de ..., se faz favor
[si fash fav**oh**r]
cupboard o armário [arm**ar**-yoo]
cure curar [k**oor**ar]
curly encaracolado [ayn-
karakool**a**doo]
current a corrente [k**oorraynt**]
curtains a cortinas
[koort**ee**nash]
cushion a almofada [almoof**a**da]
custom o hábito [**a**beetoo]
customs a alfândega [alf**a**ndiga]
cut o corte [kort]
(verb) cortar
I've cut myself cortei-me
[koort**aymi**]
cutlery os talheres [tal-y**eh**rish]
cycling o ciclismo [sikl**ee**Jmoo]
cyclist (man/woman) o/a ciclista
[sikl**ee**shta]

D

dad o papá
daily diariamente [d-yar-
yam**aynt**]
(adj) diário [d-y**ar**-yo]
damage avariar [avari-**ar**]
damaged avariado [avari-**a**do]
I'm sorry, I've damaged this
desculpe, avariei isto
[dishk**oo**lp avari-**ay ee**shtoo]
damn! raios me partam!
[**ra**-yoosh mi **partowng**]
damp (adj) húmido [**oo**meedoo]
dance a dança [**dansa**]
(verb) dançar
would you like to dance?
queres dançar? [k**eh**rish]

dangerous perigoso
[pirig**oh**zoo]
Danish (adj, language)
dinamarquês [dinamark**ay**sh]
dark (adj) escuro [shk**oo**roo]
it's getting dark está a
escurecer [sht**a**-a-shkoores**ay**r]
date*: what's the date today?
qual é a d**a**ta hoje? [kwal eh –
ohJ]
let's make a date for next
Monday vamos marc**ar** para
a próxima segunda-feira
[**va**moosh – pr**o**sima sig**oo**nda
f**ay**ra]
dates (fruit) as tâmaras
[t**a**marash]
daughter a filha [**feel**-ya]
daughter-in-law a nora
dawn a madrugada
[madroog**a**da]
at dawn de madrugada [di]
day o dia [d**ee**-a]
the day after o dia seguinte
[sig**ee**nt]
the day after tomorrow depois
de amanhã [dip**oh**-ish
daman-y**a**ng]
the day before o dia anterior
[antir-y**oh**r]
the day before yesterday
anteontem [ant-y**oh**ntayng]
every day todos os dias
[t**oh**dooz-ooJ d**ee**-ash]
all day o dia todo [t**oh**doo]
in two days' time dentro de
dois dias [d**ay**ntroo di d**oh**-iJ]
have a nice day bom dia
[bong]

day trip a excursão de um dia
[shkoors**ow**ng doong d**ee**-a]

dead morto [m**oh**rtoo]

deaf surdo [s**oo**rdoo]

deal (business) o negócio
[nig**o**s-yoo]

  it's a deal é negócio fechado
[eh – fish**a**doo]

death a morte [mort]

decaffeinated coffee o café
descafeinado [kaf**eh**
dishkafay-een**a**doo]

December Dezembro
[dez**ay**mbroo]

decide decidir [disid**ee**r]

  we haven't decided yet ainda
não decidimos [a-**ee**nda
nowng disid**ee**-moosh]

decision a decisão [disiz**ow**ng]

deck (on ship) o convés
[konv**eh**sh]

deckchair a cadeira de lona
[kad**ay**ra di l**oh**na]

deep fundo [f**oo**ndoo]

definitely de certeza [di
sirt**ay**za]

  definitely not de certeza que
não [ki nowng]

degree (qualification) a
licenciatura [lisayns-yat**oo**ra]

delay o atraso [atr**a**zoo]

deliberately de propósito [di
proop**o**zitoo]

delicatessen a charcutaria
[sharkootar**ee**-a]

delicious delicioso [dilis-y**oh**zo]

deliver entregar [ayntrig**a**r]

delivery (of mail) a distribuição
[dishtribwees**ow**ng]

Denmark a Dinamarca
[dinam**a**rka]

dental floss o fio dentário
[f**ee**-oo dent**a**r-yoo]

dentist (man/woman) o/a dentista
[dent**ee**shta]

•••••• DIALOGUE ••••••

it's this one here é este aqui [eh
ayshtak**ee**]

this one? este?

no that one não, aquele [nowng
ak**ay**l]

here aqui

yes sim [seeng]

dentures a dentadura postiça
[dentad**oo**ra poosht**ee**sa]

deodorant o desodorizante
[dizoodooriz**a**nt]

department o departamento
[dipartam**ay**ntoo]

department store os grandes
armazéns [grandz
armaz**ay**ngsh]

departure a saída [sa-**ee**da]

departure lounge a sala de
embarque [daymb**a**rk]

depend: it depends depende
[dip**ay**nd]

  it depends on ... depende
de ... [di]

deposit (payment) o depósito
[dip**o**zitoo]

description a descrição [dishkri-
s**ow**ng]

dessert a sobremesa
[sobrim**ay**za]

destination o destino
[disht**ee**noo]

develop desenvolver
 [disaynvolv**ayr**]

•••••• DIALOGUE ••••••

 could you develop these films?
 pode revelar estas películas?
 [pod riv**ilar eh**shtash pil**ee**koolash]
 yes, certainly sim, com certeza
 [seeng kong sirt**ayz**a]
 when will they be ready? quando
 ficam prontas? [kw**a**ndoo f**ee**kowng
 pr**oh**ntash]
 tomorrow afternoon amanhã à
 tarde [aman-y**a**ng a tard]
 how much is the four-hour service?
 quanto custa o serviço de quatro
 horas? [kw**a**ntoo k**oo**shtoo sirv**ee**so
 di kw**a**troo-w**o**rash]

diabetic (man/woman) o
 diabético [d-yab**eh**tikoo], a
 diabética
 diabetic foods os alimentos
 para diabéticos
 [alim**ay**ntoosh
 d-yab**eh**tikoosh]
dial marcar
dialling code o indicativo
 [indikat**ee**voo]

To phone abroad from Portugal,
dial 00, the country code (given
below), followed by the area
code (minus the initial zero)
and the number:

Australia 61	Canada 1
Ireland 353	New Zealand 64
UK 44	USA 1
	→

Portuguese Area Codes

Braga 053	Porto 02
Coimbra 039	Setúbal 065
Évora 066	Tavira 081
Faro 089	Viana do
Guarda 071	Castelo 058
Lagos 082	Vila Real 150
Lisboa 01	Viseu 032

diamond o diamante [d-yam**a**nt]
diaper a fralda
diarrhoea a diarreia [dy-arr**ay**-a]
 **do you have something for
 diarrhoea?** tem algum
 antilaxante? [tayng alg**oo**ng
 anti-lash**a**nt]
diary (for business) a agenda
 [a**ʒay**nda]
 (for personal experiences) o diário
 [oo di**a**r-yoo]
dictionary o dicionário [dis-
 yoon**a**r-yoo]
didn't* see not
die morrer [moorr**ayr**]
diesel o gasóleo [gaz**o**l-yoo]
diet a dieta [d-y**eh**ta]
 I'm on a diet estou de dieta
 [shtoh di]
 I have to follow a special diet
 tenho que seguir uma dieta
 especial [t**ay**n-yoo ki sig**eer**
 ooma – shpis-y**al**]
difference a diferença
 [difir**ay**nsa]
 what's the difference? qual é a
 diferença? [kwal eh]
different diferente [difir**ay**nt]
 this one is different este é

diferente [aysht eh]
a different table outra mesa
[**oh**tra m**ay**za]
difficult difícil [dif**ee**sil]
difficulty a dificuldade
[difikoold**a**d]
dinghy o bote de borracha [bot
di boorr**a**sha]
dining room a sala de jantar [di
Jant**a**r]
dinner (evening meal) o jant**a**r
to have dinner jantar
direct (adj) directo [dir**eh**too]
is there a direct train? há um
comboio directo? [a oong
komb**oh**-yo]
direction a direcção
[direhs**ow**ng]
which direction is it? em que
direcção fica? [ayng ki –
f**ee**ka]
is it in this direction? fica
nesta direcção? [n**eh**shta]
directory enquiries as
informações
[infoormas**oy**ngsh]

> For directory enquiries within
> Portugal, dial 118; for interna-
> tional enquiries, dial 166.

dirt a sujidade [sooJid**a**d]
dirty sujo [**soo**Joo]
disabled deficiente [difis-y**ay**nt]
is there access for the
disabled? há acesso para
deficientes? [a as**eh**soo – difis-
y**ay**ntsh]
disappear desaparecer

[dizaparis**ay**r]
it's disappeared desapareceu
[dizaparis**ay**-oo]
disappointed decepcionado
[disips-yoon**a**doo]
disappointing decepcionante
[disips-yon**a**nt]
disaster a tragédia [traJ**eh**d-ya]
disco o disco [d**ee**shkoo]
discount o desconto
[dishk**oh**ntoo]
is there a discount? pode
fazer-me um desconto? [pod
faz**ay**rm-oong]
disease a doença [dw**ay**nsa]
disgusting nojento [nooJ**ay**ntoo]
dish (meal) o prato [pr**a**too]
(bowl) a tigela [tiJ**eh**la]
dishcloth o pano de loiça
[p**a**noo di l**oh**-isa]
disinfectant o desinfectante
[dizinfit**a**nt]
disk (for computer) a disquete
[dishk**eh**t]
disposable diapers/nappies as
fraldas descartáveis [fraldaJ
dishkart**a**vaysh]
distance a distância
[disht**a**ns-ya]
in the distance ao longe [ow
lohnJ]
distilled water a água destilada
[**a**gwa dishtil**a**da]
district o bairro [b**ī**rroo]
disturb perturbar [pirtoob**a**r]
diversion (detour) o desvio
[diJv**ee**-oo]
diving board a prancha de
saltos [pr**a**nsha di s**a**ltoosh]

divorced divorciado [divoors-ya**doo**]

dizzy: I feel dizzy sinto tonturas [s**ee**ntoo tont**oo**rash]

do* fazer [faz**ay**r]

what shall we do? que vamos fazer? [ki-v**a**moosh]

how do you do it? como se faz? [**koh**moo si fash]

will you do it for me? importa-se de mo fazer? [imp**o**rtasi di moo]

•••••• DIALOGUES ••••••

how do you do? muito prazer [m**wee**ngtoo praz**ay**r]

nice to meet you muito prazer

what do you do? (work) o que é que faz? [oo ki **eh**-ki faJ]

I'm a teacher, and you? (said by man/woman) sou professor/professor**a**, e você? [soh – ee vos**ay**]

I'm a student sou estud**a**nte

what are you doing this evening? que vai fazer hoje à noite? [ki vī – **oh**J-ya n**oh**-it]

we're going out for a drink, do you want to join us? vamos tomar uma bebida, quer vir conosco? [v**a**moosh toom**a**r **oo**ma bib**ee**da kehr veer kon**oh**shkoo]

do you want cream? quer natas? [n**a**tash]

I do, but she doesn't quero, mas ela não [k**eh**roo maz-**eh**la nowng]

doctor (man/woman) o médico [m**eh**dikoo], a m**é**dica

we need a doctor precisamos de um médico [prisiz**a**moosh doong]

please call a doctor por favor, chame um médico [poor fav**oh**r sham oong]

In the case of serious illness, you can get the address of an English-speaking doctor from a British or American consular office or, with luck, from the local police or tourist office, or a major hotel.

As an EU country, Portugal has reciprocal health agreements with other member states for free health care. EU citizens will need form E111, available from main post offices. Reassuring as the EU health agreements may sound, however, some form of travel insurance is still worthwhile – and essential for North Americans and Australasians, who must pay for any medical treatment in Portugal.

In many parts of Portugal public health care lags behind much of northern Europe and you may well prefer to get private treatment. With insurance you have to pay on the spot, but will be able to claim back the cost later, along with the charges for any drugs prescribed by pharmacies. Be sure to keep all your receipts.

In an emergency dial 115.

•••••• DIALOGUE ••••••

where does it hurt? onde dói?
[ohnd doy]

right here bem aqui [bayng akee]

does that hurt now? dói agora?

yes sim [seeng]

take this to the pharmacy leve isto
à farmácia [lehv **ee**sht-wa
farm**a**s-ya]

document o documento
[dookoom**ay**ntoo]

dog o cão [kowng]

doll a boneca [boon**eh**ka]

domestic flight voo doméstico
[v**oh**oo doom**eh**shtikoo]

donkey o burro [b**oo**rroo]

don't!* não! [nowng]
don't do that! não faça isto!
[f**a**sa **ee**shtoo]

door a porta

doorman o porteiro
[poort**ay**roo]

double duplo [d**oo**ploo]

double bed a cama de casal [di
k**a**zal]

double room o quarto de casal
[kw**a**rtoo]

doughnut a fartura [fart**oo**ra]

down embaixo [aymb**ī**shoo]
down here aqui embaixo
[ak**ee**]
put it down over there deite-o
lá [d**ay**t-yoo la]
it's down there on the right é
lá embaixo, à direita [eh – a
dir**ay**ta]
it's further down the road é
nesta rua mais abaixo

[n**e**shta r**oo**-a mīz ab**ī**shoo]

downmarket (restaurant etc)
barato [bar**a**too]

downstairs embaixo
[aymb**ī**shoo]

dozen a dúzia [d**oo**z-ya]
half a dozen a meia dúzia
[m**ay**-a]

drain (in sink, in road) o cano de
esgoto [k**a**noo diJg**oh**too]

draught beer imperial [eempir-
y**a**l]

draughty: it's draughty faz
corrente de ar [fash koorr**ay**nt
dar]

drawer a gaveta [gav**ay**ta]

drawing o desenho [dis**ay**n-yoo]

dreadful horrível [ohrr**ee**vil]

dream o sonho [s**oh**n-yoo]

dress o vestido [visht**ee**doo]

dressed: to get dressed vestir-
se [visht**ee**rsi]

dressing (for cut) o penso
[p**ay**nsoo]
salad dressing o tempero
[taymp**ay**roo]

dressing gown o roupão
[rohp**ow**ng]

drink a bebida [bib**ee**da]
(verb) beber [bib**ay**r]
a cold drink uma bebida
fresca [**oo**ma – fr**ay**shka]
fancy a quick drink? vamos
tomar uma bebida? [v**a**moosh
toom**a**r **oo**ma bib**ee**da]
can I get you a drink? o que
bebe? [oo ki behb]
what would you like (to drink)?
o que gostaria de beber?

[gooshtar**ee**-ya di]
I don't drink não bebo [nowng b**ay**boo]
I'll just have a drink of water só um copo de água [saw oong k**o**poo d**a**gwa]
drinking water a água potável [**a**gwa poot**a**vil]
is this drinking water? esta água é potável? [shta – eh]

Water is drinkable from the tap anywhere in the country, and from some fresh water sources, too. Be wary, however, of pools and streams in the south of the country.

drive conduzir [kondooz**eer**]
we drove here viemos de carro [v-y**ay**moosh di k**a**rroo]
I'll drive you home levo-o a casa de carro [l**eh**voo a k**a**za di k**a**rroo]

driving
Car rental rates in Portugal are among the lowest in Europe, but bear in mind that Portugal has one of the highest accident rates, mainly because the narrow and winding roads fail to deter impatient drivers from attempting to overtake at high speeds. When driving, always keep your wits about you, keep your speed down and look out for cars overtaking in the →

opposite direction but on your side of the road. Machismo is common, and male drivers sometimes find it an affront if they are overtaken by a woman. In such situations, try not to get aggravated; if necessary pull over and let the driver overtake. Traffic drives on the right; speed limits are 60km/hr in towns and villages; 90km/hr on normal roads; 120km/hr on motorways. At road junctions, unless there's a sign to the contrary, vehicles coming from the right have priority. If you're stopped by the police, they'll want to see your documents – carry them in the car at all times.
The legal alcohol limit when driving is .05 %, but do not drink and drive.
see **motorway**

driver (of car: man/woman) o condutor [kondoot**ohr**], a condut**o**ra
(of bus: man/woman) o/a motorista [mootoor**ee**shta]
driving licence a c**a**rta de condução [di kondoos**ow**ng]
drop: just a drop, please (of drink) só um pouco, se faz favor [saw oong p**oh**koo si fash fav**ohr**]
drug o medicamento [medikam**ay**ntoo]
drugs (narcotics) a droga

drunk (adj) bêbado [b**ay**badoo]
drunken driving a condução
  enquanto embriagado
  [kondoos**ow**ng aynkw**a**ntoo
  aymbr-yag**a**doo]
dry (adj) seco [s**ay**koo]
dry-cleaner a tinturaria
  [teentoorar**ee**-a]
duck o pato [p**a**too]
**due: he was due to arrive
  yesterday** ele devia chegar
  ontem [ayl div**ee**-a shig**a**r
  ohntayng]
  when is the train due? a que
  horas é o comboio? [k-y**o**raz
  eh oo komb**oh**-yo]
dull (pain) moinho [moo-**ee**n-yoo]
dummy (baby's) a chupeta
  [shoop**ay**ta]
during durante [door**a**nt]
dust o pó [paw]
dustbin o caixote de lixo
  [kīsh**o**t di l**ee**shoo]
dusty empoeirado [aympoo-
  ayr**a**doo]
Dutch holandês [oland**ay**sh]
duty-free (goods) duty-free
duty-free shop a free-shop

Apart from standard brands of
spirits, there are no great
savings to be made at airport
duty-free shops. For national
specialities – including wine,
port, and brandy – you're
better off buying from local
grocery and liquor stores.

---

duvet o edredão [idrid**ow**ng]

E

each (every) c**a**da
  how much are they each?
  quanto é cada um?
  [kwantw**eh** – oong]
ear a orelha [or**ay**l-ya]
earache: I have earache tenho
  dor de ouvidos [t**ay**n-yoo dohr
  dohv**ee**doosh]
early cedo [s**ay**doo]
  early in the morning de manhã
  cedo [di man-y**a**ng]
  I called by earlier passei aqui
  mais cedo [pas**ay** akee mīsh]
earrings os brincos
  [br**ee**nkoosh]
east o leste [lehsht]
  in the east no leste
Easter Semana Santa [sim**a**na],
  Páscoa [p**a**shkwa]
easy fácil [f**a**sil]
eat comer [koom**ayr**]
  we've already eaten, thanks
  (said by man/woman) já
  comemos, obrigado/
  obrig**a**da [Ja koom**ay**moosh
  obrig**a**doo]

---

eating habits
Lunch is usually served from
noon to 3 p.m. and dinner from
7.30 p.m. onwards, but you
shouldn't count on being able
to eat much after 10 p.m. outside the cities and tourist
resorts.
Eating alone in a Portuguese
→

---

restaurant is considered perfectly normal, even for women, particularly at lunchtime when many Portuguese eat a full three-course meal. Evening meals are more often family affairs; it is not uncommon to see a restaurant full of children playing even at midnight.

eau de toilette a eau de toilette EC CE [say eh]
economy class classe económica [klas-ekoon**oh**mika]
Edinburgh Edimburgo [edeenb**oo**rgoo]
eels as enguias [ing**ee**-ash]
egg o ovo [**oh**voo]
eggplant a beringela [bireen**Jeh**la]
either: either … or … ou … ou … [oh]
either of them nenhum deles [nin-y**oo**ng d**ay**lish]
elastic o elástico [il**a**shtikoo]
elastic band o elástico
elbow o cotovelo [kootoov**ay**loo]
electric eléctrico [el**eh**trikoo]
electrical appliances os aparelhos eléctricos [apar**ay**l-yoosh]
electric fire o aquecedor eléctrico [akesid**ohr**]
electrician o electricista [eletris**ee**shta]
electricity a electricidade [eletrisid**a**d]
see **voltage**

elevator (in building) o elevador [elevad**ohr**]
else: something else outra coisa [**oh**tra k**oh**-iza]
somewhere else noutro sítio [**noh**troo s**ee**t-yoo]

•••••• DIALOGUE ••••••
would you like anything else? deseja mais alguma coisa? [dis**ay**Ja mīz alg**oo**ma k**oh**-iza]
no, nothing else, thanks (said by man/woman) não, mais nada, obrigado/obrigada [nowng mīsh – obrig**a**doo]

embassy a embaixada [aymbīsh**a**da]
emergency a emergência [emirJ**ay**ns-ya]
this is an emergency! isto é uma emergência! [**ee**shtoo eh **oo**ma]
emergency exit a saída de emergência [sa-**ee**da di emayrJ**ay**ns-ya]
empty vazio [vaz**ee**-oo]
end o fim [feeng]
at the end of the street no fim da rua [noo feeng da r**oo**-a]
when does it end? quando acaba? [kw**a**ndoo]
engaged (toilet, telephone) ocupado [okoop**a**doo]
(to be married) noivo [n**oh**-ivoo]
engine (car) o motor [moot**ohr**]
England a Inglaterra [inglat**eh**rra]

English (adj, language) inglês [inglaysh]
I'm English (man/woman) sou inglês/inglesa [soh]
do you speak English? fala inglês?
enjoy: to enjoy oneself divertir-se [divirteersi]

•••••• DIALOGUE ••••••

how did you like the film? gostou do filme? [goostoh doo feelm]
I enjoyed it very much; did you enjoy it? gostei imenso, você gostou? [gooshtay imaynsoo vosay gooshtoh]

enjoyable divertido [divirteedoo]
enlargement (of photo) a ampliação [ampl-yasowng]
enormous enorme [enorm]
enough suficiente [soofis-yaynt]
there's not enough ... não há suficiente ... [nowng a]
it's not big enough não é suficientemente grande [eh soofis-yayntimaynt]
that's enough, thanks (said by man/woman) está bem, obrigado/obrigada [shta bayng obrigadoo]
entrance a entrada [ayntrada]
envelope o envelope [aynvilop]
epileptic (man/woman) o epiléptico [epilehptikoo], a epiléptica
equipment o equipamento [ekipamayntoo]
error un erro [ayrroo]

especially especialmente [shpis-yalmaynt]
essential essencial [esayns-yal]
it is essential that ... é essencial que ... [eh – ki]
EU UE [oo eh]
Eurocheque o Eurocheque [ay-ooroooshehk]
see cheque
Eurocheque card o cartão Eurocheque [kartowng]
Europe a Europa [ay-ooropa]
European (adj) europeu [ay-ooroopay-oo], (f) europeia [ay-ooroopay-a]
even: even the British até os britânicos [ateh-oosh britanikoosh]
even men até mesmo os homens [ateh mayJmo osh ohmayngsh]
even if ... mesmo se ... [si]
evening a noite [noh-it]
this evening esta noite [ehshta]
in the evening à noite
evening meal o jantar [oo Jantar]
eventually no fim [noo feeng]
ever já [Ja]

•••••• DIALOGUE ••••••

have you ever been to Lamego? já esteve alguma vez em Lamego? [Ja shtayv algooma vaysh ayng lamaygoo]
yes, I was there two years ago sim, estive lá há dois anos [seeng shteev la a doh-iz anoosh]

every cada
  every day todos os dias
  [**toh**dooz-ooz d**ee**-ash]
everyone toda a gente [**toh**da a
  Jaynt]
everything tudo [**too**doo]
everywhere em toda a parte
  [ayng t**oh**da part]
exactly! exactamente!
  [ezatam**ay**nt]
exam o exame [ez**a**m]
example o exemplo
  [ez**ay**mploo]
  for example por exemplo
  [poor]
excellent excelente [ish-sil**ay**nt]
  excellent! excelente!
except excepto [ish-s**eh**too]
excess baggage o excesso de
  bagagem [ish-s**eh**soo di
  baga**Jay**ng]
exchange rate a cotação
  cambial [kootas**ow**ng
  kamby**a**l]
exciting emocionante [emoos-
  yoon**a**nt]
excuse me (to get past) com
  licença [kong lis**ay**nsa]
  (to get attention) se faz favor [si
  fash fav**ohr**]
  (to say sorry) desculpe
  [dishk**oo**lp]
exhaust (pipe) o tubo de
  escape [t**oo**boo dishk**a**p]
exhausted (tired) exausto
  [ez**ow**shtoo]
exhibition a exposição
  [shpoozis**ow**ng]
exit a saída [sa-**ee**da]

where's the nearest exit? onde
  é a saída mais próxima?
  [ohnd**eh** – mīsh pr**o**sima]
expect esperar [shpir**ar**]
expensive caro [k**a**roo]
experienced experiente [shpir-
  y**ay**nt]
explain explicar [shplik**ar**]
  can you explain that? pode
  explicar-me isso? [pod
  shplik**ar**m **ee**soo]
express (mail) o correio
  expresso [koorr**ay**-oo
  shpr**eh**soo]
  (train) o Rápido [r**a**pidoo]
extension (telephone) a extensão
  [shtens**ow**ng]
  extension 221, please
  extensão duzentos e vinte e
  um, por favor [dooz**ay**ntooz ee
  v**ee**nti-oong poor fav**ohr**]
extension lead a extensão
  [shtens**ow**ng]
extra: can we have an extra
  one? pode dar-nos mais um/
  uma? [pod d**ar**-noosh mīsh
  oong/**oo**ma]
  do you charge extra for that?
  paga-se extra por isto?
  [p**a**gasi **ay**shtra poor **ee**shtoo]
extraordinary extraordinário
  [shtra-ohrdin**ar**-yoo]
extremely extremamente
  [shtremam**ay**nt]
eye o olho [**oh**l-yoo]
  will you keep an eye on my
  suitcase for me? pode dar
  uma olhada na minha mala,
  por favor? [pod dar-oomool-

yada na m**ee**n-ya m**a**la poor fav**oh**r]

eyebrow pencil o lápis para as sobrancelhas [lapsh p**a**rash sobrans**ay**l-yash]

eye drops as gotas para os olhos [g**oh**tash p**a**rooz ol-yoosh]

eyeglasses (US) os óculos [ok**oo**loosh]

eyeliner o lápis para os olhos [lapsh p**a**rooz ol-yoosh]

eye make-up remover o desmaquilhador de olhos [dishmakil-yad**oh**r dol-yoosh]

eye shadow a sombra para os olhos

F

face a c**a**ra

factory a fábrica [f**a**brika]

Fahrenheit* Farenheit

faint (verb) desmaiar [diJmī-**a**r]

she's fainted ela desmaiou [**eh**la diJmī-**oh**]

I feel faint sinto que vou desmaiar [s**ee**ntoo ki voh desmī-**a**r]

fair (funfair, tradefair) a feira [f**ay**ra]

(adj) justo [J**oo**shtoo]

fairly bastante [basht**a**nt]

fake falso [f**a**lsoo]

fall cair [ka-**ee**r]

she's had a fall ela deu uma queda [**eh**la d**ay**-oo **oo**ma k**eh**da]

fall o Outono [oht**oh**noo] in the fall no Outono [noo]

false falso [f**a**lsoo]

family a família [fam**ee**l-ya]

famous famoso [fam**oh**zoo]

fan (electrical) a ventoinha [vayntw**ee**n-ya]

(handheld) o leque [lehk]

(sports: man/woman) o adepto [ad**eh**ptoo], a adepta

fan belt a correia da ventoinha [korr**ay**-a da vayntw**ee**n-ya]

fantastic fantástico [fant**a**shtikoo]

far longe [lohnJ]

•••••• D I A L O G U E ••••••

is it far from here? é longe daqui? [eh – dak**ee**]

no, not very far não, não é muito longe [nowng – mw**ee**ngtoo]

well how far? bem, qual é a distância? [bayng kwal eh a disht**a**ns-ya]

it's about 20 kilometres são mais ou menos vinte quilómetros [sowng mīz oh m**ay**noosh v**ee**ngt kil**o**mitroosh]

fare o bilhete [bil-y**ay**t]

farm a quinta [k**ee**nta]

fashionable na m**o**da

fast rápido [r**a**pidoo]

fat (person) gordo [g**oh**rdoo]

(on meat) a gordura [goord**oo**ra]

father o pai [pī]

father-in-law o sogro [s**oh**groo]

faucet a torneira [toorn**ay**ra]

fault o defeito [dif**ay**too]

sorry, it was my fault desculpe, foi culpa minha

[foh-i koolpa meen-ya]
it's not my fault a culpa não é
minha [nowng eh meen-ya]
faulty avariado [avariadoo]
favourite favorito [favooreetoo]
fax o fax
fax: to send a fax mandar um
fax
February Fevereiro [fivrayroo]
feel sentir [saynteer]
I feel hot estou com calor
[shtoh kong kalohr]
I feel unwell não me sinto
bem [nowng mi seentoo bayng]
I feel like going for a walk
estou com vontade de dar
um passeio [shtoh kong vontad
di dar oong pasay-oo]
how are you feeling? como se
sente? [kohmoo si saynt]
I'm feeling better sinto-me
melhor [seentoomi mil-yor]
felt-tip (pen) a caneta de feltro
[kanayta di fayltroo]
fence a vedação [vidasowng]
fender o pára-choques [para-
shoksh]
ferry o ferry-boat
festival o festival [fishtival]
fetch buscar [booshkar]
I'll fetch him vou buscá-lo [voh
booshka-loo]
will you come and fetch me
later? pode vir buscar-me
mais tarde? [pod veer
booshkarmi mīsh tard]
feverish febril [febreel]
few: a few alguns [algoonsh]
I'll give you a few dou-lhe

alguns [dohl-yalgoonsh]
a few days poucos dias
[pohkoosh dee-ash]
fiancé o noivo [noh-ivoo]
fiancée a noiva
field o campo [kampoo]
fight a briga [breega]
figs os figos [feegoosh]
fill in preencher [pri-aynshayr]
do I have to fill this in? tenho
de preencher isto? [tayn-yoo
di – eeshtoo]
fill up encher [aynshayr]
fill it up, please encha o
depósito, por favor [aynsha
oo depozitoo poor favohr]
filling (in cake, sandwich) recheio
[rishay-oo]
(in tooth) o chumbo
[shoomboo]
film o filme [feelm]

•••••• DIALOGUE ••••••

do you have this kind of film? tem
este tipo de filme? [tayng aysht
teepo]
yes, how many exposures? sim,
quantas fotografias? [seeng
kwantash footoografee-ash]
36 trinta-e-seis [treentī-saysh]

film processing a revelação de
filmes [rivilasowng di feelmsh]
filter coffee o café de filtro
[kafeh di feeltroo]
filter papers os filtros de café
[feeltroosh]
filthy nojento [nooJayntoo]
find encontrar [aynkontrar]
I can't find it não consigo

encontrar [nowng kon**see**goo]
I've found it encontrei-o
[aynkongtr**ay**-oo]
find out descobrir
[dishkoobr**eer**]
could you find out for me?
pode descobrir para mim?
[pod — meeng]
fine (weather) bom [bong]
(punishment) a multa [**moo**lta]

• • • • • • DIALOGUE • • • • • •

how are you? como está? [k**oh**moo
shta]
I'm fine, thanks (said by man/
woman) bem, obrigado/obrigada
[bayng obrig**a**doo]

is that OK? assim está bem?
[a**see**ng shta bayng]
that's fine, thanks está bem,
obrigado/obrigada [shta]

finger o dedo [d**ay**doo]
finish terminar
I haven't finished yet ainda
não terminei [a-**ee**nda nowng
termin**ay**]
when does it finish? quando é
que termina? [kw**a**ndoo eh ki
term**ee**na]
fire o fogo [f**oh**goo]
(blaze) o incêndio
[ins**ay**nd-yoo]
fire! fogo!
can we light a fire here?
podemos fazer uma fogueira
aqui? [pood**ay**moosh faz**ay**r
ooma foog**ay**ra ak**ee**]
it's on fire está a arder [shta a
ard**ay**r]

fire alarm o alarme de
incêndios [al**a**rm dins**ay**nd-
yoosh]
fire brigade os bombeiros
[bomb**ay**roosh]

> For all emergency services dial
> 115.

fire escape a saída de
emergência [sa-**ee**da
demirJ**ay**ns-ya]
fire extinguisher o extintor
[shtint**ohr**]
first primeiro [prim**ay**roo]
I was first (said by man/woman)
eu era o primeiro/a primeira
[**ay**-oo **eh**ra]
at first ao princípio [ow
prins**ee**p-yoo]
the first time a prim**ei**ra vez
[vaysh]
first on the left primeira à
esquerda [**a**-shk**ay**rda]
first aid os primeiros socorros
[prim**ay**roosh sook**o**rroosh]
first aid kit a caixa de
primeiros socorros [k**i**sha di]
first class (travel etc) primeira
classe [klas]
first floor o primeiro and**a**r
(US) o rés de chão [rehJ
doo]
first name o nome próprio
[nohm pr**o**pr-yoo]
fish o peixe [paysh]
(verb) pescar [pishk**a**r]
fishing village a aldeia de
pescadores [ald**ay**-a di

Fi

pishkad**oh**rish]

fishmonger's a peixaria [payshar**ee**-a]

fit (attack) ataque [at**a**k]

fit: it doesn't fit me não me serve [nowng mi sehrv]

fitting room a cabina de provas [kab**ee**na di pr**o**vash]

fix (repair) repar**ar**

can you fix this? (repair) pode reparar isto? [pod – **ee**shtoo]

fizzy gasoso [gaz**oh**zoo]

flag a bandeira [band**ay**ra]

flannel a toalha de c**a**ra [tw**a**l-ya di]

flash (for camera) o flash

flat (apartment) o apartamento [apartam**ay**ntoo]

(adj) plano [pl**a**noo]

I've got a flat tyre tenho um pneu furado [t**ay**n-yoo oong pn**ay**-oo foor**a**doo]

flavour o sabor [sab**oh**r]

flea a pulga [p**oo**lga]

flight o voo [v**oh**-oo]

flight number o número de voo [n**oo**miroo di]

flippers as barbatanas [barbat**a**-nash]

flood a inundação [inoondas**ow**ng]

floor (of room) o chão [showng]

(storey) o and**ar**

on the floor no chão

florist a florista [floor**ee**shta]

flour a farinha [far**ee**n-ya]

flower a flor [flohr]

flu a gripe [greep]

fluent: he speaks fluent

Portuguese ele f**a**la português fluentemente [el – poortoog**ay**sh flwentim**ay**nt]

fly a mosca [m**oh**shka]

(verb: person) ir de avião [eer dav-y**ow**ng]

fog o nevoeiro [nivw**ay**roo]

foggy: it's foggy está enevoado [shta inivw**a**doo]

folk dancing a dança folclórica [d**a**nsa foolkl**o**rika]

folk music a música folclórica [m**oo**zika]

---

folksinging

Fado is Portugal's most famous music. It is lyrical and sentimental and thought to have its origins in African slave songs. There are several **Casas de Fados** in Lisbon and in other cities. You can also hear fado songs in an **Adega Típica**.

---

follow seguir [sig**ee**r]

follow me siga-me [s**ee**gami]

food a comida [koom**ee**da]

food poisoning a intoxicação alimentar [intoksikas**ow**ng]

food shop/store a mercearia [mirs-yar**ee**-a]

foot* (of person, measurement) o pé [peh]

on foot a pé

football (game) o futebol [footb**o**l]

(ball) a bola de futebol

football match o desafio de futebol [dizaf**ee**-oo di]

for: do you have something for ...? (headache/diarrhoea etc) tem alguma coisa para ...? [tayng algooma **koh**-iza]

•••••• DIALOGUES ••••••

who's the bacalhau for? para quem é o bacalhau? [kayng eh-oo bakal-**yow**]
that's for me é para mim [eh – m**ee**ng]
and this one? e este? [ee-**ay**sht]
that's for her é para ela [**eh**la]

where do I get the bus for Castelo de São Jorge? onde posso apanhar o autocarro para o Castelo de São Jorge? [ohnd p**o**soo apan-**yar** oo owt**oo**karroo paroo kasht**eh**loo di sowng JorJ]
the bus for o Castelo de São Jorge leaves from Praça do Comércio o autocarro para o Castelo de São Jorge sai da Praça do Comércio [sī da pr**a**sa doo koom**eh**rsyo]

how long have you been here for? há quanto tempo está aqui? [a kw**a**ntoo t**ay**mpoo shta ak**ee**]
I've been here for two days, how about you? estou aqui há dois dias, e você? [shtoh ak**ee** a d**oh**-iJ dee-ash ee vos**ay**]
I've been here for a week estou aqui há uma semana [shtoh ak**ee** a **oo**ma sim**a**na]

forehead a testa [**teh**shta]
foreign estrangeiro [shtranJ**ay**roo]
foreigner (man/woman) o

estrangeiro [shtranJ**ay**roo], a estrangeira
forest a floresta [floor**eh**shta]
forget esquecer [shkis**ay**r]
I forget, I've forgotten esqueci-me [shkis**ee**mi]
fork o garfo [**gar**foo]
(in road) a bifurcação [bifoorkas**ow**ng]
form (document) o impresso [impr**eh**soo]
formal (dress) de cerimónia [di sirim**on**-ya]
fortnight a quinzena [keenz**ay**na]
fortunately felizmente [filiJm**ay**nt]
forward: could you forward my mail? pode passar a enviar-me o correio? [pod – aynv-y**a**rmi oo koorr**ay**-oo]
forwarding address a nova morada [moor**a**da]
foundation cream o creme de base [kraym di baz]
fountain a fonte [fohnt]
foyer (of hotel, theatre) o foyer [fwi-**ay**]
fracture a fractura [frat**oo**ra]
France a França [fr**a**nsa]
free livre [**lee**vr]
(no charge) gratuito [grat**oo**-eetoo]
is it free (of charge)? é gratuito? [eh]
freeway a autoestrada [owtoosht**ra**da]
see motorway
freezer o congelador

[konʃiladohr]

French (adj, language) francês [fransaysh]

French fries as batatas fritas [batatash freetash]

frequent frequente [frikwaynt]
how frequent is the bus to Évora? com que frequência há autocarros para Évora? [kong ki frikwaynsya a owtookarroosh – ehvoora]

fresh fresco [frayshkoo]

fresh orange o sumo natural de laranja [soomoo natooral di laranʃa]

Friday sexta-feira [sayshta fayra]

fridge o frigorífico [frigooreefikoo]

fried frito [freetoo]

fried egg o ovo estrelado [ohvoo shtriladoo]

friend (male/female) o amigo [ameegoo], a amiga

friendly simpático [simpatikoo]

from de [di]
when does the next train from Braga arrive? quando chega o próximo comboio de Braga? [kwandoo shayg-oo prosimoo komboh-yo di]
from Monday to Friday de segunda a sexta-feira [di sigoonda-a sayshta fayra]
from next Thursday a partir da próxima quinta-feira [a parteer da prosima keenta fayra]

• • • • • • DIALOGUE • • • • • •

where are you from? de onde é? [dohnd-eh]
I'm from Slough sou de Slough [soh di]

front a frente [fraynt]
in front em frente [ayng]
in front of the hotel em frente ao hotel [ow]
at the front na frente [na]

frost a geada [ʒ-yada]

frozen gelado [ʒiladoo]

frozen food a comida congelada [koomeeda konʃiladoo]

fruit a fruta [froota]

fruit juice o sumo de fruta [soomoo di froota]

fry fritar

frying pan a frigideira [friʒidayra]

full cheio [shay-oo]
it's full of ... está cheio de ... [shta – di]
I'm full (said by man/woman) estou satisfeito/satisfeita [shtoh satisfaytoo]

full board a pensão completa [paynsowng komplehta]

fun: it was fun foi divertido [foh-i divirteedoo]

funeral o funeral [fooneral]

funny (strange) estranho [shtranyoo]
(amusing) engraçado [ayngrasadoo]

furniture a mobília [moobeel-ya]

further mais longe [mīʒ lohnʃ]

ENGLISH ❖ PORTUGUESE | Fu

it's further down the road é mais abaixo na rua [abīshoo na **roo**-a]

how much further is it to Santarém? quantos quilómetros faltam para Santarém? [kw**a**ntoosh kil**o**mitroosh f**a**ltowng – santar**a**yng]
about 5 kilometres mais ou menos cinco quilómetros [mīz oh m**a**ynoosh s**ee**nkoo]

fuse o fusível [fooz**ee**vil]
the lights have fused as luzes fundiram-se [aɹ l**oo**zish foond**ee**rowngsi]
fuse box a caixa de fusíveis [kīsha di fooz**ee**vaysh]
fuse wire o fio de fusível [f**ee**-oo di fooz**ee**vil]
future o futuro [foot**oo**roo]
in future no futuro [noo]

G

gallon* o galão [gal**ow**ng]
game (cards, match etc) o jogo [J**oh**goo]
 (meat) a caça [k**a**sa]
garage (for fuel) a bomba de gasolina [di gazool**ee**na]
 (for repairs, parking) a garagem [gar**a**Jayng]
garden o jardim [Jard**ee**ng]
garlic o alho [**a**l-yoo]
gas o gás [gash]
gas cylinder (camping gas) a bilha de gás [b**ee**l-ya di gash]
gasoline (US) a gasolina

[gazool**ee**na]
see **petrol**
gas permeable lenses as lentes semi-rígidas [l**a**yntsh simi-r**ee**Jidash]
gas station a bomba de gasolina [b**o**hmba di gazool**ee**na]
gate o portão [poort**ow**ng]
 (at airport) o portão de embarque [daymb**a**rk]
gay o homosexual [ohmooseksw**a**l]
gay bar o gay bar
gearbox a caixa de velocidades [kīsha di viloosid**a**dsh]
gear lever a avalanca das mudanças [dash mood**a**nsash]
gears a mudança [mood**a**nsa]
general (adj) geral [Jer**a**l]
gents (toilet) a casa de banho dos homens [k**a**za di b**a**n-yoo dooz **oh**mayngsh]
genuine (antique etc) genuíno [Jinw**ee**noo]
German (adj, language) alemão [alim**ow**ng]
German measles a rubéola [roob**eh**-ola]
Germany a Alemanha [alim**a**n-ya]
get (fetch) ir buscar [eer]
will you get me another one, please? pode trazer-me outro, por favor? [pod traz**a**yrm**oh**troo poor fav**oh**r]
how do I get to ...? como vou para ...? [k**oh**moo voh]
do you know where I can get

this? sabe onde posso comprar isto? [s**a**bohnd p**o**soo – **ee**shtoo]

•••••• D I A L O G U E ••••••

can I get you a drink? posso oferecer-lhe uma bebida? [p**o**soo ofris**ay**rl-y**oo**ma bib**ee**da]

no, I'll get this one, what would you like? não, eu ofereço esta, o que gostaria? [nowng **ay**-oo ofr**ay**soo **eh**shta oo ki goosht**a**r**ee**-a]

a glass of red wine um copo de vinho tinto [oong k**o**poo di v**ee**n-yoo t**ee**nto]

get back (return) volt**a**r
get in (arrive) chegar [shig**a**r]
get off sair [sa-**ee**r]
  where do I get off? onde é que saio? [ohnd**eh** ki s**ī**-yoo]
get on (to train etc) apanhar [apan-y**a**r]
get out (of car etc) sair [sa-**ee**r]
get up (in the morning) levantar-se [livant**a**rsi]
gift a lembrança [laymbr**a**nsa]

If you are invited to dinner in a Portuguese home, don't take a bottle of wine, which is considered very much a staple of the meal. A bunch of flowers, chocolates or a small gift will be much more appreciated.

---

gift shop a loja de lembranças [l**o**Ja di laymbr**a**nsash]
gin o gin [Jeeng]

a gin and tonic, please um gin-tónico por favor [oong Jeeng t**o**nikoo poor fav**oh**r]
girl a rapariga [rapar**ee**ga]
girlfriend a namor**a**da
give* dar
  can you give me some change? pode dar-me troco? [pod d**a**rmi tr**oh**koo]
  I gave it to him dei-lhe [d**a**yl-yi]
  will you give this to ...? pode dar isto a ...? [**ee**shtoo]

•••••• D I A L O G U E ••••••

how much do you want for this? quanto quer por isto? [kw**a**ntoo kehr poor **ee**shtoo]

20 escudos vinte escudos [veent-shk**oo**doosh]

I'll give you 15 escudos dou-lhe quinze escudos [d**oh**l-yi keenz]

give back devolver [divolv**ay**r]
glad contente [kont**ay**nt]
glass (material) o vidro [v**ee**droo]
  (for drinking) o copo [k**o**poo]
  a glass of wine um copo de vinho [oong – di v**ee**n-yoo]
glasses os óculos [**o**kooloosh]
gloves as luvas [l**oo**vash]
glue a cola
go* ir [eer]
  we'd like to go to the Museu de Arte Antiga queremos ir ao Museu de Arte Antiga [kir**ay**moosh eer ow moos**ay**-oo dart**a**nt**ee**ga]
  where are you going? onde

vai? [ohnd vī]

where does this bus go? para onde vai este autocarro? [aysht owtooka**rr**oo]

let's go! vamos! [va**moosh**]

she's gone (left) ele foi-se embora [ayl f**oh**-isaymb**o**ra]

where has he gone? onde ele foi? [**oh**ndayl f**oh**-i]

I went there last week fui lá na semana passada [fwee la na sim**a**na]

hamburger to go o hamburger para levar

go away ir embora [eer aymb**o**ra]

go away! vá-se embora! [vas-aymb**o**ra]

go back (return) voltar

go down (the stairs etc) descer [dish**sayr**]

go in entrar [aynt**rar**]

go out* (in the evening) sair [sa-**eer**]

do you want to go out tonight? quer sair esta noite? [kehr – **eh**shta n**oh**-it]

go through atravessar

go up (the stairs etc) subir [soob**eer**]

goat a cabra

goat's cheese o queijo de cabra [**kay**Joo di]

God Deus [**day**-oosh]

goggles os óculos protectores [**o**kooloosh prootet**oh**rish]

gold o ouro [**oh**roo]

golf o golfe [golf]

golf course o campo de golfe

[**ka**mpoo di]

good bom [bong]

good! bem! [bayng]

it's no good não presta [nowng pr**eh**shta]

goodbye adeus [ad**ay**-oosh]

good evening boa noite [b**oh**-a n**oh**-it]

Good Friday Sexta-Feira Santa [**say**shta f**ay**ra]

Good Friday is a public holiday in Portugal. All over the country there are religious processions; almost everything will be closed and transport services greatly reduced.

good morning bom dia [bong d**ee**-a]

good night boa noite [b**oh**-a n**oh**-it]

goose o ganso [**ga**nsoo]

got: we've got to leave temos que ir [**tay**moosh ki-**eer**]

have you got any ...? tem ...? [tayng]

government o governo [goov**ay**rnoo]

gradually gradualmente [gradwalm**ay**nt]

grammar a gramática

gram(me) o grama

granddaughter a neta [**neh**ta]

grandfather o avô [av**oh**]

grandmother a avó [av**aw**]

grandson o neto [**neh**too]

grapefruit a toranja [toor**a**nJa]

grapefruit juice o sumo de

toranja [**soo**moo di tooranJa]

grapes as uvas [**oo**vash]

grass a relva [**reh**lva]

grateful agradecido
[agradis**ee**doo]

gravy o molho [**moh**l-yo]

great (excellent) óptimo [**o**timoo]
that's great! isso é optimo!
[**ee**soo eh]
a great success um grande
sucesso [oong gr**a**nd
soos**eh**soo]

Great Britain a Grã-Bretanha
[gran brit**a**n-ya]

Greece a Grécia [gr**eh**s-ya]

greedy (for food) glutão
[gloot**ow**ng]

Greek (adj, language) grego
[gr**ay**goo]

green verde [vayrd]

green card (car insurance) a c**a**rta
verde

greengrocer's o lugar [loog**a**r]

---

greeting people
The Portuguese are fairly formal
in their greetings; even the
young will greet each other with
bom dia (good day) or **boa
tarde** (good afternoon). Older
people still address each other
as **Senhor**, **Senhora** or with
other titles such as **Dona** or
Doutor. The popularity of
Brazilian soap operas has led
to many Brazilian expressions
being assimilated into collo-
quial Portuguese; you may hear →

---

younger people saying **ciao**
(which the Brazilians adopted
from Italian) on parting, for
example. You will also commonly hear the Brazilian greeting **tudo bem?** (literally: is
everything OK?) rather than the
more traditional Portuguese
como está? (how are you?).

---

grey cinzento [sinz**ay**ntoo]

grill o grelhador [gril-yad**oh**r]

grilled grelhado [gril-y**a**doo]

grocer's o merceeiro [mirs-
y**ay**roo]

ground o chão [showng]
on the ground no chão [noo]

ground floor o rés de chão
[rehJ doo]

group o grupo [gr**oo**poo]

guarantee a garantia
[garant**ee**-a]
is it guaranteed? tem
garantia? [tayng]

guest (man/woman) o convidado
[konvid**a**doo], a convid**a**da

guesthouse a pensão
[payns**ow**ng]

The main budget travel standby
is a room in a guesthouse or
pensão: these are officially
graded from one to three stars.
Most serve meals, usually in a
bargain-priced, all-inclusive
package, but they rarely
insist that you take them.
Guesthouses that don't serve →

meals are sometimes called **residenciais**, though in price and all other respects they are virtually identical. Similar to **pensões**, and generally at the cheaper end of the scale, are **hospedarias** or **casas de hóspedes** – boarding houses. Always ask to see the room before you take it, and don't be afraid to ask if there's a cheaper one – especially if you're travelling alone, when you'll frequently be asked to pay more or less the full price of a double. **Tem um quarto mais barato?** (do you have a less expensive room?) is a useful phrase.

A budget alternative is to go for rooms (**quartos** or **dormidas**) in private houses. Most commonly available in the seaside resorts, these are sometimes advertized, or more often hawked at bus and train stations. Rates should be a little below that of a guesthouse, except on the Algarve where you can pay more. It's always worth haggling over prices, especially if you're prepared to commit yourself to a longish stay.

guide (person) a guia [gee-a]
guidebook o livro-guia [leevroo–]
guided tour a excursão com

guia [shkoorsowng kong]
guitar a viola
gum (in mouth) a gengiva [JenJeeva]
gun a pistola [pishtola]
gym o ginásio [Jinaz-yoo]

H

hair o cabelo [kabayloo]
hairbrush a escova de cabelo [shkohva di]
haircut o corte de cabelo [kort]
hairdresser's (unisex, women's) o cabeleireiro [kabilayrayroo] (men's) o barbeiro [barbayroo]

It is usual to make an appointment (**marcação**) at the hairdresser's. Hairdressers expect to be tipped about 10 per cent of the bill.

hairdryer o secador de cabelo [sikadohr di kabayloo]
hair gel o gel para o cabelo [Jehl paroo]
hairgrips a mola para o cabelo
hair spray a laca
half* a metade [mitad]
   half an hour meia hora [may-a ora]
   half a litre meio litro [may-oo leetroo]
   about half that mais ou menos metade disto [mīz oh maynoosh mitad-deeshtoo]
half board a meia pensão [may-a paynsowng]

half-bottle a meia garrafa
half fare o meio bilhete
[**may**-oo bil-**yay**t]
half price metade do preço
[mit**a**d doo pr**ay**soo]
ham o fiambre [f-y**a**mbr]
hamburger o hamburger
[amb**oo**rger]
hammer o martelo [mart**eh**loo]
hand a mão [mowng]
handbag a mala de mão [di]
handbrake o travão de mão
[trav**ow**ng]
handkerchief o lenço [l**ay**nsoo]
handle (on door) o fecho
[f**ay**shoo]
(on suitcase etc) a pega [p**eh**ga]
hand luggage a bagagem de
mão [baga**J**ayng]
hang-gliding a asa-delta [aza-
d**eh**lta]
hangover a ressaca [ris**a**ka]
I've got a hangover estou de
ressaca [shtoh di]
happen acontecer [akontis**ay**r]
what's happening? o que se
passa? [oo ki si]
what has happened? o que
aconteceu? [oo
ki-akoontis**ay**-oo]
happy contente [kont**ay**nt]
I'm not happy about this não
estou contente com isso
[nowng shtoh – kong **ee**soo]
harbour o porto [p**oh**rtoo]
hard duro [d**oo**roo]
(difficult) difícil [dif**ee**sil]
hard-boiled egg o ovo cozido
[**oh**voo kooz**ee**doo]

hard lenses as lentes rígidas
[layntsh r**ee**Jidash]
hardly mal
hardly ever quase nunca [kwaz
n**oo**nka]
hardware shop a loja de
ferragens [l**o**Ja di firra**J**ayngsh]
hat o chapéu [shap**eh**-oo]
hate detestar [ditisht**a**r]
have* ter [tayr]
can I have a ...? pode dar-
me ...? [pod d**a**rmi]
do you have ...? tem ...?
[tayng]
what'll you have? o que vai
tomar? [oo ki vī toom**a**r]
I have to leave now tenho de
ir agora [t**a**yn-yoo deer]
do I have to ...? tenho de ...?
[di]
can we have some ...? posso
ter ...? [p**o**soo tayr]
hayfever a febre dos fenos
[fehbr doosh **fay**noosh]
hazelnuts as avelãs [avel**a**ngsh]
he* ele [el]
head a cabeça [kab**ay**sa]
headache a dor de cabeça [di]
headlights o far**ol**
headphones os ausculatadores
[owshkooltad**oh**rish]
health see doctor
health food shop a loja de
produtos naturais [l**o**Ja di
prood**oo**toosh natoor**ī**sh]
healthy saudável [sowd**a**vil]
hear ouvir [ohv**ee**r]

• • • • • • DIALOGUE • • • • • •

can you hear me? consegue ouvir-me? [kons**eh**g ohv**ee**r-mi]

I can't hear you, could you repeat that? não o consigo ouvir, podia repetir? [nowng oo kons**ee**goo – pood**ee**-a ripit**ee**r]

hearing aid o aparelho para a surdez [apar**ay**l-yoo – soord**ay**sh]

heart o coração [kooras**ow**ng]

heart attack o enfarte [aynf**a**rt]

heat o calor [kal**oh**r]

heater o aquecedor [akesid**oh**r]

heating o aquecimento [akesim**ay**ntoo]

heavy pesado [piz**a**doo]

heel (of foot) o calcanhar [kalkan-y**a**r]

(of shoe) o salto

could you put new heels on these? podia pôr uns saltos novos? [pood**ee**-a pohr oongsh s**a**ltoosh n**o**voosh]

heelbar o balcão para reparações rápidas de sapatos [balk**ow**ng – riparas**oy**ngsh r**a**pidash di sap**a**toosh]

height (of person) a altura [alt**oo**ra]

(mountain) a altitude [altit**oo**d]

helicopter o helicóptero [elik**o**ptiroo]

hello olá

(answer on phone) está [shta]

helmet (for motorcycle) o capacete [kapas**ay**t]

help a ajuda [aJ**oo**da]

(verb) ajud**a**r

help! socorro! [sook**oh**rroo]

can you help me? pode ajudar-me? [pod – mi]

thank you very much for your help (said by man/woman) obrigado/obrigada pela sua ajuda [obrig**a**doo – p**i**la s**oo**-a]

helpful prestável [presht**a**vil]

hepatitis a hepatite [epat**ee**t]

her*: I haven't seen her não a vi [nowng a vee]

to her para ela [**eh**la]

with her com ela [kong]

for her para ela

that's her é ela [eh]

that's her towel esta é a toalha dela [**eh**shta-**eh** – d**eh**la]

herbal tea o chá de ervas [sha d**eh**rvash]

herbs as ervas

here aqui [ak**ee**]

here is/are ... aqui está/estão ... [shta/shtowng]

here you are aqui tem [tayng]

hers* dela [d**eh**la]

that's hers isso é dela [**ee**soo eh]

hey! eh!

hi! (hello) olá! [ool**a**]

hide esconder [shkond**ay**r]

high alto [**a**ltoo]

highchair a cadeira de bébé [kad**ay**ra di beb**eh**]

highway a autoestrada [owtooshtr**a**da]

see motorway

hill o monte [mohnt]

him*: I haven't seen him não o
vi [nowng oo vee]
 to him para ele [ayl]
 with him com ele [kong]
 for him para ele
 that's him é ele [eh]

hip a anca

hire alugar [aloogar]
 for hire para alugar
 where can I hire a bike? onde
 posso alugar uma bicicleta?
 [ohnd posoo]
 see rent

his*: it's his car é o carro dele
 [eh-oo karroo dayl]
 that's his isto é dele
 [eeshtweh]

hit bater [batayr]

hitch-hike andar à boleia
 [boolay-a]

hobby o passatempo
 [–taympoo]

hold segurar [sigoorar]

hole o buraco [boorakoo]

holiday as férias [fehr-yash]
 on holiday de férias [shtoh di]

Holland Holanda [olanda]

home a casa [kaza]
 at home (in my house etc) em
 casa [ayng]
 (in my country) no meu país
 [noo may-oo pa-eesh]
 we go home tomorrow vamos
 embora amanhã [vamoosh
 aymbora aman-yang]

honest honesto [onehshtoo]

honey o mel [mehl]

honeymoon a lua-de-mel

[loo-a di]

hood (US: of car) o capot [kapoh]

hope esperar [shpirar]
 I hope so espero que sim
 [shpehroo ki seeng]
 I hope not espero que não
 [nowng]

hopefully: hopefully ... espero
 que ...

horn (of car) a buzina [boozeena]

horrible horrível [ohrreevil]

horse o cavalo [kavaloo]

horse riding andar a cavalo

hospital o hospital [oshpital]

hospitality a hospitalidade
 [oshpitalidad]
 thank you for your hospitality
 (said by man/woman) obrigado/
 obrigada pela sua
 hospitalidade [obrigadoo –
 pila soo-a]

hot quente [kaynt]
 (spicy) picante [pikant]
 I'm hot tenho calor [tayn-yoo
 kalohr]
 it's hot today está imenso
 calor hoje [shta imaynsoo –
 ohJ]

hotel o hotel [ohtehl]

A one-star hotel usually costs
about the same as a three-
star pensão (guesthouse);
sometimes establishments clas-
sified as one-star hotels are not
very different from guesthouses.
Indeed, it's not uncommon to
find a two- or three-star pensão
→

ENGLISH ❖ PORTUGUESE | Ho

offering much better quality rooms than a one-star hotel. Prices for two- and three-star hotels, though, are noticeably higher, and there's a further and more dramatic shift in rates as you move into the four- and five-star hotel league. **Estalagens** and **albergarias** are other types of hotel in the upper price ranges.

For a different type of accommodation, you could try one of the 32 government-run **pousadas** which are often converted from old monasteries or castles and located in dramatic countryside settings. They're rated in three categories, and, as with other hotels, charge different prices in low, middle and high season.

hotel room o quarto de hotel [kwar**too** doht**ehl**]
hour a hora [**o**ra]
house a casa [k**a**za]
house wine o vinho da casa [v**ee**n-yoo]
how como [k**oh**moo]
　how many? quantos? [kw**a**ntoosh]
　how do you do? muito prazer [m**wee**ngtoo praz**ay**r]

•••••• DIALOGUES ••••••

how are you? como está? [shta]
fine, thanks, and you? (said by man/woman) bem, obrigado/obrigad**a**, e você? [bayng obrig**a**doo – ee vos**ay**]

how much is it? quanto é? [kwantw**eh**]
it's 500 escudos são quinhentos escudos [sowng kin-y**ay**ntooz-shk**oo**doosh]
I'll take it vou levar [voh]

humid húmido [**oo**meedoo]
hunger a fome [fohm]
hungry: are you hungry? tens fome? [taynsh]
hurry apressar-se [apris**a**rsi]
　I'm in a hurry estou com pressa [shtoh kong pr**eh**sa]
　there's no hurry não há pressa [nowng a]
　hurry up! despacha-te! [dishp**a**shat]
hurt doer [dwayr]
　it really hurts dói-me [d**oy**mi]
husband o meu marido [m**ay**-oo mar**ee**doo]
hydrofoil o hydroplano [idroopl**a**noo]
hypermarket hipermercado [eepermerk**a**doo]

I

I* eu [**ay**-oo]
ice gelo [J**ay**loo]
　with ice com gelo [kong]
　no ice, thanks (said by man/woman) sem gelo, obrigado/obrigada [sayng – obrig**a**doo]
ice cream o gelado [Jil**a**doo]
ice-cream cone o cone de gelado [kohn di]

iced coffee o café glacé [kaf**eh** glas**ay**]

ice lolly o gelado [ʒil**a**doo]

ice rink o rinque de patinagem [r**ee**nk di patin**a**ʒayng]

ice skates os patins de gelo [pat**ee**nʒ di ʒ**ay**loo]

idea a ideia [id**ay**-a]

idiot o idiota [id-y**o**ta]

if se [si]

ignition a ignição [ignis**ow**ng]

ill doente [dwaynt]
    I feel ill sinto-me doente [s**ee**ntoomi]

illness a doença [dw**ay**nsa]

imitation (leather etc) a imitação [imitas**ow**ng]

immediately imediatamente [imed-yatam**ay**nt]

important importante [impoort**a**nt]
    it's very important é muito importante [eh m**wee**engtoo]
    it's not important não é importante [nowng]

impossible impossível [impoos**ee**vil]

impressive impressionante [impris-yoon**a**nt]

improve melhorar [mil-yor**a**r]
    I want to improve my Portuguese quero melhorar o meu português [k**eh**roo – oo m**ay**-oo poortoog**ay**sh]

in*: it's in the centre fica no centro [f**ee**ka noo s**ay**ntroo]
    in my car no meu carro [noo m**ay**-oo k**a**rroo]
    in Beja em Beja [ayng b**eh**ʒa]

in two days from now daqui a dois dias [dak**ee** a d**o**-iʒ d**ee**-ash]

in five minutes em cinco minutos [ayng s**ee**nkoo min**oo**toosh]

in May em Maio [m**ī**-oo]

in English em inglês [ingl**ay**sh]

in Portuguese em português [poortoog**ay**sh]

is he in? ele está? [el shta]

inch* a polegada [pool**e**gada]

include incluir [inklw**ee**r]
    does that include meals? isso inclui as refeições? [**ee**soo inkl**oo**-i refays**oy**ngsh]
    is that included? isso está incluído no preço? [shta inklw**ee**doo noo pr**ay**soo]

inconvenient pouco conveniente [p**oh**koo konvin-y**ay**nt]

incredible incrível [inkr**ee**vil]

Indian (adj) indiano [ind-y**a**noo]

indicator o indicador [indikad**oh**r]

indigestion a indigestão [indiʒisht**ow**ng]

indoor pool a piscina coberta [pish-s**ee**na koob**eh**rta]

indoors dentro de casa [d**ay**ntroo di k**a**za], em recinto fechado [ayng ris**ee**ntoo fish**a**doo]

inexpensive barato [bar**a**too]

infection a infecção [infehs**ow**ng]

infectious infeccioso [infehs-y**oh**zoo]

inflammation a inflamação [inflamas**ow**ng]

informal informal [infoorm**al**]

information a informação [infoormas**ow**ng]

do you have any information about ...? tem alguma informação sobre ...? [tayng alg**oo**ma – sohbr]

information desk o balcão de informações [balk**ow**ng dinfoormas**oy**ngsh]

injection a injecção [inJehs**ow**ng]

injured ferido [fir**ee**doo]

she's been injured ela ficou ferida [**eh**la fik**oh** fir**ee**da]

in-laws os sogros [oosh s**o**groosh]

inner tube (for tyre) a câmara de ar [k**a**ma-ra dar]

innocent inocente [inoos**ay**nt]

insect o insecto [ins**eh**too]

insect bite a picada de insecto [dins**eh**too]

do you have anything for insect bites? tem alguma coisa para picada de insectos? [tayng alg**oo**ma k**oh**-iza – ins**eh**toosh]

insect repellent o repele-insectos [rip**eh**l ins**eh**toosh]

inside dentro [d**ay**ntroo]

inside the hotel dentro do hotel [dwoht**eh**l]

let's sit inside vamos sentar-nos lá dentro [v**a**moosh sent**ar**-noosh]

insist insistir [insisht**eer**]

I insist insisto [ins**ee**shtoo]

insomnia a insónia [ins**o**n-ya]

instant coffee o café instantâneo [kaf**eh** inshtant**a**n-yoo]

instead em vez [ayng vaysh]

give me that one instead dê-me antes aquele [daym antsh ak**ay**l]

instead of ... em vez de ... [di]

insulin a insulina [insool**ee**na]

insurance o seguro [sig**oo**roo]

intelligent inteligente [intiliJ**ay**nt]

interested: I'm interested in ... (said by a man/woman) estou muito interessado/ interessada em ... [shtoh mw**ee**ngtoo intris**a**doo – ayng]

interesting interessante [intris**a**nt]

that's very interesting isso é muito interessante [**ee**soo eh mw**ee**engtoo]

international internacional [intayrnas-yoon**al**]

interpret interpretar [interprit**ar**]

interpreter (man/woman) o/a intérprete [int**ehr**prit]

intersection o cruzamento [kroozam**ay**ntoo]

interval (at theatre) o intervalo [interv**a**loo]

into para

I'm not into ... não me interesso por ... [nowng mintr**eh**soo poor]

introduce apresentar [aprizent**ar**]

may I introduce ...? posso
apresentar ... [po**soo**]
invitation o convite [konv**eet**]
invite convidar [konvi**dar**]
Ireland a Irlanda [eer**la**nda]
Irish irlandês [eerland**aysh**]
I'm Irish (man/woman) sou
irlandês/sou irlandesa [soh –
eerland**ay**za]
iron (for ironing) o ferro de
engomar [**feh**rroo
dayngoo**mar**]
can you iron these for me?
pode engomar-me isto? [pod
ayngoo**marm ee**shtoo]
is* é [eh]; está [shta]
island a ilha [**eel**-ya]
it* o [oo], f a
it is ... é ... [eh]; está ... [shta]
is it ...? é ...?; está ...?
where is it? onde é? [ohnd**eh**];
onde está?
it's him é ele [ayl]
it was ... era ... [**eh**ra];
estava ... [sht**a**va]
Italian (adj, language) italiano
[ital-y**a**noo]
Italy Itália [ital-ya]
itch: it itches faz comichão [fash
koomish**ow**ng]

J

jack (for car) o macaco
[ma**ka**koo]
jacket o casaco [ka**za**koo]
jam a comp**o**ta
jammed: it's jammed está
encravado [shta aynkra**va**doo]

January Janeiro [Jan**ay**roo]
jar o j**a**rro
jaw a maxila [mak**see**la]
jazz o jazz
jealous ciumento
[s-yoom**ay**ntoo]
jeans os jeans
jellyfish a alforreca [alfoor**reh**ka]
jersey a camisola [kami**zo**la]
jetty o pontão [pont**ow**ng]
jeweller's a ourivesaria
[ohrivezar**ee**-a]
jewellery a joalharia [Jwal-
yar**ee**-a]
Jewish judaico [Jood**ī**koo]
job o emprego [aymp**ray**goo]
jogging o jogging
to go jogging praticar
jogging
joke a piada [p-y**a**da]
journey a viagem [v-ya**Jay**ng]
have a good journey! boa
viagem! [**boh**-a]
jug o jarro [**Ja**rroo]
a jug of water um jarro de
água [oong – **da**gwa]
juice o sumo [**soo**moo]
July Julho [J**oo**l-yoo]
jump pular [poo**lar**]
jumper a camisola [kami**zo**la]
jump leads os cabos para ligar
a bateria [ka**boo**sh – bati**ree**-a]
junction o cruzamento
[kroozam**ay**ntoo]
June Junho [J**oo**n-yoo]

June is festival month in
Portugal. June 10th is a national
holiday (the national day of
→

Portugal and a celebration of the poet Camões). Each town and village also celebrates its own saint's day (many of which are in June) with street parties, music and dancing; all shops and many restaurants close on these holidays. Lisbon's saint's day honours Santo Antonio on June 13th. Pots of marjoram are displayed on every windowsill and the Alfama region of the city is turned into one large all-night street party, with people setting up impromptu sardine barbecues outside their houses and handing wine and food out to passers-by. São João in Porto is celebrated on June 23rd, again with dancing and drinking in the streets, but with the added tradition of the city's youth running around hitting everyone in sight with squeaky plastic hammers. Note also that any holiday which falls on a Tuesday or Thursday is likely to be preceded or followed by a bridging day to make a long weekend, so facilities could be closed for a full four days.

just (only) só [saw]
  just two só dois/duas
  just for me só para mim
  [meeng]
  just here aqui mesmo [akee mayJmoo]

not just now agora não [nowng]
we've just arrived acabámos de chegar [akabamooJ di shigar]

K

keep guardar [gwardar]
  keep the change guarde o troco [gward oo trohkoo]
  can I keep it? posso ficar com ele/ela? [posoo fikar kong ayl/ehla]
  you can keep it pode ficar com ele/ela [pod]
ketchup o ketchup
kettle a chaleira [shalayra]
key a chave [shav]
  the key for room 201, please a chave do quarto duzentos e um, faz favor [doo kwartoo doozayntooz-yoong fash favohr]
keyring o chaveiro [shavayroo]
kidneys (in body, food) os rins [reengsh]
kill matar
kilo* o quilo [keeloo]
kilometre* o quilómetro [kilomitroo]
  how many kilometres is it to ...? quantos quilómetros são até ...? [kwantoosh kilomitroosh sowng ateh]
kind (generous) amável
  that's very kind é muito amável [eh mweengtoo]

which kind do you want? que tipo deseja? [ki **tee**poo dis**ay**ʒa]
I want this/that kind desejo este/aquele tipo [aysht/ak**ay**l]

king o rei [ray]
kiosk o quiosque [k-yoshk]
kiss o beijo [**bay**ʒoo]
(verb) beijar [bay**ʒar**]
kitchen a cozinha [kooz**ee**n-ya]
kitchenette a cozinha pequena [pik**ay**na]
Kleenex® os lenços de papel [**lay**nsoosh di pap**eh**l]
knee o joelho [ʒw**ay**l-yoo]
knickers as cuecas de mulher [ash kw**eh**kaʒ di mool-**yeh**r]
knife a faca [f**a**ka]
knock bater [bat**ayr**]
knock down atropelar [atropil**ar**]
he's been knocked down ele foi atropelado [el f**oh**-i atropil**a**doo]
knock over (object) derrubar [dirroob**ar**]
(pedestrian) atropelar [atropil**ar**]
know* (somebody, a place) conhecer [koon-yis**air**]
(something) saber
I don't know não sei [nowng say]
I didn't know that não sabia isso [nowng sab**ee**-a **ee**soo]
do you know where I can find ...? sabe onde posso encontrar ...? [s**a**bohnd p**o**swaynkontr**ar**]

L

label (on clothes) a etiqueta [etik**ay**ta]
(on bottles etc) o rótulo [**ro**tooloo]
ladies' room, ladies' (toilets) o quarto de banho das senhoras [kw**ar**too di b**a**n-yoo dash sin-y**o**rash]
ladies' wear a roupa de senhoras [**roh**pa di]
lady a senhora [sin-y**o**ra]
lager a cerveja [sirvay-ʒa]
see beer
lake o lago [l**a**goo]
lamb (meat) o borrego [boorr**ay**goo]
lamp o candeeiro [kand-y**ay**roo]
lane (motorway) a faixa [f**ī**sha]
(small road) a viela [v-y**eh**la]
language a língua [l**ee**ngwa]
language course o curso de línguas [k**oo**rsoo di l**ee**ngwash]
large grande [grand]
last o último [**oo**ltimoo]
last week semana passada [sim**a**na]
last Friday sexta-feira passada [s**ay**shta-f**ay**ra]
last night ontem à noite [**oh**ntayng a n**oh**-it]
what time is the last train to Fátima? a que horas parte o último comboio para

Fátima? [kyorash part-yoo-**oo**ltimoo komb**oh**-yo]

late tarde [tard]

sorry I'm late desculpe o atraso [dishk**oo**lp oo atr**a**zoo]

the train was late o comboio estava atrasado [oo komb**oh**-yo sht**a**va atraz**a**doo]

we must go – we'll be late temos que ir – vamos atrasar-nos [t**ay**moosh ki-**ee**r – v**a**mooz-atraz**a**r noosh]

it's getting late está a ficar tarde [sht**a**-a fik**a**r]

later, later on mais tarde [mīsh]

I'll come back later volto mais tarde [v**o**ltoo]

see you later até logo [a-t**eh**]

latest o último [**oo**ltimoo]

by Wednesday at the latest quarta-feira o mais tardar [kw**a**rta-f**a**yra oo mīsh]

laugh rir [reer]

launderette a lavandaria automática [lavandar**ee**-a owtoom**a**tika]

laundromat a lavandaria automática [lavandar**ee**-a owtoom**a**tika]

laundry (clothes) a roupa para lavar [r**oh**pa]

(place) a lavandaria [lavandar**ee**-a]

lavatory os lavabos [lav**a**boosh]

law a lei [lay]

lawn o relvado [relv**a**doo]

lawyer (man/woman) o advogado [advoog**a**doo], a advogada

laxative o laxativo [lashat**ee**voo]

lazy preguiçoso [prigis**oh**zoo]

lead (electrical) o fio [f**ee**-oo]

(verb) conduzir [kondooz**ee**r]

where does this lead to? onde vai ter esta estrada? [ohnd vī tayr **eh**shta shtr**a**da]

leaf a folha [f**oh**l-ya]

leaflet o panfleto [panfl**ay**too]

leak a fuga [f**oo**ga]

(verb) ter uma fuga [tayr **oo**ma]

the roof leaks há uma fuga de água no telhado [a – d**a**gwa noo til-y**a**doo]

learn aprender [apraynd**ay**r]

least: not in the least de nenhum modo [di nin-y**oo**ong m**o**doo]

at least pelo menos [p**e**loo m**a**ynoosh]

leather o cabedal [kabid**a**l]

leave (depart) partir [part**ee**r]

(behind) deixar [daysh**a**r]

I am leaving tomorrow parto amanhã [p**a**rtoo aman-y**a**ng]

he left yesterday ele partiu ontem [ayl part**ee**-oo **oh**ntayng]

may I leave this here? posso deixar isto aqui? [p**o**soo – **ee**shtwak**ee**]

I left my coat in the bar deixei meu casaco no bar [daysh**ay** m**a**y-oo kaz**a**koo noo]

when does the bus for Lagos leave? quando parte o autocarro para Lagos? [kw**a**ndoo p**a**rtoo owtook**a**rroo – l**a**goosh] leeks o alho francês [al-yoo fransaysh]

left esquerdo [shkayrdoo]
on the left, to the left à esquerda [a shkayrda]
turn left vire à esquerda [veera]
there's none left não há mais [nowng a mīsh]

left-handed canhoto [kanyohtoo]

left luggage (office) o depósito de bagagem [dipozitoo di bagaJayng]

leg a perna [pehrna]

lemon o limão [limowng]

lemonade a limonada [limoonada]

lemon tea o chá de limão [sha di limowng]

lend emprestar [aymprishtar]
will you lend me your ...? empresta-me o seu ...? [aymprehshtamoo say-oo]

lens (of camera) a objectiva [obJeteeva]

lesbian a lésbica [lehJbika]

less* menos [maynosh]
less than menos do que [doo ki]
less expensive mais barato [mīJ baratoo]

lesson a lição [lisowng]

let (allow) deixar [dayshar]
will you let me know? diz-me depois? [deeJmi dipoh-ish]
I'll let you know depois digo-lhe [deegool-yi]
let's go for something to eat

vamos sair para comer alguma coisa [vamoosh sa-eer – koomayr algooma koh-iza]

let off: will you let me off at ...? é capaz de parar em ...? [eh kapaJ di – ayng]

letter a carta
do you have any letters for me? tem alguma carta para mim? [tayng algooma – meeng]

letterbox o marco de correio [markoo di kooray-oo]

Ordinary letterboxes follow the British pillar-box design and are also painted red; the blue letterboxes are for express mail (correio azul).

lettuce a alface [alfas]

lever a alavanca

library a biblioteca [bibl-yootehka]

licence a licença [lisaynsa]

lid a tampa

lie (verb: tell untruth) mentir [maynteer]

lie down deitar-se [daytarsi]

life a vida [veeda]

lifebelt o cinto de salvação [seentoo di salvasowng]

lifeguard o banheiro [ban-yayroo]

life jacket o colete de salvação [koolayt di salvasowng]

lift (in building) o elevador [elevadohr]
could you give me a lift? pode dar-me uma boleia? [pod

darmooma boolay-a]
would you like a lift? quer
uma boleia? [kehr]
light a luz [loosh]
(not heavy) leve [lehv]
do you have a light? (for
cigarette) tem lume? [tayng
loom]
light green verde claro [vayrd
klaroo]
light bulb a lâmpada
I need a new light bulb
preciso duma lâmpada
[priseezoo dooma]
lighter (cigarette) o isqueiro
[shkayroo]
lightning a trovoada [troovwada]
like gostar [gooshtar]
I like it gosto [goshtoo]
I like going for walks gosto de
passear a pé [di pas-yar a peh]
I like you gosto de si.[di see]
I don't like it não gosto
[nowng]
do you like ...? você gosta
de ...? [vosay goshta di]
I'd like a beer queria uma
cerveja [kiree-a ooma
sirvayJa]
I'd like to go swimming
queria ir nadar [eer]
would you like a drink?
gostaria duma bebida?
[gooshtaree-a dooma bibeeda]
**would you like to go for a
walk?** quer ir dar uma volta?
[kehr]
what's it like? como é?
[kohmoo eh]

I want one like this quero um
como este [kehroo oong
kohmwaysht]
lime a lima [leema]
lime cordial o sumo de lima
[soomoo di]
line a linha [leen-ya]
**could you give me an outside
line?** dá-me uma linha?
[damooma]
lips os lábios [lab-yoosh]
lip salve o baton para o cieiro
[batong – oo s-yayroo]
lipstick o baton [batong]
liqueur o licor [likohr]
Lisbon Lisboa [liJboh-a]
listen escutar [shkootar]
litre* o litro [leetroo]
a litre of white wine um litro
de vinho branco [di veen-yoo
brankoo]
little pequeno [pikaynoo]
just a little, thanks só um
pouco, por favor [saw oong
pohkoo por favohr]
a little milk pouco leite [layt]
a little bit more um
pouquinho mais [oong
pohkeen-yoo mīsh]
live (verb) viver [vivayr]
we live together vivemos
juntos [vivaymooJ Joontoosh]

•••••• DIALOGUE ••••••

where do you live? onde é que
vive? [ohndeh ki veev]
I live in London vivo em Londres
[veevwayng lohndrish]

lively animado [animadoo]

liver (in body, food) o fígado
[fe**e**gadoo]
loaf o pão [powng]
lobby (in hotel) o hall
lobster a lagosta [lag**oh**shta]
local local [look**a**l]
can you recommend a local
wine? pode recomendar um
vinho da região? [pod
rikoomaynd**a**r oong ve**e**n-yoo da
riJ-y**ow**ng]
can you recommend a local
restaurant? pode recomendar
um restaurante local?
[rishtawr**a**nt]
lock a fechadura [fishad**oo**ra]
(verb) fechar à chave [fish**a**r a
shav]
it's locked está fechado à
chave [shta fish**a**dwa shav]
lock out: I've locked myself out
(of room) fechei o quarto com
a chave lá dentro [fish**ay** oo
kw**a**rtoo kong – d**ay**ntroo]
locker (for luggage etc) o cacifo
[kas**ee**foo]
lollipop o chupa-chupa
[sh**oo**pa–]
London Londres [l**oh**ndrish]
long comprido [kompr**ee**doo]
how long will it take to fix it?
quanto tempo vai demorar
para consertar? [kw**a**ntoo
t**ay**mpoo vī dimoor**a**r –
konsirt**a**r]
how long does it take? quanto
tempo demora? [dim**o**ra]
a long time muito tempo
[m**wee**ngtoo]

one day/two days longer mais
um dia/dois dias [mīz oong
de**e**-a/do-iJ de**e**-ash]
long-distance call a chamada de
longa distância [sham**a**da di –
disht**a**ns-ya]
look: I'm just looking, thanks
(said by man/woman) estou só a
ver, obrigado/obrigada
[shtoh saw a vayr obrig**a**doo]
you don't look well parece
não estar bem [par**e**hs nowng
shtar bayng]
look out! cuidado! [kwid**a**doo]
can I have a look? posso ver?
[p**o**soo vayr]
look after tomar conta (de)
[toom**a**r k**oh**nta]
look at olhar (para) [ol-y**a**r]
look for procurar [prookoor**a**r]
I'm looking for ... procuro ...
[prook**oo**roo]
loose (handle etc) solto [s**oh**ltoo]
lorry o camião [kam-y**ow**ng]
lose perder [pird**ay**r]
I've lost my way perdi-me
[pird**ee**m]
I'm lost, I want to get to ...
(said by man/woman) estou
perdido/perdida, quero ir
para ... [shtoh pird**ee**doo –
k**eh**roo eer]
I've lost my bag perdi o
meu saco [pird**ee** oo m**ay**-oo
s**a**koo]
lost property (office) a secção de
perdidos e achados
[sehks**ow**ng di pird**ee**dooz ee-
ash**a**doosh]

lot: a lot, lots muito
[m**wee**ngtoo]
not a lot não muito [nowng]
a lot of people muita gente
[m**wee**ngta Jayngt]
a lot bigger muito maior
[mī-**or**]
I like it a lot gosto imenso
[**go**shtoo im**ay**nsoo]
lotion a loção [loos**ow**ng]
loud alto [**a**ltoo]
lounge (in house, hotel) a **sa**la
(in airport) a sala de espera
[dishp**eh**ra]
love o amor [am**oh**r]
(verb) amar
I love Portugal adoro Portugal
[ad**o**roo poortoog**a**l]
lovely (meal, food) delicioso
[dilis-y**oh**zoo]
(view) encantador
[aynkantad**oh**r]
(weather) excelente
[ish-sil**ay**nt]
(present) adorávil
low baixo [b**ī**shoo]
luck a sorte [sort]
good luck! boa sorte! [b**oh**-a]
luggage a bagagem [baga**J**ayng]
luggage trolley o carrinho de
bagagem [karr**ee**n-yoo di]
lump (on body) o inchaço
[insh**a**soo]
lunch o almoço [alm**oh**soo]
lungs os pulmões
[poolm**oy**ngsh]
luxurious (hotel, furnishings)
luxuoso [loosh-w**oh**zoo]
luxury o luxo [**loo**shoo]

M

machine a máquina [m**a**kina]
mad (insane) doido [d**oh**-idoo]
(angry) zangado [zang**a**doo]
Madeira (place) a Madeira
[mad**ay**ra]
(wine) o (vinho da) Madeira
[v**ee**n-yoo]

Madeira is from Portugal's
Atlantic island province. Widely
available, it comes in four main
varieties: **Sercial** (a dry aperitif), **Verdelho** (a medium-dry
aperitif), **Bual** (a medium-
sweet wine) and **Malvasia**
(Malmsey, a sweet, heavy dessert wine). Each improves with
age and special vintages are
very expensive.

magazine a revista [riv**ee**shta]
maid (in hotel) a criada [kr-y**a**da]
maiden name o nome de
solteira [nohm di soolt**ay**ra]
mail o correio [koorr**ay**-oo]
(verb) pôr no correio [pohr
noo]
is there any mail for me? há
algum correio para mim? [a
alg**oo**m – meeng]
see **post office**
mailbox o marco de correio
[m**a**rkoo di koorr**ay**-oo], a caixa
do correio [k**ī**sha doo]
see **letterbox**
main principal [prinsip**a**l]
main course o prato principal

[pra**t**oo prinsip**a**l]

main post office a central de
correios [sent**ra**l di koorr**ay**-
oosh]

main road (in town) a rua
principal [r**oo**-a prinsip**a**l]
(in country) a estrada principal
[shtr**a**da]

mains switch o disjuntor
principal [diJoont**oh**r]

make* (brand name) a m**a**rca
(verb) fazer [faz**ay**r]
I make it 500 escudos calculo
que sejam quinhentos
escudos [kalk**oo**loo ki
s**ay**Jowng kin-y**ay**ntooz-
shk**oo**doosh]
what is it made of? de que é
feito? [di k-yeh f**ay**too]

make-up a maquilhagem
[makil-ya**J**ayng]

man o homem [**oh**mayng]

manager o gerente [Jer**ay**nt]
can I see the manager? pode
chamar o gerente? [pod
sham**a**r]

manageress a gerente

manual manual [manw**a**l]

many muitos [m**wee**ngtoosh]
not many não muitos [nowng]

map o m**a**pa

You can pick up a wide range
of free brochures and maps
from the Portuguese National
Tourist Office before you go.
Once in Portugal, local tourist
offices (**turismo**) often have
→

useful local maps and leaflets
that you won't find in the national offices. However, if you're
doing any real exploration, or
driving, it's worth investing in a
good road map.

March Março [m**a**rsoo]

margarine a margarina
[margar**ee**na]

market o mercado [mirk**a**doo]

marmalade a comp**o**ta de
laranja [di lar**a**nJa]

married: I'm married (said by a
man/woman) sou casado/
casada [soh kaz**a**do]
are you married? você é
casado/casada? [vos**ay** eh]

mascara o rímel [**ree**mil]

match (football etc) o jogo
[**J**ohgoo]

matches os fósforos
[**f**oshfooroosh]

material (fabric) o tecido
[tis**ee**doo]

matter: it doesn't matter não faz
mal [n**ow**ng faJ m**a**l]
what's the matter? o que se
passa? [oo ki si]

mattress o colchão
[koolsh**ow**ng]

May Maio [m**ī**-oo]

may: may I have another one?
(different one) pode dar-me
outro/outra? [pod d**a**rmi
ohtroo]
may I come in? posso entrar?
[p**o**swayntr**a**r]

may I see it? posso vê-lo/vê-la? [**po**soo va**y**loo/**vay**la]

may I sit here? posso sentar-me aqui? [**po**soo saynt**ar**m ak**ee**]

maybe talvez [talv**ay**sh]

mayonnaise a maionese [mī-on**eh**z]

me* mim [meeng]

that's for me isto é para mim [**ee**shtw**eh** p**a**ra meeng]

send it to me envie-o/a para mim [aynv**ee**-yoo]

me too eu também [**ay**-oo tamb**ay**ng]

meal a refeição [rifays**ow**ng]

•••••• DIALOGUE ••••••

did you enjoy your meal? gostou da comida? [goosht**oh** da koom**ee**da]

it was excellent, thank you (said by man/woman) estava excelente, obrigado/obrigada [sht**a**va ish-sel**ay**nt obrig**a**doo]

mean: what do you mean? o que quer dizer? [oo ki kehr diz**ay**r]

•••••• DIALOGUE ••••••

what does this word mean? o que significa esta palavra? [oo ki signif**ee**ka **eh**shta]

it means ... in English significa ... em inglês [ayng ingl**ay**sh]

measles o sarampo [sar**a**mpoo]

meat a carne [karn]

mechanic o mecânico [mek**a**nikoo]

medicine o remédio [rim**eh**d-yoo]

Mediterranean o Mediterrâneo [miditirr**a**n-yoo]

medium médio [m**eh**d-yoo]

medium-dry meio seco [m**ay**-oo s**ay**koo]

medium-rare médio [m**eh**d-yoo]

medium-sized de tamanho médio [di tam**a**n-yoo m**eh**d-yoo]

meet encontrar [aynkontr**ar**]

nice to meet you muito prazer [m**wee**ngtoo praz**ay**r]

where shall I meet you? onde nos encontramos? [ohnd noozaynkontr**a**moosh]

meeting a reunião [r-yoon-y**ow**ng]

meeting place o local de encontro [look**a**l daynk**oh**ntroo]

melon o melão [mil**ow**ng]

men os homens [**oh**mayngsh]

mend consertar [konsirt**ar**]

could you mend this for me? pode consertar-me isto? [pod konsirt**ar**m **ee**shtoo]

menswear a roupa de homens [**roh**pa d**oh**mayngsh]

mention mencionar [maynsyoon**ar**]

don't mention it não tem de quê [nowng tayng di kay]

menu a ementa [em**ay**nta]

may I see the menu, please? posso ver a ementa, faz favor [**po**soo vayr īm**ay**nta fash fav**oh**r]

see **menu reader** page 239

message o recado [rik**a**doo]
  are there any messages for
  me? há algum recado p**a**ra
  mim? [a alg**oo**ng – meeng]
  I want to leave a message
  for ... gostava de deixar um
  recado para ... [goosht**a**va di
  daysh**a**r oong]
metal o metal [mit**a**l]
metre* o metro [m**e**htroo]
microwave (oven) microondas
  [mikroo-**oh**ndash]
midday o meio-dia [m**a**y-oo
  d**ee**-a]
  at midday ao meio-dia [ow]
middle: in the middle no meio
  [noo m**a**y-oo]
  in the middle of the night no
  meio da noite [n**oh**-it]
  the middle one o/a do meio
  [oo/a doo]
midnight a meia-noite [m**a**y-a
  n**oh**-it]
  at midnight à meia-noite
might: I might go pode ser que
  eu vá [pod sayr ki-**a**y-oo]
  I might not go pode ser que
  eu não vá [nowng]
  I might want to stay another
  day sou capaz de querer
  ficar mais um dia [soh kap**a**ʒ
  di kir**a**yr fik**a**r m**ī**sh oong
  d**ee**-a]
migraine a enxaqueca
  [aynshak**a**yka]
mild (taste) suave [swav]
  (weather) ameno [am**a**ynoo]
mile* a milha [m**ee**l-ya]
milk o leite [layt]

milkshake o batido [bat**ee**doo]
millimetre* o milímetro
  [mil**ee**mitroo]
minced meat a carne picada
  [karn pik**a**da]
mind: never mind não faz mal
  [nowng faʒ mal]
  I've changed my mind mudei
  de ideias [mood**a**y did**a**y-
  yash]

•••••• D I A L O G U E ••••••

do you mind if I open the window?
importa-se se abrir a janela?
[imp**o**rtasi s-yabr**ee**r a ʒan**e**hla]
no, I don't mind não, não me
importo [nowng mimp**o**rtoo]

mine*: it's mine é meu [eh
  m**a**y-oo]
mineral water a água mineral
  [**a**gwa]
mints as pastilhas de mentol
  [pasht**ee**l-yaʒ di]
minute o minuto [min**oo**too]
  in a minute dentro de um
  momento [d**a**yntroo doong
  moom**a**yntoo]
  just a minute só um
  momento [saw oong]
mirror o espelho retrovisor
  [shp**a**yl-yoo retrooviz**oh**r]
Miss a Senhora [sin-y**o**ra]
  Miss! se faz favor! [si fash
  fav**oh**r]
miss: I missed the bus perdi o
  autocarro [pird**ee** oo-
  owtook**a**rro]
missing falta
  there's a suitcase missing falta

uma **ma**la [**oo**ma]

mist a névoa [**ne**hvwa]

mistake o erro [**ay**rroo]

  I think there's a mistake julgo
que há um erro [Joolgoo k-ya
oong]

  sorry, I've made a mistake
desculpe, enganei-me
[dishk**oo**lp aygan**ay**m]

misunderstanding o mal-
entendido [malayntaynd**ee**doo]

mix-up: sorry, there's been a
mix-up desculpe, houve uma
confusão [**oh**vooma
konfooz**ow**ng]

mobile phone o telemóvel
[telem**o**vil]

modern moderno [mood**eh**rnoo]

modern art gallery a galeria de
arte moderna [galir**ee**-a dart
mood**eh**rna]

moisturizer o creme hidratante
[kraymeedrat**a**nt]

moment: I won't be a moment
não demoro n**a**da [nowng
dim**o**roo]

monastery o mosteiro
[moosht**ay**roo]

Monday segunda-feira
[seg**oo**nda f**ay**ra]

money o dinheiro [deen-y**ay**roo]

month o mês [maysh]

monument o monumento
[moonoom**ay**ntoo]

moon a lua [l**oo**-a]

Moor o mouro [m**oh**-ooroo]

Moorish mourisco [mor**ee**shkoo]

moped a motorizada
[mootooriz**a**da]

more* mais [mīsh]

  can I have some more water,
please? mais água, por favor
[mīz **a**gwa poor fav**oh**r]

  more expensive mais caro
[maīsh k**a**roo]

  more interesting mais
interessante [mīzintris**a**nt]

  more than 50 mais de
cinquenta [mīz di
sinkw**ay**nta]

  more than that mais do que
isso [mīz doo ki **ee**soo]

  a lot more muito mais
[m**wee**ngtoo mīsh]

•••••• D I A L O G U E ••••••

would you like some more? deseja
um pouco mais? [dis**ay**Ja oong
p**oh**koo mīsh]

no, no more for me, thanks (said by
man/woman) não, não mais para
mim, obrigado/obrigada [nowng –
meeng obrig**a**doo]

how about you? e você? [ee vos**ay**]

I don't want any more, thanks (said
by man/woman) não quero mais,
obrigado/obrigada [nowng k**eh**roo
mīsh]

morning a manhã [man-y**a**ng]

  this morning esta manhã
[**eh**shta]

  in the morning de manhã [di]

Morocco o Marrocos
[marr**o**koosh]

mosquito o mosquito
[mooshk**ee**too]

Mosquitoes can be intolerable at certain times of year and in certain areas but there seems to be no pattern to this, though the north is often cited as being particularly bad. December and January are usually mosquito-free. Mosquito-repellent lotion and coils are widely sold in towns and resorts.

which adds to the cost of a journey but has one distinct advantage for foreign visitors: because of the relatively high tolls, local drivers have been priced off the motorways, making them the least congested in Europe.
see **driving**

mosquito repellent o repele-mosquitos [rip**eh**l mooshk**ee**toosh]

most: I like this one most of all gosto mais deste [**go**shtoo mīJ daysht]

most of the time a maior parte do tempo [a mī-**o**r part doo t**ay**mpoo]

most tourists a maioria dos turistas [mī-oor**ee**-a doosh toor**ee**shtash]

mostly principalmente [prinsipalm**ay**nt]

mother a mãe [mayng]

motorbike a motocicleta [mootoosikl**eh**ta]

motorboat o barco a motor [b**a**rkwa moot**oh**r]

motorway a autoestrada [owtooshtr**a**da]

The motorway network is gradually expanding from a central spine that links Lisbon with Porto and the Algarve. The motorways are all toll roads, →

mountain a montanha [mont**a**n-ya]
  in the mountains nas montanhas [naJ mont**a**n-yash]
mountaineering o alpinismo [alpin**ee**Jmoo]
mouse o rato [r**a**too]
moustache o bigode [big**o**d]
mouth a boca [b**oh**ka]
mouth ulcer a **a**fta
move (one's car, house etc) mudar [mood**a**r]
  he's moved to another room mudou-se para outra sala [mood**oh**si para **oh**tra]
  could you move your car? podia mudar o seu carro? [pood**ee**-a]
  could you move up a little? pode chegar um pouquinho para lá? [pod shig**a**r oong pohk**ee**n-yoo]
  where has it moved to? para onde se mudou? [**oh**ndsi mood**oh**]
movie o filme [feelm]
movie theater o cinema [sin**ay**ma]

Mr o Senhor [sin-**yohr**]
Mrs a Senhora [sin-**y**ora]
much muito [m**wee**ngtoo]
  much better/worse muito
  melhor/pior [mil-**y**or/pi-**or**]
  much hotter muito mais
  quente [m**ï**sh kaynt]
  not (very) much não muito
  [nowng]
  I don't want very much não
  quero muito [k**eh**roo]
mud a lama
mug (for drinking) a caneca
  [kan**eh**ka]
  I've been mugged (said by man/
  woman) fui assaltado/
  assalt**ada** [fwee asalt**a**doo]
mum a mamã [mam**ang**]
mumps a papeira [pap**ay**ra]
museum o museu
  [mooz**ay**-oo]

> Museums, churches and monu-
> ments are open from around
> 10 a.m. to 12.30 p.m. and from
> 2 to 6 p.m., though the larger
> ones stay open through lunch-
> time. Almost all museums are
> closed on Mondays; also almost
> everything is closed on national
> public holidays and local holi-
> days.

mushrooms os cogumelos
  [kogoom**eh**loosh]
music a música [m**oo**zika]
musician (man) o músico
  [m**oo**zikoo]
Muslim (adj) muçulmano

  [moosoolm**a**noo]
mussels os mexilhões [mishil-
  y**oy**ngsh]
must: I must ... tenho de ...
  [t**ay**n-yoo di]
  I mustn't drink alcohol não
  devo beber álcool [nowng
  d**ay**voo bib**ayr a**lko-ol]
mustard a mostarda
  [moosht**a**rda]
my* o meu [m**ay**-oo], a
  minha [m**ee**n-ya], os meus
  [m**ay**-oosh], as minhas
  [m**ee**n-yash]
myself: I'll do it myself (said by
  man/woman) eu mesmo/m**e**sma
  faço isso [**ay**-oo m**ay**Jmoo –
  fasoo **ee**soo]
  by myself (said by man/woman)
  sozinho [soz**ee**n-yoo]/sozinha

N

nail (finger) a unha [**oo**n-ya]
  (metal) o prego [pr**eh**goo]
nailbrush a escova de unhas
  [shk**oh**va d**oo**n-yash]
nail varnish o verniz de unhas
  [virn**ee**J d**oo**n-yash]
name o nome [nohm]
  my name's John o meu
  nome é John [oo m**ay**-oo
  nohm eh]
  what's your name? como se
  chama? [k**oh**moo si sh**a**ma]
  what is the name of this
  street? qual é o nome desta
  rua? [kawl**eh** oo nohm d**eh**shta
  r**oo**-a]

Most Portuguese have several names: one or two Christian names and at least two surnames (the mother's last surname and the father's last surname). Portuguese names are often extremely long, especially those for distinguished families. This is because 'good' family names are retained when people get married. It is usual for the woman to add her husband's surname after her own family name. So if Maria Amaro Pires marries João Costa, she may become Maria Amaro Pires Costa.

napkin o guardanapo [gwardan**a**poo]

nappy a fralda

narrow (street) estreito [shtr**ay**too]

nasty (person) mau [mow], f má (weather, accident) grave [grav]

national nacional [nas-yoon**a**l]

nationality a nacionalidade [nas-yoonalid**a**d]

natural natural [natoor**a**l]

nausea as náuseas [n**ow**z yash]

navy (blue) azul-marinho [az**oo**l mar**ee**n-yoo]

near perto [p**eh**rtoo]
 is it near the city centre? é perto do centro da cidade? [eh – doo s**ay**ntroo da sid**a**d]
 do you go near the Paço Real?

passa perto do Passo Real? [p**eh**rtoo doo p**a**soo ri-**a**l]
 where is the nearest ...? onde fica o/a ... mais próximo/ próxima ...? [ohnd f**ee**ka oo/ a ... m**ī**sh pr**o**simoo]

nearby perto daqui [p**eh**rtoo dak**ee**]

nearly quase [kwaz]

necessary necessário [nisis**a**r-yoo]

neck o pescoço [pishk**oh**soo]

necklace o colar [kool**a**r]

necktie a gravata

need: I need ... preciso de ... [pris**ee**zoo di]
 do I need to pay? preciso de pagar?

needle a agulha [ag**oo**l-ya]

negative (film) o negativo [nigat**ee**voo]

neither: neither (one) of them nenhum deles [nin-y**oo**ng d**ay**lish]
 neither ... nor ... nem ... nem ... [nayng]

nephew o sobrinho [soobr**ee**n-yoo]

net (in sport) a rede [rayd]

Netherlands a Holanda [ol**a**nda]

network map o mapa

never nunca [n**oo**nka]

• • • • • DIALOGUE • • • • • •

have you ever been to Fátima? já esteve em Fátima? [Jasht**ay**vayng]
no, never, I've never been there não, nunca estive lá [nowng n**oo**nksht**ee**v la]

new novo [**noh**voo]
news (radio, TV etc) as notícias [nootee̍s-yash]
newsagent's a tabacaria [tabakaree-a]
newspaper o jornal [Joornal]
newspaper kiosk o quiosque de jornais [k-yoshk di Joornish]
New Year Ano Novo [anoo nohvoo]

> The Portuguese celebrate New Year's Eve (**Véspera de Ano Novo**) in parties at home, with friends or at restaurants. January 6th, **Dia de Reis**, is not as important in Portugal as in Spain, but there is a special cake baked for this day which contains a broad bean and a present; the person who gets the broad bean is supposed to pay for the cake next year. **Dia de Reis** is celebrated more in country areas, where traditionally people go from door to door, singing and improvising songs about the owner of the house and are invited in for something to eat.

Happy New Year! Feliz Ano Novo! [fileez anoo nohvoo]
New Year's Eve a véspera do dia de Ano Novo [vehshpira doo dee-a danoo]
New Zealand Nova Zelândia [nova ziland-ya]
New Zealander: I'm a New

Zealander (man/woman) sou neo-zelandês/neo-zelandesa [soh neh-o zilandaysh/neh-o zilandayza]
next próximo [prosimoo]
the next corner/street on the left a próxima esquina/rua à esquerda [shkeena/roo-a a shkayrda]
at the next stop na próxima paragem [paraJayng]
next week na próxima semana [simana]
next to próximo de [di]
nice (food, person) agradável (looks, view etc) bonito [booneetoo]
niece a sobrinha [soobreen-ya]
night a noite [noh-it]
at night à noite
good night boa noite [boh-a]

• • • • • • DIALOGUE • • • • • •

do you have a single room for one night? tem um quarto individual para uma noite? [tayn-yoong kwartwindividwal para ooma]
yes, madam sim, senhora [seeng sin-yora]
how much is it per night? quanto é por noite? [kwantweh poor]
it's 600 escudos for one night são seiscentos escudos por uma noite [sowng saysayntooshkoodoosh poor ooma]
thank you, I'll take it (said by man/woman) obrigado/obrigada, fico com ele [obrigadoo – feekoo kong ayl]

nightclub a boite [bwat]
nightdress a camisa de dormir
[kam**ee**za di doorm**ee**r]
night porter o porteiro da noite
[poort**ay**roo da n**oh**-it]
no* não [nowng]
I've no change não tenho
troco [t**ay**n-yoo tr**oh**koo]
there's no ... left não há
mais ... [a mīsh]
no way! de maneira
nenhuma! [di man**ay**ra nin-
y**oo**ma]
oh no! (upset) oh não! [nowng]
nobody* ninguém [ning**ay**ng]
there's nobody there não há
ninguém lá [nowng a – l**a**]
noise o barulho [bar**oo**l-yoo]
noisy: it's too noisy é
barulhento demais [eh barool-
y**ay**ntoo dim**ī**sh]
non-alcoholic não alcoólico
[nowng alkw**o**likoo]
none* nenhum [nin-y**oo**ng]
nonsmoking carriage a
carruagem para não
fumadores [karrwaJayng –
nowng foomad**oh**rish]
noon o meio-dia [m**ay**-oo
d**ee**-a]
no-one* ninguém [ning**ay**ng]
nor: nor do I nem eu [nayng
ay-oo]
normal normal
north o norte [nort]
in the north no norte [noo]
to the north ao norte [ow]
north of Braga ao norte de
Braga [di]

northeast o nordeste
[noord**eh**sht]
northern setentrional [setayntr-
yoon**a**l]
Northern Ireland a Irlanda do
Norte [eerl**a**nda doo nort]
northwest o noroeste
[norw**eh**sht]
Norway a Noruega [noorw**eh**ga]
Norwegian (adj) norueguês
[noorweg**ay**sh]
nose o nariz [nar**ee**sh]
nosebleed a hemorragia nasal
[emoorraJ**ee**-ya naz**a**l]
not* não [nowng]
no, I'm not hungry não, não
tenho fome [t**ay**n-yoo fohm]
I don't want anything, thank
you (said by man/woman) não
quero n**a**da, obrigado/
obrig**a**da [k**eh**roo – obrig**a**doo]
it's not necessary não é
necessário [eh neses**a**r-yoo]
I didn't know that não sabia
[sab**ee**-a]
not that one – this one esse
não – este [ays – aysht]
note (banknote) a n**o**ta
notebook o bloco de
apontamentos [blokoo
dapontam**ay**ntoosh]
notepaper (for letters) o papel de
carta [pap**eh**l di]
nothing* n**a**da
nothing for me, thanks (said by
man/woman) nada para mim,
obrigado/obrig**a**da [meeng
obrig**a**doo]
nothing else mais nada [mīJ]

novel o romance [roomans]
November Novembro [noovaymbroo]
now agora
number o número [noomiroo]
  I've got the wrong number enganei-me no número [aynganaym noo]
  what is your phone number? qual é o número do seu telefone? [kwaleh oo – doo say-oo telefohn]
number plate a chapa da matrícula [shapa da matreekoola]
nurse (man/woman) o enfermeiro [aynfirmayroo], a enfermeira
nut (for bolt) a porca
nuts a noz [nosh]

O

occupied (toilet, telephone) ocupado [okoopadoo]
o'clock* horas [orash]
October Outubro [ohtoobroo]
odd (strange) estranho [shtran-yoo]
of* de [di]
off (lights) desligado [diᴣligadoo]
  it's just off Praça do Comércio mesmo ao lado da Praça do Comércio [meᴣmoo ow ladoo da prasa doo koomehrs-yoo]
  we're off tomorrow partimos amanhã [parteemoozaman-yang]
offensive (language, behaviour) ofensivo [ofaynseevoo]

office (place of work) o escritório [shkritor-yoo]
officer (said to policeman) Senhor Guarda [sin-yohr gwarda]
often muitas vezes [mweengtaᴣ vayzish]
  not often não muitas vezes [nowng]
  how often are the buses? com que frequência há autocarros? [kong ki frikwaynsya a owtookarroosh]
oil (for car, for cooking) o óleo [ol-yoo]
ointment a pomada [poomada]
OK está bem [shta bayng]
  are you OK? você está bem? [vosay shta bayng]
  is that OK with you? está bem para si? [see]
  is it OK to ...? pode-se ...? [podsi]
  that's OK thanks (said by man/woman) está bem obrigado/obrigada [obrigadoo]
  I'm OK, thanks não quero, obrigado/obrigada [nowng kehro]
  (I feel OK) sinto-me bem [seentoom]
  is this train OK for ...? este comboio vai para ... [aysht kombohyoo vī]
  I'm sorry, OK? desculpe-me, está bem? [dishkoolpimi]
old velho [vehl-yoo]

•••••• DIALOGUE ••••••

how old are you? que idade tem?
[keedad tayng]

I'm 25 tenho vinte-e-cinco anos
[tayn-yoo veentiseenkoo]

and you? e você? [ee vosay]

old-fashioned antiquado
[antikwadoo]

old town (old part of town) a
cidade antiga [sidad anteega]

in the old town na cidade
antiga

olive oil o azeite [azayt]

olives a azeitona [azaytohna]

black/green olives as
azeitonas pretas/verdes
[azaytohnash praytash/
vayrdsh]

omelette a omeleta [omilayta]

on* sobre [sohbr]

on the street/beach na praia/
rua

is it on this road? é nesta rua?
[eh nehshta]

on the plane no avião [nwav-
yowng]

on Saturday no sábado [noo]

on television na televisão

I haven't got it on me não o
tenho comigo [nowng oo tayn-
yoo koomeegoo]

this one's on me (drink) esta
bebida sou eu que pago
[ehshta bibeeda soh ay-oo kih
pagoo]

the light wasn't on a luz não
estava acesa [looJ nowng
shtava asayza]

what's on tonight? qual é o
programa para esta noite?
[kwaleh oo proograma
parehshta noh-it]

once (one time) uma vez [ooma
vaysh]

at once (immediately)
imediatamente [imid-
yatamaynt]

one* um [oong], uma [ooma]

the white one o/a branco/
branca [oo/a brankoo]

one-way ticket o bilhete
simples [bil-yayt seemplish]

onion a cebola [sibohla]

only só [saw], somente
[somaynt]

only one só um/uma [oong/
ooma]

it's only 6 o'clock ainda são só
seis horas [a-eenda sowng saw
sayz orash]

I've only just got here acabei
de chegar [akabay di shigar]

on/off switch o interruptor de
ligar/desligar [intirrooptohr di
ligar/diJligar]

open* (adj) aberto [abehrtoo]
(verb) abrir [abreer]

when do you open? quando
abre? [kwandwabr]

I can't get it open não consigo
abrir [nowng konseegwabreer]

in the open air ao ar livre [ow
ar leevr]

opening times as horas de
abertura [orash dabirtoora]

open ticket o bilhete em aberto
[bil-yaytayng abehrtoo]

opera a ópera [**o**pira]

operation (medical) a operação [opira**sow**ng]

operator (telephone: man/woman) o/ a telefonista [telefoon**ee**shta]

For European numbers dial 099 and for the rest of the world dial 098.

opposite: the opposite direction na direcção oposta [direhs**ow**ng op**o**shta]

the bar opposite o bar do outro lado [doo **oh**troo l**a**doo]

opposite my hotel em frente ao meu hotel [ayng fraynt ow]

optician o oculista [okool**ee**shta]

or ou [oh]

orange (fruit) a laranja [laran**J**a] (colour) cor de laranja [kohr di]

orange juice (fresh) o sumo de laranja [**soo**moo] (fizzy) a laranjada com gás [laran**J**ada kong**a**sh] (diluted) o refresco de laranja [rif**ray**shkoo di]

orchestra a orquestra [ork**eh**shtra]

order: can we order now? (in restaurant) podemos pedir agora? [pood**ay**moosh pid**ee**r]

I've already ordered, thanks (said by man/woman) já pedi, obrigado/obrigada [**J**a pid**ee** obrig**a**doo]

I didn't order this não pedi isto [nowng – **ee**shtoo]

out of order avariado [avar-y**a**doo]

ordinary vulgar [voolg**a**r]

other outro [**oh**troo]

the other one o outro [oo]

the other day outro dia [d**ee**-a]

I'm waiting for the others estou a esperar outras pessoas [stoh a shpir**a**r **oh**trash pis**oh**-ash]

do you have any others? tem mais algum/alguma? [tayng mīsh alg**oo**ng/alg**oo**ma]

otherwise doutro modo [d**oh**troo m**o**doo]

our* nosso [n**o**soo], nossa [n**o**sa], nossos [n**o**soosh], nossas [n**o**sash]

ours* nosso, nossa, nossos, nossas

out: he's out saiu [sa-**ee**-oo]

three kilometres out of town a três quilómetros da cidade [traysh kil**o**mitroo**J** da sid**a**d]

outdoors fora de casa [di k**a**za]

outside do lado de fora [doo l**a**doo di]

can we sit outside? podemos sentar-nos lá fora? [pood**ay**moosh saynt**a**rnoosh]

oven o forno [f**oh**rnoo]

over: over here aqui [ak**ee**]

over there ali [al**ee**]

over five hundred mais de quinhentos/quinhentas [mīsh di]

it's over terminado [tirmin**a**doo]

overcharge: you've overcharged me você vendeu-me mais caro [vosay venday-oomi mīsh karoo]

overcoat o sobretudo [soobritoodoo]

overlooking: I'd like a room overlooking the courtyard queria um quarto que dê para o pátio [kiree-a oong kwartoo ki day paroo pat-yoo]

overnight (travel) de noite [di noh-it]

overtake ultrapassar [ooltrapasar]

owe: how much do I owe you? quanto lhe devo? [kwantoo l-yi dayvoo]

own: my own ... o meu próprio ... [oo may-oo propr-yoo]

are you on your own? (to man/woman) está sozinho/sozinha? [shta sawzeen-yoo]

I'm on my own (said by man/woman) estou sozinho/sozinha [shtoh]

owner (man/woman) o dono [dohnoo], a dona

oysters as ostras [ohshtrash]

P

pack fazer as malas [fazayr aJ malash]

a pack of ... um pacote de ... [oong pakot di]

package (parcel) a encomenda [aynkoomaynda]

package holiday a excursão organizada [shkoorsowng organizada]

packed lunch o almoço embalado [almohsw-aymbaladoo]

packet: a packet of cigarettes o maço de cigarros [masoo di sigarroosh]

padlock o cadeado [kad-yadoo]

page (of book) a página [paJina] could you page Mr ...? pode chamar o Sr ...? [pod shamar oo sin-yohr]

pain a dor [dohr] I have a pain here tenho uma dor aqui [tayn-yoo ooma dohr akee]

painful doloroso [dooloorohzoo]

painkillers os analgésicos [analJehzikoosh]

paint a tinta [teenta]

painting a pintura [pintoora]

pair: a pair of ... um par de ... [oong di]

Pakistani (adj) paquistanês [pakishtanaysh]

palace o palácio [palas-yoo]

pale pálido [palidoo] pale blue azul claro [azool klaroo]

pan a panela [panehla]

panties as cuecas [kwehkash]

pants (underwear) as cuecas [kwehkash] (US) as calças [kalsash]

pantyhose os collants [koolansh]

paper o papel [papehl]

(newspaper) o jornal [Joornal]
a sheet of paper uma folha de
papel [**oo**ma foh**l**ya di]
paper handkerchiefs os lenços
de papel [l**ay**nsoosh]
paragliding o parapentismo
[parapaynt**ee**Jmoo]
parcel a encomenda
[aynkoom**ay**nda]
pardon (me)? (didn't understand/
hear) desculpe? [dishk**oo**lp],
como? [k**oh**moo]
parents os pais [pīsh]
parents-in-law os sogros
[s**oh**groosh]

park o jardim público
[Jard**ee**ng p**oo**blikoo]
(verb) estacionar [shtas-
yoon**ar**]
can I park here? posso
estacionar aqui? [p**o**soo –
ak**ee**]

Parking is extremely difficult in
city and town centres: only the
top hotels have their own car
parks and you can expect to
spend ages looking for a space,
often ending up on the outskirts
of town and having to walk to the
centre.

parking lot o parque de
estacionamento [park di shtas-
yoonam**ay**ntoo]
part a parte [part]
partner (boyfriend/girlfriend) o
companheiro [kompan-
y**ay**roo], a companh**ei**ra

party (group) o grupo [gr**oo**poo]
(celebration) a festa [f**eh**shta]
pass (in mountains) o
desfiladeiro [dishfilad**ay**roo]
passenger (man/woman) o
passageiro [pasaJ**ay**roo], a
passag**ei**ra
passport o passaporte
[pasap**or**t]

It is advisable to carry an ID
card with you at all times but as
a tourist you are unlikely to be
fined if caught without one.

past*: in the past no passado
[noo pas**a**doo]
just past the information office
logo a seguir ao escritório
de informações [l**o**goo a
sig**ee**r owshkrit**o**r-yoo
dinfoormas**oy**ngsh]
path o caminho [kam**ee**n-yoo]
pattern o desenho [diz**ay**n-yoo]
pavement o passeio [pas**ay**-oo]
on the pavement no passeio
[noo]
pavement café o café de
esplanada [kaf**eh** dishplan**a**da]
pay pagar
can I pay, please? por favor,
queria pagar [poor fav**oh**r
kir**ee**-a]
it's already paid for já está
pago [Ja shta p**a**goo]

•••••• DIALOGUE ••••••

who's paying? quem vai pagar?
[kayng vī]

I'll pay eu pago [**ay**-oo pa**g**oo]
no, you paid last time, I'll pay não,
você pagou da última vez, eu
pago [nowng vos**ay** pag**oh** da-
ooltima v**ay**sh]

pay phone o telefone público
[telef**oh**n p**oo**blikoo]
peaceful tranquilo
[trankw**ee**loo]
peach o pêsscgo [**pay**sigoo]
peanuts os amendoins
[amayndw**ee**nsh]
pear a pêra [**pay**ra]
peas as ervilhas [irv**ee**l-yash]
peculiar (taste, custom) estranho
[shtr**a**n-yoo]
pedestrian crossing o passagem
de peões [pasa**J**ayng di
p-yoyngsh], a pasadeira de
peões [pasad**ay**ra]

> You should be particularly
> careful when crossing the road,
> because pedestrian crossings
> are often ignored by drivers.

pedestrian precinct a zona para
peões [**z**ohna p**a**ra p-yoyngsh]
peg (for washing) a m**o**la
(for tent) a cavilha [kav**ee**l-ya]
pen a caneta [kan**ay**ta]
pencil o lápis [lapsh]
penfriend (man/woman) o/a
correspondente
[koorrishpond**ay**nt]
penicillin a penicilina
[penisil**ee**na]
penknife o canivete [kaniv**eh**t]

pensioner (man/woman) o
reformado [rifoorm**a**doo], a
reform**a**da
people a gente [Jaynt]
the other people in the hotel
as outras pessoas no hotel
[az**oh**trash pis**oh**-ash nwoht**ehl**]
too many people gente
demais [dim**ī**sh]
pepper (spice) a pimenta
[pim**ay**nta]
(vegetable) o pimento
[pim**ay**ntoo]
peppermint (sweet) a hortelã-
pimenta [ortil**a**ng pim**ay**nta]
per: per night por noite [poor
n**oh**-it]
how much per day? quanto é
por dia? [kwantw**eh**
poor d**ee**-a]
per cent por cento [s**ay**ntoo]
perfect perfeito [pirf**ay**too]
perfume o perfume [pirf**oo**m]
perhaps talvez [talv**ay**sh]
perhaps not talvez não [nowng]
period (of time, menstruation) o
período [pir**ee**-oodoo]
perm a permanente
[pirman**ay**nt]
permit a licença [lis**ay**nsa]
person a pessoa [pis**oh**-a]
personal stereo o walkman®
petrol a gasolina [gazool**ee**na]

> Four-star petrol (**super**) is
> relatively expensive: about 25
> per cent more than in Britain,
> and nearly twice the US →

equivalent. Unleaded petrol (**sem chumbo**) is now widely available, and most rental cars run on it.

petrol can a lata de gasolina [di gazool**ee**na]

petrol station a bomba de gasolina [b**oh**mba di]

pharmacy a farmácia [farm**a**s-ya]

For minor health complaints you should go to a **farmácia**; in larger towns there's usually one where English is spoken. Pharmacists are highly trained and can dispense many drugs that would be available only with a prescription in Britain or North America.

---

phone o telefone [telef**oh**n] (verb) telefonar [telefoon**a**r]

International calls can be made direct from almost any phone booth, but in most of them you'll need a good stock of coins and a great deal of patience as the international lines are often blocked and you need to insert a large amount to make the connection. In busy tourist areas, it's easier to use **credifones**, which you can use with phonecards available from post offices – note that there →

---

are two different types of phonecards, each only valid in the corresponding credifone. You'll find payphones in bars and cafés (and, increasingly, in Turismo offices and newsagents), usually indicated by the sign of a red horse on a white circle over a green background and the legend **Correio de Portugal – Telefone**. Otherwise, you could go to the main post office, which is very likely to have phone cabins – just tell the clerk the number you want to phone, and pay for your call afterwards. Except in Lisbon and Porto, most telephone offices are closed in the evening, but there is no cheap-rate period anyway for international calls. Reverse charge (collect) calls can be made from any phone, dialling 099 for a European connection and 098 for the rest of the world.

---

phone book a lista telefónica [**lee**shta telef**oh**nika]

phone box a cabina telefónica [kab**ee**na]

phonecard o cartão de telefone [kart**ow**ng di telef**oh**n]

phone number o número de telefone [n**oo**miroo]

photo a fotografia [footoografee-a]

excuse me, could you take a

photo of us? faz favor, pode tirar-nos uma fotografia? [fash fav**oh**r pod tir**a**rnooz **oo**ma]

phrasebook o livro de expressões [l**ee**vroo dishpris**oy**ngsh]

piano o piano [p-y**a**noo]

pickpocket (man/woman) o/a carteirista [kartayr**ee**shta]

pick up: will you be there to pick me up? estarás lá para apanhar-me? [shtara**J** – apan**ya**rmi]

picnic o piquenique [pikin**ee**k]

picture (drawing, painting) a pintura [peent**oo**ra] (photograph) a fotografia [footoograf**ee**-a]

pie a tarte [tart]

piece o pedaço [pid**a**soo] a piece of ... um bocado de ... [oong book**a**doo di]

pilchards as sardinhas [sard**ee**n-yash]

pill a pílula [p**ee**loola] I'm on the pill estou a tomar a pílula [shtoh a toom**a**r]

pillow a almofada [almoof**a**da]

pillow case a fronha da almofada [fr**oh**n-ya]

pin o alfinete [alfin**ay**t]

pineapple o ananás [anan**a**sh]

pineapple juice o sumo de ananás [s**oo**moo danan**a**sh]

pink cor de rosa [kohr di r**o**za]

pipe (for smoking) o cachimbo [kash**ee**mboo] (for water) o cano [k**a**noo]

pipe cleaner o desentupidor de cachimbo [dizayntoopid**oh**r di kash**ee**mboo]

pity: it's a pity é uma pena [eh **oo**ma p**ay**na]

pizza a pizza

place o lugar [loog**a**r] at your place na sua casa [s**oo**-a k**a**za] at his place na casa dele [dayl]

plain (not patterned) liso [l**ee**zoo]

plane o avião [av-y**ow**ng] by plane de avião [dav-y**ow**ng]

plant a planta

plaster cast o gesso [**J**ay**s**oo]

plasters o adesivo [adiz**ee**voo]

plastic o plástico [pl**a**shtikoo]

plastic bag o saco de plástico [s**a**koo di]

plate o prato [pr**a**too]

platform o cais [k**ī**sh] which platform is it for Fátima? qual é o cais para Fátima? [kwal**eh** oo]

play (verb) jogar [**J**oog**a**r] (in theatre) a peça de teatro [p**eh**sa di t-y**a**troo]

playground o pátio de recreio [p**a**t-yoo di rikr**ay**-oo]

pleasant agradável

please se faz favor [si fash fav**oh**r], por favor [poor] yes please sim, por favor [seeng] could you please ...? por favor, pode ...? [pod] please don't por favor, não faça isto [nowng f**a**sa **ee**shtoo]

pleased: pleased to meet you
(said to man/woman) muito
prazer em conhecê-lo/
conhecê-la [m**wee**ngtoo
praz**ay**r ayng koon-yis**ay**loo]
pleasure: my pleasure de n**a**da
[di]
plenty: plenty of ... muito ...
[m**wee**ngtoo]
there's plenty of time temos
muito tempo [t**ay**mooJ –
t**ay**mpoo]
that's plenty, thanks (said by
man/woman) ch**e**ga, obrig**a**do/
obrig**a**da [sh**ay**ga obrig**a**doo]
pliers o alic**a**te [alik**a**t]
plug (electrical) a tom**a**da
[toom**a**da]
(for car) a vela [v**eh**la]
(in sink) a t**a**mpa do r**a**lo [doo
r**a**loo]
plumber o canalizador
[kanalizad**ohr**]
p.m.* da tarde [tard]
poached egg o **o**vo escalf**a**do
[**oh**voo shkalf**a**doo]
pocket o bolso [oo b**oh**lsoo]
point: two point five dois
v**í**rgula c**i**nco [d**oh**-iJ
v**ee**rgoola s**ee**nkoo]
there's no point não v**a**le a
p**e**na [nowng v**a**l-ya p**ay**na]
points (in car) os platin**a**dos
[platin**a**doosh]
poisonous veneno**s**o
[vinin**oh**zoo]
police a pol**í**cia [pool**ee**s-ya]
call the police! ch**a**mem a
pol**í**cia! [sh**a**mayng]

There are three different
authorities with which you
might come into contact, though
in an emergency, the first policeman you see will be able to help
you. In major towns, the police
force most likely to be of assistance will be the **PSP** (**Polícia
de Segurança Pública**), responsible among other things
for incidents involving tourists.
They wear distinctive blue
uniforms, a beret and a
badge on their jackets identify-
ing themselves. The **Polícia
Judiciária** is the force responsible for investigating crime.
The **GNR** (**Guarda Nacional
Republicana**) police the rural
areas, patrol the motorways,
and are responsible for oversee-
ing all ceremonial occasions;
ordinarily they wear blue-grey
uniforms. You can't count on
English being spoken by most of
the local police personnel.
For all emergency services dial
115.

policeman o pol**í**cia [oo
pool**ee**s-ya]
police station o P**o**sto da
Pol**í**cia [p**oh**shtoo]
policewoman a mulher-pol**í**cia
[mool-y**eh**r]
polish (for shoes) a pom**a**da para
calç**a**dos [poom**a**da para
kals**a**doosh]

polite bem-educado [bayng idook**a**doo]
polluted contaminado [kontamin**a**doo]
pony o pónei [p**o**nay]
pool (for swimming) a piscina [pish-s**ee**na]
poor (not rich) pobre [p**o**br]
   (quality) mau [mow], f má
pop music a música pop [m**oo**zika]
pop singer (man/woman) o cantor pop [kant**oh**r], a cant**o**ra pop
popular popular [poopool**a**r]
population a população [poopoolas**ow**ng]
pork a carne de porco [karn di p**oh**rkoo]
port (for boats) o porto [p**oh**rtoo]
   (drink) o vinho do Porto [v**ee**n-yoo doo]

Port is produced from grapes grown in the valley of the Douro and is stored in huge wine lodges at Vila Nova de Gaia, a riverside suburb of Porto. You can visit these for tours and free tastings. Alternatively, you can try any of 300 types and vintages of port at the **Instituto do Vinho do Porto** (Port Wine Institute) in Lisbon and Porto. Even if your quest for port isn't serious enough to do either, be sure to try the dry white aperitif ports, still little known outside the country.

porter (in hotel) o porteiro [poort**ay**roo]
portrait o retrato [ritr**a**too]
Portugal Portugal [poortoog**a**l]
Portuguese (adj) português [poortoog**ay**sh]
   (language) português
   (man) o português
   (woman) a portuguesa
   the Portuguese os portugueses [poortoog**ay**zish]
posh (restaurant, people) chique [sheek]
possible possível [poos**ee**vil]
   is it possible to ...? é possível ...? [eh]
   as ... as possible tão ... quanto possível [t**ow**ng ... kwantoo]
post (mail) o correio [koorr**ay**-oo]
   (verb) pôr no correio [pohr noo]
   could you post this for me? podia-me pôr isto no Scorreio? [poode**e**-ami – **ee**shtoo noo]
postbox a caixa do correio [k**i**sha doo]
postcard o postal [poosht**a**l]
postcode o código postal [k**o**digoo poosht**a**l]
poster (for room) o poster
   (in street) o cartaz [kart**a**sh]
poste restante a posta-restante [p**o**shta risht**a**nt]
post office os correios [koorr**ay**-oosh]

Post offices are indicated by the letters **CTT** (**Correios e Telecomunicações**) and are normally open Monday to Friday from 9 a.m. to 6 p.m; larger ones are sometimes open on Saturday mornings as well and the main Lisbon branches have much longer opening hours. You can have poste restante (general delivery) mail sent to you at any post office in the country. Letters should be marked **Posta Restante**, and ideally your name should be written in capitals and underlined. To collect, you need to take along your passport – look for the counter marked **encomendas**. If you are expecting mail, ask the postal clerk to check for letters under your first name and any other initials (including Ms, etc) as well as under your surname.

To send mail abroad, you are best advised to use the more expensive **correio azul** (express mail).

potato a bat**a**ta
potato chips as batatas fritas [bat**a**tash fr**ee**tash]
pots and pans as panelas e tachos [pan**eh**lazee t**a**shoosh]
pottery (objects) a loiça de barro [l**oh**-isa di b**a**rroo]
pound* (money, weight) a libra [l**ee**bra]

power cut o corte de energia [kort denir**Jee**-a]
power point a tomada [toom**a**da]
practise: I want to practise my Portuguese quero praticar o meu português [k**eh**roo pratik**a**roo m**a**y-oo poortoog**ay**sh]
prawn a g**a**mba
prefer: I prefer ... prefiro ... [prif**ee**roo]
pregnant gr**á**vida
prescription (for medicine) a receita [ris**ay**ta]
see **pharmacy**
present (gift) o presente [priz**ay**nt]
president (of country: man/woman) o/a presidente [prizid**ay**nt]
pretty bonito [boon**ee**too]
it's pretty expensive é muito caro [m**wee**ngtoo k**a**roo]
price o preço [pr**ay**soo]
priest o padre [padr]
prime minister (man/woman) o primeiro ministro [prim**ay**roo min**ee**shtroo], a prim**ei**ra min**i**stra
printed matter os impressos [impr**eh**soosh]
priority (in driving) a prioridade [pr-yoorid**a**d]
prison a cadeia [kad**ay**-a]
private privado [priv**a**doo]
private bathroom a casa de banho privativa [k**a**za di ban-yoo privat**ee**va]
probably provavelmente

[proovavilm**ay**nt]

problem o problema
[proobl**ay**ma]

no problem! tudo bem!
[t**oo**doo bayng]

program(me) o programa
[proogr**a**ma]

promise: I promise prometo
[proom**ay**too]

**pronounce: how is this
pronounced?** como se
pronuncia? [k**oh**moo si
proonoons**ee**-a]

properly (repaired, locked etc) bem
[bayng]

protection factor (of suntan lotion)
o factor de protecção [fat**oh**r
di prootehs**ow**ng]

Protestant protestante
[prootisht**a**nt]

public convenience a casa de
banho pública [k**a**za di ban-
yoo p**oo**blika]

public holiday o feriado [fir-
y**a**doo]

pudding (dessert) a sobremesa
[sobrim**ay**za]

pull puxar [poosh**a**r]

pullover o pullover

puncture o furo [f**oo**roo]

purple roxo [r**oh**shoo]

purse (for money) a carteira
[kart**ay**ra]

(US) a mala de mão [di]

push empurrar [aympoorr**a**r]

pushchair o carrinho de bebé
[karr**ee**n-yoo di beb**eh**]

put* pôr [pohr]

where can I put ...? onde

posso pôr ...? [ohnd p**o**soo]

**could you put us up for the
night?** pode dar-nos
acomodação para uma
noite? [pod d**a**rnooz
akoomoodas**ow**ng para **oo**ma]

pyjamas o pijama [piᴊ**a**ma]

Q

quality a qualidade [kwalid**a**d]

quarantine a quarentena
[kwaraynt**ay**na]

quarter a quarta parte [kw**a**rta
part]

quayside: on the quayside no
cais [noo kīsh]

question a pergunta [pirg**oo**nta]

queue a bicha [b**ee**sha]

quick rápido [r**a**pidoo]

that was quick! que rápido
que foi! [kī – foh-i]

what's the quickest way there?
qual é o caminho mais
rápido para lá? [kwal**eh** oo
kam**ee**n-yoo mīsh r**a**pidoo]

quickly depressa [dipr**eh**sa]

quiet (place, hotel) silencioso
[silayns-y**oh**zoo]

quiet! cale-se! [k**a**lsi]

quite (fairly) bastánte [basht**a**nt]

(very) muito [m**wee**ngtoo]

that's quite right está certo
[shta s**eh**rtoo]

quite a lot bastante

R

rabbit o coelho [kw**ay**l-yoo]

race (for runners, cars) a corrida [koorr**ee**da]

racket (tennis, squash) a raqueta [rak**eh**ta]

radiator (of car, in room) o radiador [rad-yad**oh**r]

radio o rádio [r**a**d-yoo]
on the radio no rádio [noo]

rail: by rail por caminho de ferro [poor kam**ee**n-yoo di f**eh**rroo]

railway o caminho de ferro

rain a chuva [sh**oo**va]
in the rain à chuva
it's raining está a chover [sht**a**-a shoov**ay**r]

raincoat o impermeável [impirm-y**a**vil]

rape a violação [v-yoolas**ow**ng]

rare (uncommon) raro [r**a**roo]
(steak) mal passado [pas**a**doo]

rash (on skin) a erupção [eroops**ow**ng]

raspberry a framboesa [frambw**ay**za]

rat a ratazana

rate (for changing money) o câmbio [k**a**mb-yoo]

rather: it's rather good é bastante bom/boa [eh basht**a**nt bong/b**oh**-a]
I'd rather ... prefiro ... [prif**ee**roo]

razor (electric) a máquina de barbear [m**a**kina di barb-y**ar**]

razor blades as lâminas p**a**ra

barbear [l**a**minash]

read ler [layr]

ready pronto [pr**oh**ntoo]
are you ready? (said to man/woman) estás pronto/pronta? [sht**a**sh pr**oh**ntoo]
I'm not ready yet (said by man/woman) ainda não estou pronto/pronta [a-**ee**nda nowng shtoh]

•••••• DIALOGUE ••••••

when will it be ready? quando estará pronto? [kw**a**ndoo shtar**a**]
it should be ready in a couple of days deve ficar pronto em dois dias [dehv fik**ar** – ayng d**oh**-iJ d**ee**-ash]

real verdadeiro [virdad**ay**roo]

really realmente [r-yalm**ay**nt]
I'm really sorry lamento imenso [lam**ay**ntoo im**ay**nsoo]
that's really great isso é fantástico [eesw**eh** fant**a**shtikoo]
really? (doubt) de verdade? [di vird**a**d]
(polite interest) sim? [seeng]

rear lights as luzes de trás [l**oo**zish di trash]

rearview mirror o espelho retrovisor [shp**ay**l-yoo ritroviz**oh**r]

reasonable (prices etc) razoável [razw**a**vil]

receipt o recibo [ris**ee**boo]

recently há pouco [a p**oh**koo]

reception (in hotel, for guests) a recepção [risehs**ow**ng] at reception na recepção

reception desk o balcão da recepção [balk**ow**ng]

receptionist (man/woman) o/a recepcionista [risehs-yoon**ee**shta]

recognize reconhecer [rikoon-yis**ay**r]

recommend: could you recommend ...? podia recomendar ...? [pood**ee**-a rikoomaynd**ar**]

record (music) o disco [d**ee**shkoo]

red vermelho [virm**ay**l-yoo]

red wine o vinho tinto [v**ee**n-yoo t**ee**ntoo]

refund o reembolso [ri-aymb**oh**lsoo]

can I have a refund? pode dar-me o reembolso? [pod d**ar**moo]

region a região [riJ-y**ow**ng]

registered: by registered mail por correio registado [poor koorr**ay**-oo riJisht**a**doo]

registration number a matrícula [matr**ee**koola]

relative (noun: male/female) o/a parente [par**ay**nt]

religion a religião [riliJ-y**ow**ng]

remember: I remember lembro-me [l**ay**mbroomi]

I don't remember não me lembro [n**ow**ng mi l**ay**mbroo]

do you remember? lembra-se? [l**ay**mbrasi]

rent (noun: for apartment etc) o aluguer [aloog**ehr**]

(verb: car etc) alugar

to rent para alugar

•••••• DIALOGUE ••••••

I'd like to rent a car queria alugar um carro [kir**ee**-a – oong k**a**rroo]

for how long? por quanto tempo? [poor kw**a**ntoo t**ay**mpoo]

two days dois dias [d**oh**-iJ d**ee**-ash]

this is our range esta é a nossa gama [**eh**shteh-a n**o**sa]

I'll take the ... fico com o ... [f**ee**koo kongoo]

is that with unlimited mileage? é com quilometragem ilimitada? [eh kong kilomitr**a**Jayng]

it is sim [seeng]

can I see your licence, please? posso ver a sua carta de condução, por favor? [p**o**soo vayr a s**oo**-a k**a**rta dl kondoos**ow**ng poor fav**ohr**]

and your passport e o seu passaporte [yoo s**ay**-oo pasap**or**t]

is insurance included? o seguro está incluído? [oo sig**oo**roo shta inklw**ee**doo]

yes, but you pay the first 15,000 escudos sim, mas tem de pagar os primeiros quinze contos [seeng mash tayŋg ki pag**ar** oosh prim**ay**roosh keenz k**oh**ntoosh]

can you leave a deposit of 10,000 escudos? pode deixar um depósito de dez contos? [pod daysh**ar** oong dip**o**zitoo di dehsh]

rented car o carro de aluguer [k**a**rroo daloog**ehr**]

repair **reparar**

can you repair this? pode reparar isto? [pod riparar **ee**shtoo]

repeat **repetir** [ripit**ee**r]

could you repeat that? podia repetir? [pood**ee**-a]

reservation **a reserva** [riz**eh**rva]

I'd like to make a reservation queria fazer uma reserva [kir**ee**-a faz**ayr oo**ma]

•••••• DIALOGUE ••••••

I have a reservation tenho uma reserva [**tay**n-yoo **oo**ma]

yes sir, what name please? sim senhor, que nome, por favor? [seeng sin-**yoh**r ki nohm poor fav**oh**r]

reserve (verb) **reservar** [rizir**var**]

•••••• DIALOGUE ••••••

can I reserve a table for tonight? posso reservar uma mesa para esta noite? [p**o**soo – **oo**ma m**ay**za para **eh**shta n**oh**-it]

yes madam, for how many people? sim senhora, para quantas pessoas? [seeng sin-y**o**ra para kw**a**ntash pis**oh**-ash]

for two para duas [d**oo**-ash]

and for what time? e para que hora? [i – ki-**o**ra]

for eight o'clock para as oito horas [az**oh**-itorash]

and could I have your name, please? pode dizer-me o seu nome, por favor? [pod diz**ayr**moo s**ay**-oo nohm poor fav**oh**r]

see **alphabet** for spelling

rest: **I need a rest** preciso dum descanso [pris**ee**zoo doong dish**kan**soo]

the rest of the group o resto do grupo [**reh**shtoo doo gr**oo**poo]

restaurant **o restaurante** [rishtowr**a**nt]

Portugal is full of affordable restaurants, and servings tend to be huge. Your main course is likely to be accompanied by a huge portion of both chips and rice. You'll often find that the smarter the restaurant, the smaller the portion. It is perfectly acceptable to ask for a half portion, **uma meia dose** [**oo**ma m**ay**-a doz] or **uma dose** between two. Meals are often listed like this on the menu. It is worth checking out the **ementa turística**, too – not necessarily a 'tourist menu' as such, but more like the French **menu de jour**. Smarter restaurants, however, sometimes resent the law that compels them to offer the **ementa turística**, responding with stingy portions.

You will often be brought a variety of starters to nibble while ordering your meal; these are sometimes part of a set cover charge, but more often you will be charged for as much as →

you eat – in some places right down to each individual portion of butter. If you do not want starters, tell the waiter to take them away as soon as you take a seat.

Portuguese waiters tend to rely on a high level of honesty amongst their customers, paticularly in local bars. The most common way of working out the bill at the end of an evening is simply to count up the empty bottles and plates on the table.

Apart from straightforward restaurants – **restaurantes** – you could end up eating a meal in one of several other venues. A **tasca** is a small neighbourhood tavern, a **casa de pasto** is a cheap local dining room usually with a set three-course menu, mostly served only at lunchtime. A **cervejaria** (literally: beer house) is more informal than a restaurant, with people dropping in at all hours for a beer and a snack. In Lisbon they are often wonderful old tiled caverns, specialising in seafood. Also specialising in seafood is a **marisqueira**, occasionally very upmarket, though as often as not a regular restaurant with a superior fishy menu.

restaurant car a carruagem restaurante [karrwaJayng rishtowrant]
rest room a casa de banho [kaza di ban-yoo] see toilet
retired: I'm retired (said by man/ woman) estou reformado/ reformada [shtoh rifoormadoo]
return: a return to ... um bilhete de ida e volta a ... [oong bil-yayt deeda ee]
return ticket o bilhete de ida e volta see ticket
reverse charge call a chamada paga no destinátario [shamada – noo dishtinatar-yoo]
reverse gear a marcha atrás [marshatrash]
revolting repugnante [ripoognant]
rib a costela [kooshtehla]
rice o arroz [arrohsh]
rich (person) rico [reekoo] (food) forte [fort]
ridiculous ridículo [rideekooloo]
right (correct) certo [sehrtoo] (not left) direito [diraytoo]
you were right tinhas razão [teen-yaJ razowng]
that's right está certo [shta]
this can't be right isto não pode estar certo [eeshtoo nowng pod shtar]
right! está bem! [bayng]
is this the right road for ...? esta é a estrada certa para ...? [ehshta eh a shtrada]

on the right à direita [dir**ay**ta]

turn right vire à direita [veer]

right-hand drive com volante à direita [kong vool**a**nt]

ring (on finger) o anel [an**eh**l]

I'll ring you eu telefono-lhe [**ay**-oo telef**oh**nool-yi]

ring back voltar a telefonar [telefoon**ar**]

ripe (fruit) maduro [mad**oo**roo]

rip-off: it's a rip-off isso é um roubo [**ee**soo eh oong r**oh**boo]

rip-off prices os preços exorbitantes [**pray**sooz ezoorbit**a**ntsh]

risky arriscado [arrishk**a**doo]

river o rio [r**ee**-oo]

road (in town) a rua [r**oo**-a]

(in country) a estrada [shtr**a**da]

is this the road for ...? é esta a estrada para ...? [**eh**shta]

it's just down the road é aqui perto [eh ak**ee** p**eh**rtoo]

road accident o acidente de viação [asid**ay**nt di v-yas**ow**ng]

road map o mapa das estradas [daz shtr**a**dash]

roadsign o sinal

rob: I've been robbed (said by man/woman) fui roubado/ roubada [fwee rohb**a**doo]

rock a rocha [r**o**sha]

(music) a música rock [m**oo**zika]

on the rocks (with ice) com gelo [kong J**ay**loo]

roll (bread) o paposseco [papoos**ay**koo]

roof (of house) o telhado [til-

ya**doo**]

(of car) o tejadilho [tiJad**ee**l-yoo]

roof rack o porta-bagagens no tejadilho [p**o**rta baga**J**ayngsh]

room o quarto [kw**a**rtoo]

in my room no meu quarto [noo m**ay**-oo]

•••••• DIALOGUE ••••••

do you have any rooms? tem quartos vagos? [tayng kw**a**rtoosh v**a**goosh]

for how many people? para quantas pessoas? [kw**a**ntash pis**oh**-ash]

for one/for two para uma/para duas [**oo**ma/ – d**oo**-ash]

yes, we have rooms free sim, temos quartos vagos [seeng t**ay**moosh]

for how many nights will it be? para quantas noites? [n**oh**-itsh]

just for one night só para uma noite [saw – n**oh**-it]

how much is it? quanto é o quarto? [kwantw**eh**]

... with bathroom and ... without bathroom ... com casa de banho e ... sem casa banho [kong k**a**za di b**a**n-yoo ee ... sayng]

can I see a room with bathroom? posso ver um quarto com casa de banho? [p**o**sso vayr oong]

OK, I'll take it está bem, fico com ele [shta bayng f**ee**koo kong ayl]

room service o serviço de quartos [sirv**ee**soo di kw**a**rtoosh]

rope a corda
rosé (wine) rosé [roozay]
roughly (approximately)
  aproximadamente
  [aproosimadamaynt]
round: it's my round é a minha
  rodada [eh a meen-ya roodada]
roundabout (for traffic) a rotunda
  [rootoonda]
round trip ticket o bilhete de ida
  e volta [bil-yayt deeda ee]
  see ticket
route o trajecto [trajehtoo]
  what's the best route? qual é o
  melhor trajecto? [kwal eh-oo
  mil-yor]
rubber (material, eraser) a
  borracha [boorrasha]
rubber band o elástico
  [ilashtikoo]
rubbish (waste) o lixo [leeshoo]
  (poor quality goods) o refugo
  [rifoogoo]
  rubbish! (nonsense) que
  disparate! [ki dishparat]
rucksack a mochila [moosheela]
rude grosseiro [groosayroo]
ruins as ruínas [rweenash]
rum o rum [roong]
  a rum and Coke® uma cuba
  livre [ooma kooba leevr]
run (verb: person) correr
  [koorrayr]
  how often do the buses run?
  de quanto em quanto tempo
  há autocarros? [di kwantoo
  ayng kwantoo taympoo a
  owtookarroosh]
  I've run out of money o meu

dinheiro acabou [oo may-oo
  din-yayroo akaboh]
rush hour a hora de ponta [ora
  di pohnta]

S

sad triste [treesht]
saddle a sela [sehla]
safe (adj) seguro [sigooroo]
safety pin o alfinete de
  segurança [alfinayt di
  sigooransa]
sail a vela [vehla]
  (verb) velejar [viliJar]
sailboard a prancha de
  windsurf [pransha di]
sailboarding praticar windsurf
  [pratikar]
salad a salada
salad dressing o tempero da
  salada [taympayroo]
sale: for sale à venda [vaynda]
salmon o salmão [salmowng]
salt o sal
same: the same o mesmo
  [mayJmoo]
  the same as this igual a este
  [igwal a aysht]
  the same again, please o
  mesmo, por favor [poor
  favohr]
  it's all the same to me tanto
  faz [tantoo fash]
sand a areia [aray-a]
sandals as sandálias [sandal-
  yash]
sandwich a sandes [sandsh]
sanitary napkins/towels os

pensos higiénicos [**pay**nsooz iJ-**yeh**nikoosh]
sardine a sardinha [sard**ee**n-ya]
Saturday sábado [**sa**badoo]
sauce o molho [**moh**l-yoo]
saucepan a panela [pan**eh**la]
saucer o pires [**peer**sh]
sauna a sauna [**sow**na]
sausage a salsicha [sals**ee**sha]
say* dizer [diz**ay**r]
   how do you say ... in Portuguese? como se diz ... em português? [**koh**moo si deez ... ayng poortoog**ay**sh]
   what did he say? o que é que ele disse? [oo k-yeh kayl dees]
   he said ... ele disse ...
   could you say that again? pode repetir? [pod ripit**eer**]
scarf (for neck) o lenço de pescoço [**lay**nsoo di pishk**oh**soo]
   (for head) o lenço de cabeça [kab**ay**sa]
scenery a paisagem [pīza**J**ayng]
schedule (US) o horário [oo or**ar**-yoo]
scheduled flight o voo regular [**voh**-oo rigool**ar**]
school a escola [shk**o**la]
scissors: a pair of scissors a tesoura [tiz**oh**ra]
scooter a motoreta [mootoor**ay**ta]
scotch o whisky [w**ee**shkee]
Scotch tape® a fita gomada [f**ee**ta goom**a**da]
Scotland a Escócia [shk**o**s-ya]
Scottish escocês [shkoos**ay**sh]

I'm Scottish (man/woman) sou escocês/escocesa [soh – shkoos**ay**za]
scrambled eggs os ovos mexidos [**o**voosh mish**ee**doosh]
scratch o arranhão [arran-**yow**ng]
screw o parafuso [paraf**oo**zoo]
screwdriver a chave de fendas [shav di f**ay**ndash]
sea o mar
   by the sea à beira-mar [**bay**ra]
seafood os mariscos [mar**ee**shkoosh]
seafood restaurant a marisqueira [marishk**ay**ra]
seafront a praia [prī-a]
   on the seafront junto à praia [**Joo**ntwa]
seagull a gaivota [gī**vo**ta]
search procurar [prookoor**ar**]
seashell a concha do mar [**koh**nsha doo]
seasick: I feel seasick (said by man/woman) estou enjoado/enjoada [shtoh aynJ**wa**doo]
   I get seasick enjoo sempre [aynJ**oh**-oo saympr]
seaside: by the seaside à beira do mar [**bay**ra doo]
seat o assento [as**ay**ntoo]
   is this seat taken? este lugar está ocupado? [aysht loog**ar** shta okoop**a**doo]
seat belt o cinto de segurança [**see**ntoo di sigoor**a**nsa]
sea urchin o ouriço-do-mar

[ohreesoo doo]

seaweed a **a**lga

secluded retirado [ritir**a**doo]

second (adj) segundo
[sig**oo**ndoo]
(of time) o segundo
just a second! espere um
momento! [shp**ay**roong
moom**ay**ntoo]

second class (travel) segunda
classe [sig**oo**nda klas]

second floor o segundo andar
[sig**oo**ndoo]
(US) o primeiro andar
[prim**ay**roo]

second-hand em segunda mão
[ayng sig**oo**nda mowng]

see* ver [vayr]
can I see? posso ver? [p**o**soo]
have you seen the ...? viu o/
a ...? [v**ee**-oo]
I saw him this morning vi-o
esta manhã [v**ee**-oo **eh**shta
man-y**a**ng]
see you! até logo! [at**eh**
l**o**goo]
I see (I understand) percebo
[pirs**ay**boo]

self-catering apartment o
aparthotel [apartoht**eh**l]

self-service o self-service

sell vender [vaynd**ay**r]
do you sell ...? vende ...?
[vaynd]

Sellotape® a fita gomada
[f**ee**ta goom**a**da]

send mand**a**r
I want to send this to England
quero mandar isto para

Inglaterra [k**eh**roo – **ee**shtoo
paringlat**eh**rra]

senior citizen (man/woman) o
cidadão de terceira idade
[sidad**ow**ng di tirs**ay**ra id**a**d], a
cidadã de terceira idade
[sidad**a**ng]

separate separado [sipar**a**doo]

separated: I'm separated (said by
man/woman) estou separado/
separada [sht**oh**]

separately (pay, travel)
separadamente
[siparadam**ay**nt]

September Setembro
[sit**ay**mbroo]

septic séptico [**seh**ptikoo]

serious sério [**seh**r-yoo]

service charge (in restaurant) a
taxa de serviço [t**a**sha di
sirv**ee**soo]

service station a estação de
serviço [shtas**ow**ng]

serviette o guardanapo
[gwardan**a**poo]

set menu a ementa fixa
[em**ay**nta f**ee**ksa]

several vários [var-y**oo**sh]

sew coser [kooz**ay**r]
could you sew this back on?
podia coser-me isto?
[pood**ee**-a kooz**ay**rm **ee**shtoo]

sex o sexo [**seh**xoo]

sexy sexy [**seh**xi]

shade: in the shade à sombra
[s**oh**mbra]

shallow (water) pouco
profundo [p**oh**koo
proof**oo**ndoo]

shame: what a shame! que pena! [ki p**ay**na]

shampoo o champô [shamp**oh**] shampoo and set lavagem e mise [lava**j**ayng i m**ee**zi]

share (room, table etc) partilhar [partil-y**ar**]

sharp (knife) afiado [af-y**a**doo] (taste) ácido [**a**sidoo] (pain) agudo [ag**oo**doo]

shattered (very tired) estafado [shtaf**a**doo]

shaver a máquina de barbear [m**a**kina di barb-y**ar**]

shaving foam a espuma de barbear [shp**oo**ma]

shaving point a tomada para a máquina de barbear [toom**a**da p**a**ra m**a**kina]

she* ela [**eh**la] is she here? ela está aqui? [shta ak**ee**]

sheet (for bed) o lençol [layns**o**l]

shelf a prateleira [pratil**ay**ra]

shellfish os mariscos [mar**ee**shkoosh]

sherry o vinho de Xerêz [v**ee**n-yoo di shir**ay**sh]

ship o navio [nav**ee**-o] by ship de navio [di]

shirt a camisa [kam**ee**za]

shit! merda! [m**eh**rda]

shock o choque [shok] I got an electric shock from the ... apanhei um choque eléctrico do ... [apan-y**ay** oong – el**eh**trikoo doo]

shock-absorber o amortecedor [amoortisid**oh**r]

shocking chocante [shook**ant**]

shoe os sapatos [sapat**oosh**] a pair of shoes um par de sapatos [oong par di]

shoelaces os atacadores [atakad**oh**rish]

shoe polish a graxa para sapatos [gr**a**sha p**a**ra sap**a**toosh]

shoe repairer o sapateiro [sapat**ay**roo]

shop a loja [l**o**ja]

Shops are usually open from around 8.30 a.m. to 7 p.m. and close for lunch from around 12.30 to 2.30 p.m. However, many shops in the big cities are open from around 9 a.m. to 6 p.m., and often don't close for lunch. Most shops are shut on Sunday and many close at 12.30 p.m. on Saturday, even in the main shopping district in Lisbon. Modern shopping malls, which are springing up around the larger cities, are likely to be open seven days a week from around 9 a.m. to as late as 11 p.m. or even midnight.

---

shopping: I'm going shopping vou às compras [voh ash k**oh**mprash]

shopping centre o centro comercial [s**ay**ntroo komayrs-y**al**]

shop window a montra [m**oh**ntra]

shore (of sea, lake) a margem
[marɹayng]

short (person) baixo [bīshoo]
(time, journey) curto [koortoo]

shortcut o atalho [atal-yoo]

shorts os calções [kalsoyngsh]

should: what should I do? que
devo fazer? [ki dayvoo fazayr]
he should be back soon ele
deve voltar logo [ayl dehv
vooltar logoo]
you should ... devia [divee-a]
you shouldn't ... não devia ...
[nowng]

shoulder o ombro [ohmbroo]

shout gritar

show (in theatre) o espetáculo
[shpitakooloo]
could you show me? podia
mostrar-me? [poodee-a
mooshtrarmi]

shower (in bathroom) o duche
[dooish]
(of rain) o aguaceiro
[agwasayroo]
with shower com duche
[kong]

shower gel o gel de duche [ɹehl
di doosh]

shrimp a gamba

shut (verb) fechar [fishar]
when do you shut? a que
horas fecha? [k-yorash
fehsha]
when does it shut? a que
horas fecha?
it's shut está fechado/
fechada [shta fishadoo]
I've shut myself out fechei a

porta e deixei a chave
dentro [fishay – i dayshay a
shav dayntroo]
shut up! cale-se! [kalisi]

shutter (on camera) o obturador
[obtooradohr]
(on window) os postigos
[pooshteegoosh]

shy tímido [teemidoo]

sick (unwell) doente [dwaynt]
I'm going to be sick (vomit)
vou vomitar [voh voomitar]

side o lado [ladoo]
the other side of the street o
outro lado da rua [oo ohtroo
– roo-a]

sidelights as luzes de presença
[aɹ looziɹ di prizaynsa]

side salad a salada a
acompanhar [akompan-yar]

side street a rua secundária
[roo-a sikoondar-ya]

sidewalk o passeio [pasay-oo]

sight: the sights of ... os
centros de interesse de ...
[oosh sayntroosh dintrays di]

sightseeing: we're going
sightseeing vamos ver os
lugares de interesse
[vamoosh vayr oosh loogarish]

sightseeing tour o circuito
turístico [sirkoo-eetoo
tooreeshtikoo]

sign (roadsign etc) o sinal

signal: he didn't give a signal
(driver, cyclist) ele não deu um
sinal [ayl nowng day-oo oong]

signature a assinatura
[asinatoora]

signpost o poste indicador [posht indikad**ohr**]

silence o silêncio [sil**ayn**s-yoo]

silk a seda [**say**da]

silly tolo [t**oh**loo]

silver a prata

silver foil o papel de alumínio [pap**eh**l daloom**ee**n-yoo]

similar semelhante [simil-y**ant**]

simple (easy) simples [s**ee**mplish]

since: since last week desde a semana passada [d**ay**Jda sim**a**na]

since I got here desde que cheguei [d**ay**Jd ki shig**ay**]

sing cant**ar**

singer (man/woman) o cantor [kant**ohr**], a cant**ora**

single: a single to ... uma bilhete simples p**ara** ... [**oo**ng bil-y**ayt** s**ee**mplish]

I'm single (said by man/woman) sou solteiro/solt**eira** [soh soolt**ay**roo]

single bed a cama individual [individw**al**]

single room o quarto individual [kw**ar**too]

single ticket o bilhete simples [bil-y**ayt** s**ee**mplish]

sink (in kitchen) a lava-louça [l**a**va l**oh**sa]

sister a irmã [eerm**ang**]

sister-in-law a cunhada [koon-y**a**da]

sit: can I sit here? posso sentar-me aqui? [p**o**soo saynt**ar**mi ak**ee**]

is anyone sitting here? está alguém sentado aqui? [shta alg**ay**ng saynt**a**doo ak**ee**]

sit down sentar-se [saynt**ar**si]

sit down sente-se [s**ay**ntsi]

size o tamanho [tam**a**n-yoo]

skin a pele [pehl]

skin-diving mergulhar [mirgool-y**ar**]

skinny magricela [magris**eh**la]

skirt a saia [s**ī**-ya]

sky o céu [s**eh**-oo]

sleep dormir [doorm**eer**]

did you sleep well? dormiu bem? [doorm**ee**-oo bayng]

sleeper (on train) a carruagem-cama [karrw**a**Jayng k**a**ma]

sleeping bag o saco de dormir [s**a**koo di doorm**eer**]

sleeping car (on train) a carruagem-cama [karrw**a**Jayng k**a**ma]

sleeping pill o comprimido para dormir [komprim**ee**doo p**a**ra doorm**eer**]

sleepy: I'm feeling sleepy estou com sono [shtoh kong s**oh**noo]

sleeve a manga

slide (photographic) o diapositivo [d-yapoozit**ee**voo]

slip (garment) a combinação [kombinas**ow**ng]

slippery escorregadio [shkoorrigad**ee**-oo]

slow lento [l**ay**ntoo]

slow down! (driving) mais devagar! [mīJ divag**ar**]

slowly devag**ar**

very slowly muito devag**ar**

[m**wee**ngtoo]
could you speak more slowly?
pode fa**l**ar mais devagar?
[pod – mīJ]
small pequeno [pik**ay**noo]
smell: it smells (smells bad)
cheira mal [sh**ay**ra]
smile sorrir [soor**ree**r]
smoke o fumo [f**oo**moo]
do you mind if I smoke?
import**a**-se que fume?
[imp**o**rtasi ki f**oo**mi]
I don't smoke não fumo
[nowng]
do you smoke? fuma? [f**oo**ma]
snack: just a snack só um snack
[saw oong]
sneeze o espirro [shp**ee**rroo]
snorkel o snorkel
snow a neve [nehv]
it's snowing está a nevar
[shta]
so: **it's so good!** é tão bom! [eh
towng bong]
it's so expensive! é tão caro!
[k**a**roo]
not so much não tanto [nowng
t**a**ntoo]
it's not so bad não é tão mau/
má [eh towng mow]
so am I, so do I eu também
[**ay**-oo tamb**ay**ng]
so-so mais ou menos
[mīzohm**ay**noosh]
soaking solution (for contact
lenses) a solução para as
lentes de contacto
[sooloos**ow**ng p**a**raJ layntsh di
kont**a**too]

soap o sabonete [saboon**ay**t]
soap powder o detergente
[deterJ**ay**nt]
sober sóbrio [s**o**br-yoo]

> soccer
> Soccer is Portugal's national
> sport. Even the smallest village
> has a **campo de futebol** for
> local players, while on a
> national level, spectator loyalty
> is largely split between the
> two teams who win most of the
> domestic trophies, Porto and
> Benfica. Support seems to defy
> geography, with many people in
> the north proclaiming undying
> love for the Lisbon team,
> Benfica, and vice versa. Most
> football matches have a relaxed
> family atmosphere and there is
> rarely any crowd trouble.

sock a peúga [p-y**oo**ga]
socket (electrical) a tomada
[toom**a**da]
soda (water) a s**o**da
sofa o sofá [soof**a**]
soft (material etc) mole [mol]
soft-boiled egg o ovo quente
[**oh**voo kaynt]
soft drink a bebida não
alcoólica [bib**ee**da nowng alko-
olika]
soft lenses as lentes
gelatinosas [layntsh
Jilatin**o**zash]
sole (of shoe, of foot) a s**o**la
could you put new soles on

these? pode pôr-lhes solas
novas? [pod pohrl-yish solash
novash]
some: can I have some water?
pode trazer-me água?
[trazayrm]
can I have some of this? pode
dar-me um pouco disto?
[darmoong pohkoo deeshtoo]
somebody, someone alguém
[algayng]
something alguma coisa
[algooma koh-iza]
something to eat alguma
coisa para comer [koomair]
sometimes às vezes [ash
vayzish]
somewhere nalguma parte
[nalgooma part]
son o filho [feel-yoo]
song a canção [kansowng]
son-in-law o genro [Jaynroo]
soon em breve [ayng brev]
I'll be back soon estarei de
volta em breve [shtaray di
vohltayng]
as soon as possible logo que
possível [logoo ki pooseevil]
sore: it's sore dói-me [doymi]
sore throat a dor de garganta
[dohr di]
sorry: (I'm) sorry tenho muita
pena [tayn-yoo mweengta
payna]
sorry? (didn't understand) como?
[kohmoo]
sort: what sort of ...? que tipo
de ...? [ki teepoo di]
soup a sopa [sohpa]

sour (taste) azedo [azaydoo]
south o sul [sool]
in the south no sul [noo]
South Africa a Africa do Sul
[doo]
South African (adj) sul-africano
[soolafrikanoo]
I'm South African (man/woman)
sou sul-africano/sul-africana
[soh]
southeast o sudeste [soodehsht]
southwest o sudoeste
[soodwehsht]
souvenir a lembrança
[laymbransa]
Spain a Espanha [shpan-ya]
Spanish espanhol [shpan-yol]
spanner a chave de porcas
[shav di porkash]
spare part a peça
sobresselente [pehsa
sobrisilaynt]
spare tyre o pneu
sobresselente [p-nay-oo]
spark plug a vela [vehla]
sparkling wine o vinho
espumante [veen-
yooshpoomant]
speak: do you speak English?
fala inglês? [inglaysh]
I don't speak ... não falo ...
[nowng faloo]

•••••• DIALOGUE ••••••

can I speak to Roberto? posso
falar com o Roberto? [posoo –
kong oo]
who's calling? quem fala? [kayng]
it's Patricia é Patricia [eh]

I'm sorry, he's not in, can I take a message? desculpe, ele não está, quer deixar um recado? [dishko**oo**lp ayl nowng shta kehr daysh**a**r oong rik**a**doo]

no thanks, I'll call back later não, obrigada, ligarei mais tarde [ligar**ay** mīsh tard]

please tell him I called por favor, diga-lhe que telefonei [poor fav**oh**r dee**ga**l-yi ki telefoon**ay**]

spectacles os óculos [**o**kooloosh]

speed a velocidade [viloosid**a**d]

speed limit o limite de velocidade [lim**ee**t di]

speedometer o velocímetro [viloos**ee**mitroo]

spell: how do you spell it? como é que se soletra? [k**oh**moo eh ki si sool**eh**tra]

see alphabet

spend gastar [gash**ta**r]

spider a aranha [ar**a**n-ya]

spin-dryer o secador de roupa [sikad**oh**r di r**oh**pa]

splinter a pua [p**oo**-a]

spoke (in wheel) o raio [r**ī**-oo]

spoon a colher [kool-y**eh**r]

sport o desporto [dishp**oh**rtoo]

sprain: I've sprained my ... torci o ... [toors**ee** oo]

spring (season) a Primavera [primav**eh**ra]

(of car, seat) a m**o**la

square (in town) a praça [pr**a**sa]

squash o squash

stairs a escada [shk**a**da]

stale (bread) duro [d**oo**roo]

stall: the engine keeps stalling o motor está sempre a falhar [oo moot**oh**r shta s**ay**mpra fal-y**a**r]

stamp o selo [s**ay**loo]

•••••• DIALOGUE ••••••

a stamp for England, please um selo para Inglaterra, faz favor [oong s**ay**loo para inglat**eh**rra fash fav**oh**r]

what are you sending? o que vai enviar? [oo ki vī aynv-y**a**r]

this postcard este postal [aysht poosht**a**l]

You can buy stamps at post offices (**correios**) or at tobacco-nists' and souvenir stands.

standby standby

star a estrela [shtr**ay**la]

(in film: man/woman) o actor principal [at**oh**r prinsip**a**l], a actriz principal [atr**ee**sh]

start o começo [koom**ay**soo]

(verb) começar [koomis**a**r]

when does it start? quando começa? [kwandoo koom**eh**sa]

the car won't start o carro não pega [oo karroo nowng p**eh**ga]

starter (of car) o motor de arranque [moot**oh**r darr**a**nk]

(food) a entrada [ayntr**a**da]

starving: I'm starving (said by man/woman) estou morto/morta de fome [shtoh m**oh**rtoo – di fohm]

state (country) o estado
[sht**a**doo]
the States (USA) os Estados
Unidos [sht**a**dooz oon**ee**doosh]
station a estação [shtas**ow**ng]
statue a estátua [sht**a**twa]
stay: where are you staying? (to
man/woman) onde está
hospedado/hospedada?
[ohndsht**a** oshpid**a**doo]
I'm staying at ... (said by man/
woman) estou hospedado/
hospedada em ... [shtoh –
ayng]
I'd like to stay another two
nights gostaria de ficar mais
duas noites [gooshtar**ee**-a di
fik**a**r mīsh d**oo**-aJ n**oh**-itsh]
steak o bife [beef]
steal roubar [rohb**a**r]
my bag has been stolen
roubaram-me a mala
[rohb**a**rowng m-ya m**a**la]
steep (hill) íngreme [**ee**ngrim]
steering a direcção
[direhs**ow**ng]
step: on the step no degrau
[digr**ow**]
stereo a aparelhagem (de
som) [aparil-ya**J**ayng (di song)]
sterling as libras esterlinas
[l**ee**braz ishtirl**ee**nash]
steward (on plane) o comissário
de bordo [koomis**a**r-yoo di
b**o**rdoo]
stewardess a hospedeira
[oshpid**ay**ra]
sticking plaster o adesivo
[adiz**ee**voo]

sticky tape a fita-cola [f**ee**ta
k**o**la]
still: I'm still here ainda estou
aqui [a-**ee**nda shtoh ak**ee**]
is he still there? ele ainda está
aí? [ayl – shta a-**ee**]
keep still! fique quieto! [feek
k-y**eh**too]
sting: I've been stung (said by
man/woman) fui picado/picada
[fwee pik**a**doo]
stockings as meias [m**ay**-ash]
stomach o estômago
[sht**oh**magoo]
stomach ache a dor de
estômago [dohr disht**oh**magoo]
stone (rock) a pedra [p**eh**dra]
stop parar
please, stop here (to taxi driver
etc) pare aqui, por favor [par
ak**ee** poor fav**oh**r]
do you stop near ...? pára
perto de ...? [p**eh**rtoo di]
stop it! pare com isso! [kong
eesoo]
stopover a paragem [para**J**ayng]
storm a tempestade
[taympisht**a**d]
straight (whisky etc) puro
[p**oo**roo]
it's straight ahead sempre em
frente [s**ay**mprayng fraynt]
straightaway em seguida [ayng
sig**ee**da]
strange (odd) esquisito
[shkiz**ee**too]
stranger (man/woman) o estranho
[shtr**a**n-yoo], a estranha
I'm a stranger here sou de

fora [soh di]

strap (on watch) a pulseira
[pools**ay**ra]
(on dress) a alça [**a**lsa]
(on suitcase) a correia
[koor**ray**-a]

strawberry o morango
[moor**a**ngoo]

stream o ribeiro [rib**ay**roo]

street a rua [**roo**-a]
on the street na rua

streetmap o mapa da cidade
[sid**a**d]

string o cordel [koord**eh**l]

strong forte [fort]

stuck emperrado [aympirr**a**doo]
it's stuck está emperrado
[shta]

student (male/female) o/a
estudante [shtood**a**nt]

stupid estúpido [shto**o**pidoo]

suburb os arredores
[arred**o**rish]

subway (US) o metro [m**eh**troo]

suddenly subitamente
[soobitam**ay**nt]

suede a camurça [kam**oo**rsa]

sugar o açúcar [as**oo**kar]

suit o fato [f**a**too]
it doesn't suit me (jacket etc)
não me fica bem [nowng mi
f**ee**ka bayng]
it suits you fica-lhe bem
[f**ee**kal-yi]

suitcase a mala

summer o Verão [vir**ow**ng]
in the summer no Verão [noo]

sun o sol
in the sun ao sol [ow]

out of the sun à sombra
[s**oh**mbra]

sunbathe tomar banho de sol
[to**o**mar b**a**n-yoo di]

sunblock (cream) o creme écran
total [kraym ekr**a**ng toot**a**l]

sunburn a queimadura de sol
[kaymad**oo**ra di]

sunburnt queimado de sol
[kaym**a**doo]

Sunday domingo [doom**ee**ngoo]

sunglasses os óculos de sol
[**o**kooloosh di]

sun lounger a cadeira
reclinável [kad**ay**ra reklin**a**vil]

sunny: it's sunny está (a fazer)
sol [shta (a faz**ay**r) sol]

sunroof o tejadilho de abrir
[tiJad**ee**l-yoo dabr**ee**r]

sunset o pôr do sol [pohr doo]

sunshade o chapéu de sol
[shap**eh**-oo di]

sunshine a luz do sol [looJ doo]

sunstroke a insolação
[insoolas**ow**ng]

suntan o bronzeado [bronz-
y**a**doo]

suntan lotion a loção de
bronzear [loos**ow**ng di bronz-
y**a**r]

suntanned bronzeado [bronz-
y**a**doo]

suntan oil o óleo de bronzear
[**o**l-yoo di]

super óptimo [**o**timoo]

supermarket o supermercado
[soopermerk**a**doo]

supper o jantar [J**a**ntar]

supplement (extra charge) o

suplemento [sooplim**ay**ntoo]
sure: are you sure? tem a
certeza? [tayng a sirt**ay**za]
sure! claro! [kl**a**roo]
surname o apelido [apil**ee**doo]
swearword a asneira [aɹn**ay**ra]
sweater a camisola [kamiz**o**la]
sweatshirt a sweatshirt
Sweden a Suécia [sw**eh**s-ya]
Swedish (adj, language) sueco
[sw**eh**koo]
sweet (taste) doce [dohs]
(dessert) a sobremesa
[sobrim**ay**za]
sweets os rebuçados
[riboos**a**doosh]
swelling o inchaço [insh**a**soo]
swim nadar
I'm going for a swim vou
nadar [voh]
let's go for a swim vamos
nadar [v**a**moosh]
swimming costume o fato de
banho [f**a**too di b**a**n-yoo]
swimming pool a piscina [pish-
s**ee**na]
swimming trunks os calções de
banho [kals**oy**ngsh di b**a**n-yoo]
Swiss (adj) suíço [sw**ee**soo]
switch o interruptor
[intiroopt**oh**r]
switch off (engine, TV) desligar
[diɹlig**a**r]
(lights) apagar
switch on (engine, TV) ligar
(lights) acender [asaynd**ay**r]
Switzerland a Suíça [sw**ee**sa]
swollen inchado [insh**a**doo]

T

table a mesa [m**ay**za]
a table for two uma mesa
para duas pessoas [**oo**ma –
d**oo**-ash pis**oh**-ash]
tablecloth a toalha de mesa
[tw**a**l-ya di m**ay**za]
table tennis o ténis de mesa
[t**eh**nish]
table wine o vinho de mesa
[v**ee**n-yoo]
tailback (of traffic) a fila de
carros [f**ee**la di k**a**rroosh]
tailor a alfaiataria [alfi-atar**ee**-a]
take (lead) levar
(accept) aceitar [asayt**a**r]
can you take me to the ...?
pode levar-me ao ...? [pod
lev**a**rmow]
do you take credit cards?
aceita cartões de crédito?
[as**ay**ta kart**oy**ngsh di
kr**eh**ditoo]
fine, I'll take it está bem, fico
com ele [shta bayng f**ee**koo
kong ayl]
can I take this? (leaflet etc)
posso levar isto? [p**o**soo –
eeshtoo]
how long does it take? quanto
tempo leva? [kw**a**ntoo
t**ay**mpoo l**eh**va]
it takes three hours leva três
horas [trayz**o**rash]
is this seat taken? este lugar
está ocupado? [aysht loog**a**r
shta okoop**a**doo]
hamburger to take away o

hamburger para levar
can you take a little off here?
(to hairdresser) pode cortar um
pouco aqui? [pod koort**ar** oong
p**oh**koo ak**ee**]
talcum powder o pó de talco
[paw di t**a**lkoo]
talk fal**ar**
tall alto [**a**ltoo]
tampons o tampão [tamp**ow**ng]
tan o bronzeado [bronz-y**a**doo]
  to get a tan bronzear-se
  [bronz-y**ar**si]
tank (of car) o depósito
  [dip**o**zitoo]
tap a torneira [toorn**ay**ra]
tape (for cassette) a fita [f**ee**ta]
tape measure a fita métrica
  [m**eh**trika]
tape recorder o gravador
  [gravad**oh**r]
taste o sabor [sab**oh**r]
  can I taste it? posso provar?
  [p**o**soo]
taxi o t**á**xi
  will you get me a taxi? pode
  chamar-me um táxi? [pod
  sham**ar**moong]
  where can I find a taxi? onde
  posso encontrar um táxi?
  [ohnd p**o**swaynkontr**ar**]

•••••• DIALOGUE ••••••

to the airport/to the Borges Hotel,
please para o aeroporto/Hotel
Borges, se faz favor [par**oo**-
ayroop**oh**rtoo/oht**eh**l bor**j**ish si fash
fav**oh**r]
how much will it be? quanto vai

custar? [kw**a**ntoo v**ī** koosht**ar**]
two thousand escudos dois contos
[d**oh**-ish k**oh**ntoosh]
that's fine right here, thanks aqui
está bem, obrigado/obrigada
[ak**ee** shta bayng obrig**a**doo]

Lisbon's taxis are inexpensive
as long as your destination is
within the city limits. All taxis
have meters, which are generally
switched on, and tips are not
expected.

---

taxi-driver o pracista
  [pras**ee**shta]
taxi rank a praça de táxis
  [pr**a**sa di t**a**xish]
tea (drink) o chá [sha]
  tea for one/two, please chá
  para um/dois, por favor
  [oong/d**oh**-ish poor fav**oh**r]

Tea is a big drink in Portugal
and you'll find wonderfully
elegant **casas de chá** (literally:
tea houses) dotted around the
country. Tea is usually served
without milk; **um chá com leite**
is tea with milk, **um chá com
limão** tea with lemon, but **um
chá de limão** is an infusion of
hot water with a lemon rind.

---

teabags os saquinhos de chá
  [sak**ee**n-yooj di sha]
teach: could you teach me?
  pode ensinar-me? [pod
  aynsin**ar**mi]

teacher (man/woman) o professor [proofes**oh**r], a profess**o**ra

team a equipa [ek**ee**pa]

teaspoon a colher de chá [kool-**yehr** di sha]

tea towel o pano de cozinha [**pa**noo di koo**zee**n-ya]

teenager o/a adolescente [adoolish-s**ay**nt]

telegram o telegr**a**ma

telephone o telefone [telef**oh**n] see phone

television a televisão [televiz**ow**ng]

> The Portuguese are avid television watchers; it's rare to find a bar, café or restaurant without a television on the corner, even in fairly upmarket places.

tell: could you tell him ...? pode dizer-lhe ...? [pod diz**ay**rl-yi]

temperature (weather) a temperatura [taympirat**oo**ra] (fever) a febre [**fehb**r]

tennis o ténis [**teh**nish]

tennis ball a bola de ténis [di]

tennis court o campo de ténis [**ka**mpoo]

tennis racket a raqueta de ténis [rak**eh**ta]

tent a tenda (de campismo) [**tay**nda (di kamp**ee**Jmoo)]

term (at university, school) o período escolar [pir**ee**-oodoo shkool**a**r]

terminus (rail) o terminal [tirmin**al**]

terrible terrível [tirr**ee**vil]

terrific (weather) esplêndido [shpl**ay**ndidoo] (food, teacher) excelente [ish-sel**ay**nt]

than* do que [doo ki] smaller than mais pequeno do que [mīsh pik**ay**noo]

thanks, thank you (said by man/woman) obrigado/obrig**a**da [obrig**a**doo]

thank you very much muito obrigado/obrigada [m**wee**ngtoo]

thanks for the lift obrigado/obrigada pela boleia [p**i**la bool**ay**-a]

no thanks não obrigado/obrigada [nowng]

•••••• DIALOGUE ••••••

thanks (said by man/woman) obrigado/obrigada

that's OK, don't mention it está bem, não se preocupe com isso [shta bayng nowng si pri-ook**oo**p kong **ee**soo]

that*: that ... esse/essa ... [ays/**eh**sa] (further away) aquele/aquela ... [ak**ay**l/ak**eh**la]

that one esse/essa/isso [**ee**soo] (further away) aquele/aquela/aquilo [ak**ee**loo]

I hope that ... espero que ... [shp**eh**ro ki]

that's nice! que bom! [bong]

is that ...? isso é ...? [eh]
that's it (that's right) certo
[se**h**rtoo]
the* o [oo], a
(pl) os [oosh], as [ash]
theatre o teatro [t-y**a**troo]
their* deles [d**ay**lish], delas
[de**h**lash]
theirs* deles, delas
them* os [oosh]
(feminine) as [ash]
for them para eles/elas [aylsh/
e**h**lash]
with them com eles/elas
[kong]
to them para eles/elas
who? – them quem? – eles/
elas [kayng]
then (at that time) então
[aynt**ow**ng]
(after that) depois [dip**oh**-ish]
there ali [al**ee**], lá
over there ali adiante [ad-
y**a**nt]
up there ali acima [as**ee**ma]
is there/are there ...? há ...? [a]
there is/there are ... há ...
there you are (giving something)
tome lá [tohm]
thermometer o termómetro
[tirm**oh**mitroo]
Thermos flask® o termo
[t**ay**rmoo]
these*: these men estes
homens [**ay**shtiz**oh**mayngsh]
these women estas mulheres
[e**h**shtaɹ mool-ye**h**rish]
I'd like these queria estes/
estas [kir**ee**-a **ay**shtish/

e**h**shtash]
they* (male) eles [**ay**lish]
(female) elas [e**h**lash]
thick espesso [shp**ay**soo]
(stupid) estúpido [sht**oo**pidoo]
thief (man/woman) o ladrão
[ladr**ow**ng], a ladra
thigh a coxa [k**oh**sha]
thin fino [f**ee**noo]
(person) magro [m**a**groo]
thing a coisa [k**oh**-iza]
my things as minhas coisas
[aɹ m**ee**n-yash k**oh**-izash]
think pensar [payns**a**r]
I think so acho que sim
[**a**shoo ki seeng]
I don't think so acho que não
[nowng]
I'll think about it vou pensar
[voh]
third party insurance o seguro
contra terceiros [sig**oo**roo
k**oh**ntra tirs**ay**roosh]
thirsty: I'm thirsty tenho sede
[t**ay**n-yoo sayd]
this*: this boy este menino
[aysht min**ee**noo]
this girl esta menina [e**h**shta
min**ee**na]
this one este [aysht]/esta
[e**h**shta]/isto [**ee**shtoo]
this is my wife esta é a minha
mulher [eh a m**ee**n-ya mool-
y**eh**r]
is this ...? isto é ...?
[**ee**shtweh]
those*: those ... esses/essas ...
[**ay**sish/e**h**sash]
(further away) aqueles/

aquelas ... [ak**ay**lish/ak**eh**lash]
which ones? – those quais? –
esses/essas [kw**ī**sh]
(further away) quais? – aqueles/
aquelas
thread o fio [f**ee**-oo]
throat a garg**a**nta
throat pastilles as pastilhas
p**a**ra a garg**a**nta [pasht**ee**l-
yash]
through por, através de
[atrav**eh**J di]
does it go through ...? (train,
bus) p**a**ssa em ...? [**ay**ng]
throw atir**a**r
throw away deit**a**r f**o**ra
[dayt**a**r]
thumb o poleg**a**r [poolig**a**r]
thunderstorm a trovo**a**da
[troovw**a**da]
Thursday quinta-feira [k**ee**nta
f**ay**ra]
ticket o bilhete [bil-y**ay**t]

•••••• DIALOGUE ••••••

a return to Setúbal um bilhete de
ida e v**o**lta p**a**ra Setúbal [oong –
deed**ī** – sit**oo**bal]
coming back when? quando v**o**lta?
[kw**a**ndoo]
today/next Tuesday hoje/na
pr**ó**xima t**e**rça-feira [ohJ/na
pr**o**sima t**ay**rsa f**ay**ra]
that will be 500 escudos são
quinhentos escudos [sowng keen-
y**ay**ntooz-shk**oo**doosh]

It's always cheaper to buy bus
and tram tickets in advance
(**pré-comprados**) in one of the
kiosks around Lisbon and other
major cities – these can be
return or multiple tickets. You
can also buy multiple, return or
single tickets for the underground, and the same rule ap-
plies – the more trips you buy
at once, the cheaper it will be.

ticket office (bus, rail) a
bilheteira [bil-yit**ay**ra]
tide a maré [mar**eh**]
tie (necktie) a grav**a**ta
tight (clothes etc) apert**a**do
[apirt**a**doo]
it's too tight está demasiado
apert**a**do [shta dimaz-y**a**doo]
tights os collants [kool**a**nsh]
till a caixa [k**ī**sha]
time* o tempo [t**ay**mpoo]
what's the time? que horas
são? [k-y**o**rash sowng]
this time esta vez [**eh**shta
vaysh]
last time a última vez
[**oo**ltima]
next time a próxima vez
[pr**o**sima]
three times três vezes [traysh
v**ay**zish]
timetable o horário [oo or**a**r-yoo]
tin (can) a l**a**ta
tinfoil o papel de alumínio
[pap**eh**l daloom**ee**n-yoo]
tin-opener o abre-latas

[abrilatash]

tiny minúsculo [minooshkooloo]

tip (to waiter etc) a gorgeta [goorJayta]

> Simple cafés and restaurants don't charge for service, though people generally leave small change as a tip in these places. In more upmarket restaurants, you'll either be charged or should leave around 10 per cent. Hotels include a service charge, but porters and maids expect something; cab drivers don't.

tired cansado [kansadoo]
I'm tired (said by man/woman) estou cansado/cansada [shtoh]

tissues os lenços de papel [laynsoosh di papehl]

to: to Lisbon/London para Lisboa/Londres [liJboh-a/lohndrish]

to Portugal/England para Portugal/Inglaterra [poortoogal/inglatehrra]

we're going to the museum/to the post office vamos ao museo/aos correios [vamooz ow moosay-oo/owsh koorray-oosh]

toast (bread) a torrada [toorrada]

today hoje [ohJ]

toe o dedo do pé [daydoo doo peh]

together juntos [Joontoosh]

we're together (in shop etc) viemos juntos [v-yaymoosh Joontoosh]

toilet a casa de banho [kaza di ban-yoo]
where is the toilet? onde é a casa de banho? [ohndeh]
I have to go to the toilet tenho de ir à casa de banho [taynyoo deer]

> Ladies' toilets often charge (or a small tip might be expected) and they are usually clean. The gents' toilets may look more aesthetic (lots of ironwork) and are free, but are usually unattractive inside. A sign that says retretes will head you in the right direction, then it's homens for men and senhoras for women.

toilet paper o papel higiénico [papehl iJ-yehnikoo]

tomato o tomate [toomat]

tomato juice o sumo de tomate [soomoo di toomat]

tomato ketchup o ketchup

tomorrow amanhã [aman-yang]
tomorrow morning amanhã de manhã [aman-yang di man-yang]
the day after tomorrow depois de amanhã [dipoh-ish daman-yang]

toner (cosmetic) o tónico [tonikoo]

tongue a língua [leengwa]

tonic (water) a água tónica
[**a**gwa]

tonight esta noite [**eh**shta
n**oh**-it]

tonsillitis a amigdalite
[ameegdal**eet**]

too (excessively) demasiado
[dimaz-y**a**doo]
(also) também [tamb**ayng**]
too hot demasiado quente
[k**ay**nt]
too much demais [dim**ī**sh]
me too eu também [**ay**-oo
tamb**ayng**]

tooth o dente [d**ay**nt]

toothache a dor de dentes [dohr
di d**ay**ntsh]

toothbrush a escova de dentes
[shk**oh**va]

toothpaste a pasta de dentes
[p**a**shta]

top: on top of ... em cima de ...
[ayng s**ee**ma di]
at the top no alto [noo **a**ltoo]
at the top of ... no topo de ...
[t**oh**poo di]

top floor o piso superior
[p**ee**zoo soopir-y**oh**r]

topless topless

torch a lanterna [lant**eh**rna]

total o total [toot**a**l]

tour a excursão [shkoors**ow**ng]
is there a tour of ...? há
alguma excursão/visita
guiada a ...? [alg**oo**ma –
viz**ee**ta gee-**a**da]

tour guide (man/woman) o guia
turístico [g**ee**-a
toor**ee**shtikoo], a guia

turística

tourist (man/woman) o/a turista
[toor**ee**shta]

tourist information office o
turismo [toor**ee**ʃmoo]

In Portugal itself you'll find a
tourist office in almost any
town or village of any size. The
vast majority are exceptionally
helpful and friendly. Aside from
the help they can give you in
finding a room (some will make
bookings, others simply supply
lists), they often have useful
local maps and leaflets that
you won't find in the national
offices. Local tourist office
opening hours are generally
Monday to Saturday from 9 a.m.
to 12.30 p.m. and from 2 to 6
p.m., though in Porto, Lisbon,
the Algarve and other resorts
they often stay open later than
this, and open on Sunday too.
In more out-of-the-way towns
and villages, offices will be
closed at weekends.

tour operator o operador
turístico [opirad**ohr**
toor**ee**shtikoo]

towards para

towel a toalha [tw**a**l-ya]

town a cidade [sid**a**d]
in town na cidade
just out of town junto à
cidade [j**oo**ntwa]

town centre o centro da cidade

[**say**ntroo]

town hall a câmara municipal [moonisip**al**]

toy o brinquedo [breenk**ay**doo]

track (US) o cais [kīsh]
see **platform**

tracksuit o fato de treino [f**a**too di tr**ay**noo]

traditional tradicional [tradis-yoon**al**]

traffic o trânsito [tr**a**nzitoo]

traffic jam o engarrafamento [ayngarrafam**ay**ntoo]

traffic lights os semáforos [sim**a**fooroosh]

trailer (for carrying tent etc) o reboque [rib**o**k]
(US) a roulotte [rool**o**t]

trailer park o parque de campismo [park di kamp**ee**Jmoo]

train o comboio [komb**oy**-oo]
by train de comboio [di]

CP, the Portuguese railway company, operates all trains. Most are designated **Regional**, which means they stop at most stations en route and have first-and second-class cars. The next category up, **Intercidades**, are twice as fast and twice as expensive, and you should reserve your seat in advance if using them. The fastest, most luxurious and priciest services are the **Rápidos** (known as **Alfa**), which speed between →

Lisbon, Coimbra, and Porto – sometimes they have only first-class seats. Both these latter classes charge supplements for rail pass holders.

Always turn up at the station with time to spare since long queues often form at the ticket desk. If you end up on the train without first buying a ticket you could be liable for a huge supplement, or be kicked off the train at the next stop.

Train travel is inexpensive and most travellers simply buy a ticket every time they make a journey. If you're planning on a lot of train travel, using a rail pass will probably save you money.

•••••• DIALOGUE ••••••

is this the train for Fátima? é este o comboio para Fátima? [eh **ay**shtoo]

sure com certeza [kong sirt**ay**za]

no, you want that platform there não, tem que ir à plataforma de lá [nowng tayng ki-**eer** – di]

trainers (shoes) os sapatos de treino [sap**a**toosh di tr**ay**noo]

train station a estação de comboios [shtas**ow**ng di komb**oy**-oosh]

tram o eléctrico [el**eh**trikoo]

translate traduzir [tradooz**eer**]
could you translate that? pode traduzir isto? [pod – **ee**shtoo]

translation a tradução
[tradoos**ow**ng]

translator (man/woman) o
tradutor [tradoot**ohr**], a
tradut**or**a

trash (waste) o lixo [l**ee**shoo]

trashcan o caixote de lixo
[k**ī**shot di l**ee**shoo]

travel viajar [v-ya**ı**ar]
we're travelling around
estamos a viajar por aí
[sht**a**mooz – poor a-**ee**]

travel agent's a agência de
viagens [a**ı**aynsya di
v-ya**ı**ayngsh]

traveller's cheque o cheque de
viagem [shehk di v-ya**ı**ayng]

tray a travessa [trav**eh**sa]

tree a árvore [**a**rvoori]

tremendous bestial [bisht-y**al**]

trendy à m**o**da

trim: just a trim, please (to
hairdresser) queria só cortar as
pontas, por favor [kir**ee**-a
saw koort**ar** ash p**o**ntash poor
fav**ohr**]

trip (excursion) a excursão
[shkoors**ow**ng]
I'd like to go on a trip to ...
gostava de ir numa viagem
a ... [gosht**a**va deer n**oo**ma v-
ya**ı**ayng]

trolley o carrinho [karr**ee**n-yoo]

trouble: I'm having trouble
with ... tenho tido problemas
com ... [t**ay**n-yoo t**ee**doo
prool**ay**mash kong]

trousers as calças [k**a**lsash]

true verdadeiro [virdad**ay**roo]

that's not true não é verdade
[nowng eh vird**ad**]

trunk (US: of car) o porta-
bagagens [p**o**rta-bag**a**ıayngsh]

trunks (swimming) os calções de
banho [kals**oy**ngsh di b**a**n-yoo]

try tent**ar**
can I try it? posso
experimentar? [p**o**soo
shpirimaynt**ar**]
(food) posso provar? [proov**ar**]

try on experiment**ar**
can I try it on? posso
experimentar? [p**o**soo
shpirimaynt**ar**]

T-shirt a T-shirt

Tuesday terça-feira [t**ay**rsa
f**ay**ra]

tuna o atum [at**oo**ng]

tunnel o túnel [t**oo**nil]

turn: turn left/right vire à
esquerda/direita [v**ee**ra
shk**ay**rda/dir**ay**ta]

turn off: where do I turn off?
onde devo virar? [ohnd
d**ay**voo]
can you turn the heating off?
pode desligar o
aquecimento? [pod di**ı**lig**ar** oo
akesim**ay**ntoo]

turn on: can you turn the heating
on? pode ligar o
aquecimento?

turning (in road) a curva [k**oo**rva]

TV TV [tay-vay]

tweezers a pinça [p**ee**nsa]

twice duas vezes [d**oo**-a**ı**
v**ay**zish]
twice as much o dobro [oo

dohbroo]

twin beds as camas separadas [kamash siparadash]

twin room o quarto com duas camas [kwartoo kong doo-ash]

twist: I've twisted my ankle torci o meu tornozelo [toorsee oo may-oo toornoozayloo]

type o tipo [teepoo]
a different type of ... um tipo diferente de ... [oong – difIraynt di]

typical típico [teepikoo]

tyre o pneu [p-nay-oo]

U

ugly feio [fay-oo]

UK Reino Unido [raynooneedoo]

ulcer a úlcera [oolsira]

umbrella o guarda-chuva [gwarda shoova]

uncle o tio [tee-oo]

unconscious inconsciente [inkonsh-syaynt]

under (in position) debaixo de [dibIshoo di]
(less than) menos de [maynoosh di]

underdone (meat) mal passado [pasadoo]

underground (railway) o metro [mehtroo]

underpants as cuecas [kwehkash]

understand: I understand já percebi [ja pirsibee]
I don't understand não

percebo [nowng pirsayboo]
do you understand? está a compreender? [shta a komprayndayr]

unemployed desempregado [dizaymprigadoo]

United States os Estados Unidos [shtadooz ooneedoosh]

university a universidade [oonivirsidad]

unleaded petrol a gasolina sem chumbo [gazooleena sayng shoomboo]

unlimited mileage quilometragem ilimitada [kilomitraJayng ilimitada]

unlock abrir [abreer]

unpack desfazer as malas [dishfazayr aJ malash]

until até a [ateh]

unusual pouco vulgar [pohkoo voolgar]

up acima [aseema]
up there lá em cima [ayng seema]
he's not up yet (not out of bed) ele ainda não está levantado [ayl a-eenda nowng shta levantadoo]
what's up? (what's wrong?) o que aconteceu? [oo ki akontisay-oo]

upmarket sofisticado [soofishtikadoo]

upset stomach o desarranjo intestinal [dizarranJoo intishtinal]

upside down de pernas para o ar [di pehrnash proo ar]

upstairs lá em cima [ayng
seema]
urgent urgente [oorJaynt]
us* nos [noosh]
  with us connosco
  [konohshkoo]
  for us para nós [nosh]
USA os Estados Unidos
  [shtadooz ooneedoosh]
use usar [oozar]
  may I use ...? posso usar ...?
  [posoo]
useful útil [ootil]
usual usual [oozwal]
  the usual (drink etc) o de
  sempre [oo di saympr]

V

vacancy: do you have any
  vacancies? (hotel) têm vagas?
  [tay-ayng vagash]
  see room
vacation as férias [fehr-yash]
  on vacation de férias [shtoh di]
vaccination a vacinação
  [vasinasowng]
vacuum cleaner o aspirador
  [ashpiradohr]
valid (ticket etc) válido [validoo]
  how long is it valid for? até
  quando é válido? [ateh
  kwandoo]
valley o vale [val]
valuable (adj) valioso [val-
  yohzoo]
  can I leave my valuables here?
  posso deixar aqui os meus
  artigos de valor? [posoo

dayshar akee ooJ may-ooz
  arteegoosh di valohr]
value o valor
van a furgoneta [foorgoonayta]
vanilla a baunilha [bowneel-ya]
  a vanilla ice cream um gelado
  de baunilha [oong Jiladoo di]
vary: it varies varia [varee-a]
vase a jarra [Jarra]
veal a vitela [vitehla]
vegetables os legumes
  [ligoomish]
vegetarian (man/woman) o
  vegetariano [viJitar-yanoo], a
  vegetariana

Vegetarians should note that
chicken or ham is often not
considered meat by the
Portuguese; cheese omelettes
sometimes come with ham
included, and vegetable soup is
often made with chicken or pork
stock, with lumps of bacon
floating in it. Most restaurants
do good salads if requested, but
again look out for the ham.

vending machine a máquina de
  venda [makina di vaynda]
very muito [mweengtoo]
  very little for me muito pouco
  para mim [pohkoo para
  meeng]
  I like it very much gosto muito
  disso [goshtoo – deesoo]
vest (under shirt) a camisola
  interior [kamizola intir-yohr]
via via [vee-a]

video (film) o vídeo [veed-yoo]
video recorder o videogravador [veed-yoogravadohr]
view a vista [veeshta]
villa a vivenda [vivaynda]
village a aldeia [alday-a]
vinegar o vinagre [vinagr]
vineyard a vinha [veen-ya]
visa o visto [veeshtoo]
visit visitar [vizitar]
   I'd like to visit ... gostaria de visitar ... [gooshtaree-a di]
vital: it's vital that ... é imprescindível que ... [eh impresh-sindeevil ki]
vodka o vodka
voice a voz [vosh]
voltage a tensão [taynsowng]

> The voltage in Portugal is 220V. You will need an adapter for a two-pin (round) plug.

vomit vomitar [voomitar]

W

waist a cintura [sintoora]
waistcoat o colete [koolayt]
wait esperar [shpirar]
   wait for me espere por mim [shpehr poor meeng]
   don't wait for me não espere por mim [nowng]
   can I wait until my wife/partner gets here? posso esperar até a minha mulher/companheira chegar? [pos shpirar ateh a meen-ya mool-

yehr/kompan-yayra shigar]
   can you do it while I wait? pode fazer isso enquanto espero? [pod fazayr eesoo aynkwantoo shpehroo]
   could you wait here for me? pode esperar-me? [pod shpirarmi]
waiter o empregado de mesa [aympregadoo di mayza]
   waiter! se faz favor! [si fash favohr]
waitress a empregada de mesa [aympregada di mayza]
   waitress! se faz favor!
wake: can you wake me up at 5.30? pode acordar-me às cinco meia? [pod akoordarmi ash seenkwee may-a]
wake-up call a chamada para despertar [shamada para dishpirtar]
Wales o País de Gales [pa-eej di galish]
walk: is it a long walk? é muito longe a pé? [eh mweengtoo lohnj a peh]
   it's only a short walk é perto a pé [pehrtoo]
   I'll walk vou a pé [voh]
   I'm going for a walk vou dar um passeio [oong pasay-oo]
Walkman® o walkman®
wall (outside) o muro [mooroo]
   (inside) a parede [parayd]
wallet a carteira [kartayra]
wander: I like just wandering around gosto de andar a ver [goshtoo dandar a vayr]

want: I want a ... queria um ... [kir**ee**-a oong]

I don't want any ... não quero ... [nowng k**eh**roo]

I want to go home quero ir para casa [eer p**a**ra k**a**za]

I don't want to não quero

he wants to ele quer [ayl kehr]

what do you want? o que deseja? [oo ki dis**ay**Ja]

ward (in hospital) a enfermaria [aynfirmar**ee**-a]

warm quente [kaynt]

I'm so warm tenho tanto calor [t**ay**n-yoo t**a**ntoo kal**oh**r]

was*: he was (ele) era [(ayl) **eh**ra]; (ele) estava [sht**a**va]

she was (ela) era [(**eh**la)]; (ele) estava

it was era; estava

wash lavar

(oneself) lavar-se [–si]

can you wash these? pode lavar isto? [pod – **ee**shtoo]

washer (for bolt etc) a anilha [an**ee**l-ya]

washhand basin o lavatório [lavat**o**r-yoo]

washing (clothes) a roupa para lavar [r**oh**pa]

washing machine a máquina de lavar [m**a**kina di]

washing powder o detergente [deterJ**ay**nt]

washing-up liquid o detergente líquido [l**ee**kidoo]

wasp a vespa [v**ay**shpa]

watch (wristwatch) o relógio (de pulso) [ril**o**J-yoo (di p**oo**lsoo)]

will you watch my things for me? pode tomar conta das minhas coisas? [pod toom**a**r k**oh**nta daJ m**ee**n-yash k**oh**-izash]

watch out! cuidado! [kwid**a**doo]

watch strap a correia de relógio [koorr**ay**-a di ril**o**J-yoo]

water a água [**a**gwa]

may I have some water? pode dar-me um pouco de água? [pod d**a**rmoong p**oh**koo d**a**gwa]

waterproof (adj) à prova de água [d**a**gwa]

waterskiing o esqui aquático [shkee akw**a**tikoo]

wave (in sea) a onda [**oh**nda]

way: it's this way é por aqui [eh por ak**ee**]

it's that way é por ali [al**ee**]

is it a long way to ...? é muito longe até ...? [mw**ee**ngtoo lohnJ at**eh**]

no way! de maneira nenhuma! [di man**ay**ra nin-y**oo**ma]

•••••• DIALOGUE ••••••

could you tell me the way to ...? pode indicar-me o caminho para ...? [podindik**a**rmoo kam**ee**n-yoo]

go straight on until you reach the traffic lights siga em frente até chegar ao semáforo [s**ee**gayng fr**ay**nt at**eh** shigar ow sem**a**fooroo]

turn left vire à esquerda [v**ee**ra shk**ay**rda]

take the first on the right vire na

primeira à direita [veer na
primayra dirayta]
see where

we* nós [nosh]
weak fraco [frakoo]
weather o tempo [taympoo]

•••••• DIALOGUE ••••••

what's the weather forecast? qual é
a previsão do tempo? [kwaleh a
privizowng doo taympoo]
it's going to be fine vai estar bom
[vī shtar bong]
it's going to rain vai chover
[shoovayr]
it'll brighten up later vai melhorar
mais tarde [mil-yoorar mīsh tard]

wedding o casamento
[kazamayntoo]
wedding ring a aliança
[al-yansa]
Wednesday quarta-feira [kwarta
fayra]
week a semana [simana]
a week (from) today de hoje a
uma semana [dohJ a ooma]
a week (from) tomorrow de
amanhã a uma semana
[daman-yang]
weekend o fim de semana
[feeng di]
at the weekend no fim de
semana [noo]
weight o peso [payzoo]
weird esquisito [shkizeetoo]
he's weird ele é esquisito
[ayl eh]
welcome: welcome to ... bem

vindo a ... [bayng veendwa]
you're welcome (don't mention it)
não tem de quê [nowng tayng
di kay]
well: I don't feel well não me
sinto muito bem [mi seentoo
mweengtoo bayng]
she's not well ela não está
bem [ehla – shta]
you speak English very well
fala inglês muito bem
[inglaysh]
well done! muito bem!
this one as well este também
[aysht tambayng]
well well! (surprise) ah sim!
[seeng]

•••••• DIALOGUE ••••••

how are you? como está? [kohmo
shta]
very well, thanks, and you? (said by
man/woman) muito bem,
obrigado/obrigada, e você?
[obrigadoo – ee vosay]

well-done (meat) bem passado
[bayng pasadoo]
Welsh galês [galaysh]
I'm Welsh (man/woman) sou
galês/galesa [soh – galayza]
were*: we were éramos
[ehramoosh]; estávamos
[shtavamoosh]
you were você era [vosay
ehra]; você estava [shtava]
they were (eles/elas) eram
[(aylsh/ehlash) ehrowng];
(eles/elas) estavam
[shtavowng]

west o oeste [wesht]
in the west no oeste [noo]
West Indian (adj) antilhano
[antil-y**a**noo]
wet molhado [mool-y**a**doo]
what? o quê? [oo kay]
what's that? o que é isso? [oo
k-yeh **ee**soo]
what should I do? o que
devo fazer? [oo kay d**ay**voo
faz**ay**r]
what a view! que vista linda!
[ki v**ee**shta l**ee**nda]
what bus do I take? que
autocarro devo tomar? [ki
owtook**a**rroo d**ay**voo toom**a**r]
wheel a roda
wheelchair a cadeira de rodas
[kad**ay**ra di r**o**dash]
when? quando? [kw**a**ndoo]
when we get back quando
nós voltarmos [nosh
voolt**a**rmoosh]
when's the train/ferry? quando
é o comboio/ferry?
[kw**a**ndweh o komb**oy**-oo]
where? onde? [ohnd]
I don't know where it is não
sei onde está [nowng say
ohndsht**a**]

•••••• DIALOGUE ••••••

where is the cathedral? onde fica a
catedral? [ohnd f**ee**ka]
it's over there fica ali adiante
[f**ee**kalee ad-y**a**nt]
could you show me where it is on
the map? pode mostrar-me onde
está no mapa? [pod mooshtr**a**rmi

ohndsht**a** noo m**a**pa]
it's just here está bem aqui [shta
bayng ak**ee**]
see way
which: which bus? qual
autocarro? [kwal owtook**a**rroo]

•••••• DIALOGUE ••••••

which one? qual deles? [kwal
d**ay**lish]
that one aquele [ak**ay**l]
this one? este? [aysht]
no, that one não aquele ali [nowng
– al**ee**]

while: while I'm here enquanto
estou aqui [aynkw**a**ntoo shtoh
ak**ee**]
whisky o whisky [w**ee**shkee]
white branco [br**a**nkoo]
white wine o vinho branco
[v**ee**n-yoo]
who? quem? [kayng]
who is it? quem é? [kayng**eh**]
the man who ... o homem
que ... [**oh**mayng ki]
whole: the whole week toda a
semana [t**oh**da sim**a**na]
the whole lot tudo isto
[t**oo**doo **ee**shtoo]
whose: whose is this? de quem
é isto? [di kayng eh **ee**shtoo]
why? porquê? [poork**ay**]
why not? porque não?
[nowng]
wide largo [l**a**rgoo]
wife: my wife a minha mulher
[m**ee**n-ya mool-y**eh**r]
will*: will you do it for me? fá-lo
para mim? [f**a**loo para meeng]

wind o vento [**vay**ntoo]

window a janela [Jan**eh**la]
(of shop) a montra [m**oh**ntra]

near the window ao pé da
janela [ow peh]

in the window (of shop) na
montra

window seat o lugar ao pé da
janela [loog**ar** ow peh da
Jan**eh**la]

windscreen o pára-brisas [para-
br**eeza**sh]

windscreen wiper o limpa pára-
brisas [**lee**mpa]

windsurfing o windsurf

windy: it's so windy está muito
vento [shta m**wee**ngtoo
vayntoo]

wine o vinho [**vee**n-yoo]

can we have some more wine?
pode trazer mais vinho? [pod
traz**ay**r mish]

The best-known Portuguese
table wines are reds from the
Dão region. Among other
smaller regions offering interesting red wines are Colares
(near Sintra), Bucelas in the
Estremadura (crisp, dry whites),
Valpaças from Trás-os-Montes,
Reguengos from Alentejo and
Lagoa from the Algarve.
The light, slightly sparkling
vinhos verdes – 'green wines',
in age not colour – are produced
in quantity in the Minho.
They're drunk early and don't →

mature or improve with age, but
are great with meals, especially
shellfish. There are red and rosé
vinhos verdes, though the
whites are the most successful
– Casal Garcia is the one you'll
find most often in restaurants.
Otherwise, Portuguese rosé
wines are known abroad mainly
through the spectacularly suc
cessful export of Mateus Rosé.
Portugal also produces a
range of sparkling champagne-
method wines: **espumantes
naturais**. These are designated
bruto (extra-dry), **seco** (fairly
dry), **meio seco** (quite sweet)
or **doce** (very sweet). The best
of these come from the Bairrada
region, northwest of Coimbra,
though Raposeira wines are the
most commonly available.
Even the most basic of restaurants usually have a decent selection of wines, many of which
are available in half-bottles, too.
The **vinho da casa** (house
wine) is nearly always remark-
ably good value.

wine list a lista dos vinhos
[**lee**shta dooJ **vee**n-yoosh]

winter o Inverno [inv**eh**rnoo]
in the winter no Inverno [noo]

winter holiday as férias de
inverno [**feh**r-yash dinv**eh**rnoo]

wire o arame [ar**am**]
(electric) o fio [**fee**-oo]

wish: best wishes com os melhores cumprimentos [kong ooJ mil-yorish koomprimayntoosh]

with com [kong]

I'm staying with ... estou na casa do/da ... [shtoh na kaza doo]

without sem [sayng]

witness a testemunha [tishtimoon-ya]

will you be a witness for me? quer ser minha testemunha? [kehr sayr meen-ya]

woman a mulher [mool-yehr]

---

women

Portugal is rarely a dangerous place for women travellers, and only in the following few areas do you need to be particularly wary: parts of Lisbon (particularly the Cais do Sodré and the Bairro Alto by night), streets immediately around the train stations in the larger towns (traditionally the red light districts), and the Algarve, where aggressive males congregate on the pick-up. People may initially wonder why you're travelling on your own – especially inland and in the mountains, where Portuguese women never travel unaccompanied – but once they have accepted that you are a crazy foreigner you're likely to be welcomed.

---

wonderful (weather, holiday, person) maravilhoso [maravil-yohzoo]

(meal) excelente [ish-selaynt]

won't*: it won't start não pega [nowng pehga]

wood (material) a madeira [madayra]

woods (forest) o bosque [boshk]

wool a lã [lang]

word a palavra

work o trabalho [trabal-yoo]

it's not working não funciona [nowng foons-yohna]

I work in ... trabalho em ... [ayng]

world o mundo [moondoo]

worry: I'm worried (said by man/ woman) estou preocupado/ preocupada [shtoh pri-okoopadoo]

worse: it's worse está pior [shta p-yor]

worst o pior [oo]

worth: is it worth a visit? vale a pena uma visita? [val a payna ooma vizeeta]

would: would you give this to ...? pode dar isto a ...? [pod dar eeshtwa]

wrap: could you wrap it up? pode embrulhá-lo? [aymbrool-yaloo]

wrapping paper o papel de embrulho [papehl daymbrool-yoo]

wrist o pulso [poolsoo]

write escrever [shkrivayr]

could you write it down?
pode escrever isso? [pod –
eesoo]
how do you write it? como é
que escreve isso? [**koh**moo eh
kishkr**eh**v]

writing paper o papel de c**a**rta
[pap**eh**l di]

wrong: it's the wrong key não é
esta a chave [nowng eh **eh**shta
shav]
this is the wrong train este
não é o comboio [aysht nowng
eh oo komb**oy**-oo]
the bill's wrong a conta está
enganada [**koh**ntashta
aygan**a**da]
sorry, wrong number
desculpe, enganei-me no
número [dishk**oo**lp
aygan**ay**mı noo n**oo**miroo]
sorry, wrong room desculpe,
enganei-me no quarto
[kw**a**rtoo]
there's something wrong
with ... passa-se qualquer
coisa com ... [p**a**sasi kwalk**eh**r
k**oh**-iza kong]
what's wrong? o que se
passa? [oo ki si]

X

X-ray o raio X [**ra**-yoo sheesh]

Y

yacht o iate [yat]
yard* a jarda [J**a**rda]
year o ano [**a**noo]
yellow amarelo [amar**eh**loo]
yes sim [seeng]
yesterday ontem [**oh**ntayng]
yesterday morning ontem de
manhã [di man-y**a**ng]
the day before yesterday
anteontem [anti**oh**ntayng]
yet ainda [a-**ee**nda], já [J**a**]

•••••• DIALOGUE ••••••

is it here yet? já está aqui? [J**a** shta
ak**ee**]
no, not yet não, ainda não [nowng
a-**ee**nda nowng]
you'll have to wait a little longer yet
ainda terá que esperar um
pouquinho [tira kishpirar oong
pohk**ee**n-yoo]

yoghurt o iogurte [yoog**oo**rt]
you* (pol) você [vos**ay**]
(more formal: to man/woman) o
senhor [oo sin-y**oh**r], a
senhora
(fam) tu [too]
this is for you isto é para si
[**ee**shtweh p**a**ra see]
(fam) isto é para ti
with you consigo [kons**ee**goo]
(fam) contigo [kont**ee**goo]

The most usual way of
addressing people you don't
know is to use: **o senhor** (to a →

man), **a senhora** (to a woman),
os senhores (to more than one
man) and **as senhoras** (to more
than one woman).
Você usually indicates greater
familiarity with the other
person. It is used between people who feel on an equal foot-
ing.
Tu indicates intimacy. It is used
among family members, close
friends, and between people
who belong to a particular
group (for example children,
students).

could you put a new zip on?
pode pôr um fecho éclair
novo? [pod pohr oong –
n**oh**voo]
zipcode o código postal
[k**o**digoo poosht**a**l]
zoo o jardim zoológico
[Jard**ee**ng zwol**o**Jikoo]
zucchini a courgette

young jovem [J**o**vayng]
your* (pol) seu [s**ay**-oo], sua
[s**oo**-a]
(more formal: to man/woman) do
senhor [sin-y**oh**r], da
senhora [sin-y**o**ra]
(fam) teu [t**ay**-oo], tua [t**oo**-a]
yours* (pol) seu [s**ay**-oo], sua
[s**oo**-a]
(more formal: to a man/woman) do
senhor [doo sin-y**oh**r], da
senhora [sin-y**o**ra]
(fam) teu [t**ay**-oo], tua [t**oo**-a]
youth hostel o albergue da
juventude [alb**eh**rg da
Joovaynt**oo**d]

Z

zero zero [z**eh**roo]
zip o fecho éclair®
[**fay**shwaykl**eh**r]

Portuguese-English

COLLOQUIALISMS

The following are words you might well hear. You shouldn't be tempted to use any of the stronger ones unless you are sure of your audience.

bestial! [bisht-yal] fantastic!

burro m [boorroo] thickhead

cabrão! [kabrowng] bastard!

está nas suas sete quintas [shta nash soo-ash seht keentash] he's/
   she's in his/her element

estou-me nas tintas [shtoh-mi nash teentash] I don't give a damn

filho da puta! [poota] son-of-a-bitch!

gajo m [gaJoo] bloke

grosso [grohsoo] pissed

imbecil [imbeseel] stupid

isso é canja [eesweh kanJa] piece of cake (literally: this is chicken soup)

louco [lohkoo] nutter

maçada [masada] bother

maluco [malookoo] barmy, nuts

merda! [mehrda] shit!

não faz mal [nowng faJ] it doesn't matter

não me diga! [nowng mi deega] you don't say!

ora essa! [ora ehsa] don't be stupid!

porreiro! [poorrayroo] bloody good!

que chatice! [ki shatees] oh no!, blast!

que disparate! [dishparat] rubbish!, nonsense!

que droga! [droga] blast!

raios o partam! [ra-yooz oo partowng] damn you!

rua! [roo-a] get out of here!

sacana! bastard!

tolo [tohloo] silly

vá à fava! go away!

vá para o caralho! [paroo karal-yoo] fuck off!

vá para o diabo! [d-yaboo] go to hell!

vá para o inferno! [infehrno] go to hell!

A

a the; to; her; it; to it; you

à to the

a abrir brevemente open soon

abaixo [abīshoo] below; down
  mais abaixo [mīz] further
  down

abcesso m [absehsoo] abscess

aberto [abehrtoo] open; opened

aberto até às 19 horas open
  until 7 p.m.

aberto das ... às ... horas open
  from ... to ... o'clock

abertura f [abirtoora] opening

aborrecer [aboorrisayr] to
  annoy; to bore

aborrecido [aboorriseedoo]
  annoying; bored; annoyed

abre-garrafas m [abrigarrafash]
  bottle-opener

abre-latas m [abrilatash] can-
  opener, tin-opener

Abril [abreel] April

abrir [abreer] to open; to
  unlock

a/c c/o

acabar to finish

acalmar-se [–si] to calm down

acampar to camp

acaso: por acaso [poor akazoo]
  by chance

aceitar [asaytar] to accept; to
  take

acelerador m [asiliradohr]
  accelerator

acenda os médios switch on
  dipped headlights

acenda os mínimos switch on
  your parking lights

acender [asayndayr] to switch
  on; to light

acento m [asayntoo] accent

aceso [asayzoo] on, switched
  on

acesso m [asehsoo] access

acetona f [asitohna] nail polish
  remover

acho: acho que não [ashoo ki
  nowng] I don't think so
  acho que sim [seeng] I think
  so

acidente m [asidaynt] accident;
  crash

acidente de viação [di v-ya-
  sowng] road accident

ácido [asidoo] sour; sharp

acima [aseema] up; above

acompanhar [akompan-yar] to
  accompany

aconselhar [akonsil-yar] to
  advise

acontecer [akontisayr] to
  happen
  o que aconteceu? [oo
  ki-akontisay-oo] what has
  happened?, what's up?,
  what's wrong?
  o que é que está a acontecer?
  [oo k-yeh kishta] what's
  happening?

acordado [akoordadoo] awake

acordar [akoordar] to wake, to
  wake up
  ele já acordou? [ayl Ja
  akoordoh] is he awake?

acordo: de acordo com [d-ya-
  kohrdoo kong] according to

A.C.P. [a say pay] Portuguese Motoring Organization

acreditar to believe

acrílico m [akreelikoo] acrylic

actor principal m [atohr preensipal], actriz principal f [atreesh] film star

adaptador m [adaptadohr] adapter

adega f cellar; old-style bar

adepta f [adehpta], adepto m [adehptoo] fan

adesivo m [adizeevoo] sticking plaster, plaster, Bandaid®

adeus [aday-oosh] goodbye, bye

adeuzinho! [aday-oozeen-yoo] cheerio!

adiantado [ad-yantadoo] in advance

adiante: fica ali adiante [feekalee ad-yant] it's over there

adoecer [ad-wisayr] to fall ill

adolescente m/f [adoolish-saynt] teenager

adorar [adoorar] to adore

adorável [adooravil] lovely

adulta f [adoolta], adulto m [adooltoo] adult

advogada f [advoogada], advogado m [advoogadoo] lawyer

aeroporto m [a-ayroopohrtoo] airport

afiado [af-yadoo] sharp

afogador m choke

África f Africa

África do Sul [doo sool] South Africa

africano (m) [afrikanoo] African

afta f mouth ulcer

afundar [afoondar] to sink

agência f [aɹayns-ya] agency

agência de viagens [di v-ya-ɹayngsh] travel agency

agenda f [aɹaynda] diary (for business)

agitar bem antes de usar shake well before using

agora [agora] now
agora não [nowng] not just now

Agosto [agohshtoo] August

agradável [agradavil] nice, pleasant

agradecer [agradisayr] to thank

agradecido [agradiseedoo] grateful

água f [agwa] water

aguaceiro m [agwasayroo] shower

água de colónia [di] eau de toilette

água destilada f [agwa dishtilada] distilled water

água fria [free-a] cold water

água potável [pootavil] drinking water

aguardar [agwardar] to wait for

agudo [agoodoo] sharp

agulha f [agool-ya] needle

ah sim! [seeng] well well!

aí [a-ee] there

ainda [a-eenda] yet, still
ainda mais ... [mīsh] even more ...
ainda não [nowng] not yet

ainda são só ... [sowng saw] it's only ...

ajuda f [aJooda] help

ajudar to help

al. avenue

alameda f [alamayda] avenue

alarme m [alarm] alarm

alarme de incêndios [dinsayndyoosh] fire alarm

alavanca f lever

alavanca das mudanças [daJ moodansash] gear lever

albergaria f [albirgaree-a] luxury hotel

albergue da juventude m [albehrg da Joovayntood] youth hostel

albergue juvenil youth hostel

alça f [alsa] strap

alcunha f [alkoon-ya] nickname

aldeia f [alday-a] village

aldeia de pescadores [di pishkadohrish] fishing village

alemã (f) [alimang] German

Alemanha f [aliman-ya] Germany

alemão (m) [alimowng] German

além de [alayng di] apart from

alérgico a ... [alehrJikoo] allergic to ...

Alfa high-speed train

alfabeto m [alfabehtoo] alphabet

alfaiataria f [alfi-ataree-a], alfaiate m [alfi-at] tailor

alfândega f [alfandiga] Customs

alfinete m [alfinayt] brooch; pin

alfinete de segurança m [di sigooransa] safety pin

alforreca f [alfoorrehka] jellyfish

alga f seaweed

algodão m [algoodowng] cotton

algodão em rama [ayng] cotton wool

alguém [algayng] anybody; somebody, someone

algum [algoong], alguma [algooma] some

alguma coisa [koh-iza] anything else, something else

algumas [algoomash], alguns [algoonsh] a few, some

ali [alee] (over) there

ali acima [aseema] up there

ali adiante [ad-yant] over there

é por ali [eh poor] it's that way

aliança f [al-yansa] wedding ring

alicate m [alikat] pliers

alicate de unhas [doon-yash] nail clippers

alimento m [alimayntoo] food

alimentos para diabéticos mpl [alimayngtoosh para d-yabehtikoosh] diabetic foods

almoçar [almoosar] to have lunch

almoço m [almohsoo] lunch

almoço embalado [almohswaymbaladoo] packed lunch

almofada f [almoofada] cushion; pillow

alojamento m [alooJamayntoo] accommodation

alpinismo m [alpin**ee**Jmoo] mountaineering

altitude f [altit**oo**d] height

alto [**a**ltoo] high; tall; loud
no alto [noo] at the top

altura f [alt**oo**ra] height

altura máxima maximum headroom

alugam-se quartos rooms to let, rooms for rent

alugar [aloog**ar**] to hire, to rent

aluga-se [al**oo**ga-si] for hire, to rent

aluguer m [aloog**eh**r] rent

aluguer de automóveis [dowtoom**o**vaysh] car hire, car rental

aluguer de barcos boat hire

aluguer de barracas sunshades for hire

aluguer de cadeiras beach chairs for hire

aluguer de gaivotas pedal boat hire

aluguer de parassóis beach umbrellas for hire

alvorada f [alvoor**a**da] dawn

ama f childminder

amanhã [aman-y**a**ng] tomorrow

amanhã à tarde [tard] tomorrow afternoon

amanhã de manhã [di man-y**a**ng] tomorrow morning

amar to love

amarelo [amar**eh**loo] yellow

amargo [am**a**rgoo] bitter

amável [am**a**vil] kind; generous

ambos [**a**mboosh] both

ambulância f [ambool**a**ns-ya] ambulance

ameno [am**ay**noo] mild

América f America

americano [amirik**a**noo] American

amiga f [am**ee**ga] friend

amigdalite f [ameegdal**ee**t] tonsillitis

amigo m [am**ee**goo] friend

amor m [am**oh**r] love

amortecedor m [amoortisid**oh**r] shock-absorber

amperes mpl [amp**eh**rish] amps

ampliação f [ampl-yas**ow**ng] enlargement

ampolas bebíveis fpl [amp**oh**laJ bib**ee**vaysh] ampoules

analgésicos mpl [analJ**eh**zeekoosh] painkillers

análises de sangue fpl [anal**i**ziJ di sang] blood tests

anca f hip

âncora f anchor

andar (m) floor, storey; to walk

andar à boleia [bool**ay**-a] to hitchhike

andar a cavalo [kav**a**loo] horse-riding

andar a pé [peh] to walk

anel m [an**eh**l] ring

anilha f [an**ee**l-ya] washer

animado [anim**a**doo] lively

aniversário de casamento m [anivirs**a**r-yoo di kazam**ay**ntoo] wedding anniversary

aniversário natalício [natal**ee**s-yoo] birthday

ano m [anoo] year

Ano Novo [nohvoo] New Year

anteontem [anti-ohntayng] the day before yesterday

antepassado m ancestor

anterior: dia anterior m [dee-a antir-yohr] the day before

antes [antsh] before

antibióticos mpl [antib-yotikoosh] antibiotics

anticongelante m [–konJilant] antifreeze

antigo [anteegoo] ancient, old

antiguidade f [antigweedad] antique

anti-histamínicos mpl [–eesh-tameenikoosh] antihistamines

antilaxante m [anti-lashant] medicine for diarrhoea

antiquado [antikwadoo] old-fashioned

anti-séptico m [–sehptikoo] antiseptic

anúncio m [anoons-yoo] advertisement

ao [ow] to the; at the

ao norte de north of

ao ouvir o sinal... when you hear the tone ...

ao pé de [ow peh di] near

ao preço de custo cost price

aos [owsh] to the; at the

apagar to switch off

apagar os máximos headlights off

apanhar [apan-yar] to get on, to catch; to pick up

apanhar banhos de sol [ban-yooJ di] to sunbathe

apara-lápis m pencil sharpener

aparelhagem (de som) f [aparel-yaJayng (di song)] stereo; audio equipment

aparelho m [aparayl-yoo] device

aparelho auditivo hearing aid

aparelho para a surdez [soordaysh] hearing aid

aparelhos eléctricos mpl [aparayl-yooz elehtrikoosh] electrical appliances

apartamento m [apartamayntoo] apartment, flat

aparthotel m [apartohtehl] self-catering apartment

a pé [peh] on foot

apelido m [apileedoo] surname; family name

apendicite f [apendiseet] appendicitis

apertado [apirtadoo] tight

apertar to hold tight; to fasten

apertar o cinto de segurança fasten your seatbelt

apetecer [apitisayr] to feel like

apetece-me [apitehsimi] I feel like

apetite m [apiteet] appetite

apinhado [apeen-yadoo] crowded

aprender [aprayndayr] to learn

apresentar [aprizentar] to introduce

apressar-se [aprisarsi] to hurry

à prova de água [dagwa] waterproof

aproximadamente [aproosimadamaynt] approximately, roughly

aquecedor m [akesid**ohr**] heater

aquecedor eléctrico [el**eh**trikoo] electric fire

aquecimento m [akesim**ay**ntoo] heating

aquecimento central [sayntral] central heating

aquela [ak**eh**la], aquele [ak**ay**l] that, that one (further away)

aquelas [ak**eh**lash], aqueles [ak**ay**lish] those (further away)

aqui [ak**ee**] (over) here

aqui embaixo [aymb**ī**shoo] down here

aqui está/estão ... [shta/ sht**ow**ng] here is/are ...

aqui mesmo [m**ay**Jmoo] just here

é por aqui [eh por] it's this way

aquilo [ak**ee**loo] that; that one (further away)

aqui tem [ak**ee** tayng] here you are

ar m air

árabe [**a**rabi] Arab; Arabic os Árabes the Arabs

arame m [ar**a**m] wire

aranha f [ar**a**n-ya] spider

arco-íris m [arkoo-**ee**reesh] ˙ rainbow

ar condicionado m [kondis- yoon**a**doo] air conditioning

arder [ard**ay**r] to burn

areia f [ar**ay**-a] sand

armário m [arm**a**r-yoo] cupboard

armazém m [armaz**ay**ng] warehouse; big store

aroma artificial/natural artificial/ natural fragrance

arq. architect

arqueologia f [ark-yolooJ**ee**-a] archaeology

arquitecto m [arkit**eh**too] architect

arraial m [arrī-**a**l] local fair with fireworks, singing and dancing

arranhão m [arran-y**ow**ng] scratch

arranjos mpl [arr**a**nJoosh] repairs

arredores mpl [arred**o**rish] suburb

arriscado [arrishk**a**doo] risky

arte f [art] art

artesanato m [artizan**a**too] handicrafts, crafts

artifis-y**a**l] artificial

artigos de bébé mpl [art**ee**gooJ di beb**eh**] baby goods

artigos de campismo [kamp**ee**Jmoo] camping equipment

artigos de casa [k**a**za] household goods

artigos de desporto [dishp**oh**rtoo] sports goods

artigos de luxo [l**oo**shoo] luxury goods

artigos de viagem [v-ya**J**ayng] travel goods

artigos em cabedal [ayng kabid**a**l] leather goods

artigos em cortiça [koort**ee**sa] cork goods

artigos em pele [pehl] leather goods

artigos regionais regional
goods, typical goods from
the region

artista m/f [arteeshta] artist

árvore f [arvoori] tree

as [ash] the; them; you

às to the; at the

asa f wing

asa-delta f [aza-dehlta] hang-
gliding

ascensor m [ashsaynsohr] lift,
elevator

a senhora [sin-yora] you

asma f [aJma] asthma

asneira f [aJnayra] nonsense;
swearword

aspirador m [ashpiradohr]
vacuum cleaner

aspirina f [ashpireena] aspirin

assaltado [asaltadoo] mugged

assar to bake; to roast

as senhoras [ash sin-yorash] you

assento m [asayntoo] seat

assim [aseeng] this way
assim está bem [shta bayng]
that'll do nicely
assim está bem? is that OK?

assinado signed

assinar to sign

assinatura f [asinatoora]
signature

às vezes [aJ vayzish]
sometimes

atacadores mpl [atakadohrish]
shoelaces

atalho m [atal-yoo] shortcut

ataque m [atak] fit; attack

ataque cardíaco [kardee-akoo]
heart attack

até [ateh] until

até amanhã [aman-yang] see
you tomorrow

até já [Ja] see you soon

até logo! [logoo] see you!, see
you later!

até mesmo ... [mayJmoo] even
...

atenção please note; caution;
warning

atenção ao comboio beware of
the train

atenção: portas automáticas
warning: automatic doors

aterragem f [atirraJayng] landing

aterragem de emergência
emergency landing

aterrar to land

atirar to throw

Atlântico m Atlantic

atletismo m [atleteeJmoo]
athletics

atraente [atra-aynt] attractive

atrás [atrash] at the back,
behind
atrás de ... [di] behind ...

atrasado [atrazadoo] late,
delayed
estar atrasado [shtar] to be
late

atraso m [atrazoo] delay

através de [atravehJ di] through

atravessar to go through, to
cross

atravesse go, walk

atropelar [atropilar] to knock
over, to knock down

auscultador m [owshkooltadohr]
receiver

auscultadores mpl
[owshkooltadohrish]
headphones

australiano (m) [owshtral-yanoo]
Australian

autobanco m [owtoobankoo]
cash dispenser, cashpoint,
ATM

autocarro m [owtookarroo]
coach, bus

autoçarro do aeroporto
[dwayroopohrtoo] airport bus

autoestrada f [owtooshtrada]
motorway, highway,
freeway

automático [owtoomatikoo]
automatic

automóvel m [owtoomovil] car

Automóvel Clube de Portugal
Portuguese Motoring
Organization

av. avenue

avance go, walk

avaria f [avaree-a] breakdown

avariado [avari-adoo] damaged;
faulty; out of order

avariar [avari-ar] to damage; to
break down

avarias [avaree-ash] breakdown
service

ave f [avi] bird

à venda [vaynda] for sale

avenida f [avineeda] avenue

avião m [av-yowng] plane,
aircraft, airplane
de avião [dav-yowng] by
plane; by air

aviso m [aveezoo] warning; notice

avô m [avoh] grandfather

avó f [avaw] grandmother

azedo [azaydoo] sour

azul [azool] blue

azulejaria f [azoolayJaree-a] tile
maker's workshop

azul-marinho [azool mareen-yoo]
navy blue

B

bagagem f [bagaJayng] luggage,
baggage

bagagem de mão f [di mowng]
hand luggage

baía f [ba-ee-a] bay

baile m [bīli] dance

bairro m [bīrroo] district

baixo [bīshoo] low; short

balcão m [balkowng] counter

balcão de informações
[dinfoormasoyngsh]
information desk

balcão da recepção [risehsowng]
reception desk

balcão para reparações rápidas
de sapatos [riparasoyngsh
rapidash di sapatoosh] heelbar

balde m [bowld] bucket

banco m [bankoo] bank; stool

banco de poupança [di
pohpansa] savings bank

banda f band

bandeira f [bandayra] flag

banheira f [ban-yayra] bathtub,
bath

banheiro m [ban-yayroo]
lifeguard

banheiros [ban-yayroosh] toilets

banho m [ban-yoo] bath

banho de sol: tomar banho de sol [toomar – di] to sunbathe

barata (f) cockroach; cheap, inexpensive

barato [baratoo] cheap, inexpensive

barba f beard

barbatanas fpl [barbatanash] flippers

barbeiro m [barbayroo] men's hairdresser's, barber's shop

barco m [barkoo] boat

barco a motor [barkwa mootohr] motorboat

barco a remos [raymoosh] rowing boat

barco a vapor steamer

barco à vela sailing boat

barcos de aluguer boats for hire

barraca f beach hut

barro: louça de barro f [lohsa di barroo] earthenware

barulhento [barool-yayntoo] noisy

barulho m [barool-yoo] noise

bastante [bashtant] fairly; rather; quite (a lot)

bata (à porta) knock

batechapas bodywork repairs

bater [batayr] to hit, to knock

bateria f [batiree-a] battery (for car)

baton m [batong] lipstick

baton para o cieiro [oo s-yayroo] lip salve

bêbado [baybadoo] drunk

bebé m [bebeh] baby

beber [bibayr] to drink

bebida f [bibeeda] drink

beco sem saída cul-de-sac, dead end

bege beige

beijar [bayJar] to kiss

beijo m [bayJoo] kiss

beira: à beira do mar [bayra doo] at/by the seaside

beira-mar: à beira-mar by the sea

belga (m/f) Belgian

Bélgica f [behlJika] Belgium

beliche m [bileesh] berth, bunk; couchette; bunk beds

belo [behloo] beautiful

bem [bayng] fine, I'm fine, well, OK; properly

bem! good!

bem aqui [akee] right here

está bem [shta] that's fine

estás bem? [shtash] are you all right?

você está bem? [vosay] are you OK?

bem-educado [bayng idookadoo] polite

bem passado [pasadoo] well-done

bem-vindo [veendoo] welcome

bem vindo a ... welcome to ...

bengaleiro m [bengalayroo] cloakroom, checkroom

berço m [bayrsoo] cot

bestial! [bisht-yal] fantastic!, tremendous!

bexiga f [bisheega] bladder

biberão m [bibirowng] baby's bottle

biblioteca f [bibl-yoot**eh**ka] library

bicha f [b**ee**sha] queue, line

bicicleta f [bisikl**eh**ta] bicycle, bike

bifurcação f [bifoorkas**ow**ng] fork (in road)

bigode m [big**o**d] moustache

bilha de gás f [b**ee**l-ya di gash] gas cylinder

bilhete m [bil-y**ay**t] fare; ticket; single ticket, one-way ticket

bilhete de entrada [daynt**ra**da] admission ticket

bilhete de excursão [dishkoors**ow**ng] excursion ticket

bilhete de ida [d**ee**da] single ticket, one-way ticket

bilhete de ida e volta [d**ee**dī] return ticket, round trip ticket

bilhete de lotaria [di lootar**ee**-a] lottery ticket

bilhete em aberto [bil-y**ay**tayng ab**eh**rtoo] open ticket

bilheteira f [bil-yit**ay**ra] box office, ticket office

bilhetes tickets

bilhete simples m [bil-y**ay**t s**ee**mplish] single ticket, one-way ticket

bloco de apartamentos m [bl**o**koo dapartam**ay**ntoosh] apartment block

bloco de apontamentos [dapontam**ay**ntoosh] notebook

blusa f [bl**oo**za] blouse

boa [b**oh**-a] good

boa noite [n**oh**-it] good evening; good night

Boas Festas! [b**oh**-ash f**eh**shtash] merry Christmas and a happy New Year!

boa sorte! [s**oh**rt] good luck!

boa tarde [tard] good afternoon; good evening

boate f [bwat] nightclub; disco

boa viagem! [v-ya**J**ayng] have a good journey!

boca f [b**oh**ka] mouth

bocadinho m [bookad**ee**n-yoo] a small bit

bocado m [book**a**doo] piece

bochecha f [boosh**ay**sha] cheek

bóia f [b**o**-ya] buoy

boite f [bwat] nightclub; disco

bola f ball

bola de futebol [di footb**o**l] football

boleia f [bool**ay**-a] lift; ride dar (uma) boleia a to give a lift to

bolha f [b**oh**l-ya] blister

bolinha f [bol**ee**n-ya] ball (small)

bolso m [oo b**oh**lsoo] pocket

bom [bong] good; fine

bom apetite! [bong apit**ee**t] enjoy your meal!

bomba f [b**oh**mba] bomb; pump

bomba de ar air pump

bomba de gasolina [di gazool**ee**na] garage, filling station, gas station; petrol pump

bombeiros mpl [bomb**ay**roosh] fire brigade

bom dia [bong d**ee**-a] good
  morning
boné m [boon**eh**] cap, hat
boneca f [boon**eh**ka] doll
bonito [boon**ee**too] beautiful;
  nice; pretty
borboleta f [borbool**ay**ta]
  butterfly
borda f edge
borracha f [boorr**a**sha] rubber;
  eraser
bosque m [boshk] woods, forest
bota f boot (footwear)
botão m [boot**ow**ng] button
botas de borracha fpl
  wellingtons
bote de borracha m [bot di
  boorr**a**sha] dinghy
braço m [br**a**soo] arm
branco [br**a**nkoo] white
Brasil m [braz**ee**l] Brazil
brasileiro (m) [brazil**ay**roo]
  Brazilian
breve [brev] brief
  em breve soon
briga f [br**ee**ga] fight
brigar to fight
brilhante [breel-y**a**nt] bright;
  brilliant
brincadeira f [breenkad**ay**ra] joke
brincos mpl [breenkoosh]
  earrings
brinquedo m [breenk**ay**doo] toy
brisa f [br**ee**za] breeze
britânico [brit**a**nikoo] British
brochura f [brosh**oo**ra] leaflet
bronquite [bronk**ee**t] bronchitis
bronzeado (m) [bronz-y**a**doo]
  tan; suntan; suntanned

bronzeador m suntan lotion
bronzear [brohnz-y**a**r] to tan
bronzear-se [–si] to get a tan
bugigangas mpl [booJig**a**ngash]
  bric-a-brac
bule m [bool] teapot
buraco m [boor**a**koo] hole
burro (m) [b**oo**rroo] donkey;
  thickhead; stupid
bus bus lane
buscar [boosh**ka**r] to collect; to
  fetch
bússola f [b**oo**soola] compass
buzina f [booz**ee**na] horn

C

c/ with
cá here
cabeça f [kab**ay**sa] head
cabedais mpl [kabid**i**sh] leather
  goods
cabedal m [kabid**a**l] leather
cabeleireiro m [kabilayr**ay**roo]
  hairdresser's
cabeleireiro de homens
  [d**oh**mayngsh] men's
  hairdresser
cabeleireiro de senhoras [di sin-
  y**o**rash] ladies' salon
cabeleireiro unisexo
  [oonis**eh**ksoo] unisex salon
cabelo m [kab**ay**loo] hair
cabide m [kab**ee**d]
  coathanger
cabina f [kab**ee**na] cabin
cabina de provas [di pr**o**vash]
  fitting room
cabina telefónica [kab**ee**na

telefo**h**nika] phone box,
phone booth

cabos para ligar a bateria mpl
[ka**boosh** – batir**ee**-a] jump
leads

cabra f goat

cabrão! [kabr**ow**ng] bastard!

cabrona! bastard!

caça f [ka**sa**] game (meat);
hunting

caçarola f [kasar**o**la] saucepan

cachimbo m [kash**ee**mboo] pipe
(for smoking)

cacifo m [kas**ee**foo] locker

cada each, every

cadeado m [kad-ya**doo**] padlock

cadeia f [kad**ay**-a] prison; chain

cadeira f [kad**ay**ra] chair

cadeira de bebé [di beb**eh**]
highchair

cadeira de lona [l**oh**na]
deckchair

cadeira de rodas [r**o**dash]
wheelchair

cadeira reclinável [reklin**a**vil] sun
lounger

cadeirinha de bebé f [kadayr**ee**n-
ya di beb**eh**] pushchair,
buggy

caderneta f [kadayrn**ay**ta] book
of tickets

café m [kaf**eh**] café; coffee

café de esplanada [dishplan**a**da]
pavement café

cãibra f [k**ay**mbra] cramp

cair [ka-**eer**] to fall

cais m [k**ī**sh] quay; quayside;
platform, (US) track

caixa f [k**ī**sha] box; cash desk;

till; cashier; cashpoint,
ATM; savings bank; building
society

caixa automático
[owtoom**a**teekoo] cashpoint,
cash dispenser, ATM

caixa de fusíveis [di fooz**ee**vaysh]
fusebox

caixa de mudanças
[mood**a**nsash] gearbox

caixa de primeiros socorros
[prim**ay**roosh sook**o**rroosh]
first-aid kit

caixa de velocidades
[viloosid**a**dsh] gearbox

caixa do correio [doo koorr**ay**-oo]
postbox; mailbox

caixa fechada till closed

caixote de lixo m [k**ī**sh**o**t di
l**ee**shoo] bin, dustbin,
trashcan

calçado m [kals**a**doo] footwear

calcanhar m [kalkan-**yar**] heel (of
foot)

calças fpl [k**a**lsash] trousers,
(US) pants

calções mpl [kals**oy**ngsh] shorts

calções de banho [di ban-yoo]
swimming trunks

calculadora f [kalkoolad**oh**ra]
calculator

caldeira f [kald**ay**ra] boiler

calendário m [kalend**a**r-yoo]
calendar

cale-se! [k**a**lsi] quiet!; shut up!

calmo [k**a**lmoo] calm

calor m [kal**oh**r] heat
está imenso calor [shta
im**ay**nsoo] it's hot

ter calor [tayr] to be hot

cama f bed

cama de bebé [di bebeh] cot

cama de campanha [kampan-ya] campbed

cama de casal [di kazal] double bed

cama de solteiro [sooltayroo] single bed

cama dupla [doopla] double bed

cama e pequeno almoço [ee pikaynoo almohsoo] bed and breakfast

cama individual f [individwal] single bed

câmara f camera

câmara de ar f [dar] inner tube

câmara de vídeo f [di veed-yoo] camcorder

câmara municipal f [moonisipal] town hall

camarim m [kamareeng] dressing room

camarote m [kamarot] cabin

camas separadas fpl [kamash siparadash] twin beds

câmbio m [kamb-yoo] bureau de change, exchange; exchange rate

câmbio do dia [doo dee-a] current exchange rate

camião m [kam-yowng] lorry

caminho m [kameen-yoo] path

caminho de ferro railway

Caminhos de Ferro Portugueses Portuguese Railways

camioneta f [kam-yoonayta] coach, bus; light truck

camisa f [kameeza] shirt

camisa de dormir [di doormeer] nightdress

camisaria f [kamizaree-a] shop selling shirts

camisola f [kamizola] jersey, jumper, sweater

camisola interior [intir-yohr] vest (under shirt)

campainha f [kampa-een-ya] bell

campismo m [kampeeJmoo] camping

campo m [kampoo] field; countryside, country

campo de futebol [di footbol] football ground

campo de golfe [golf] golf course

campo de ténis [tehnish] tennis court

camurça f [kamoorsa] suede

canadiano (m) [kanad-yanoo] Canadian

canal m canal; channel

Canal da Mancha English Channel

canalizador m [kanalizadohr] plumber

canção f [kansowng] song

cancelado [kansiladoo] cancelled

cancelar [kansilar] to cancel

candeeiro m [kand-yayroo] lamp

caneca f [kanehka] mug

caneta f [kanayta] pen

caneta de feltro [di fayltroo] felt-tip pen

caneta esferográfica [shfiroografika] ballpoint pen

canhoto [kan-yohtoo] left-
handed
canivete m [kaniveht] penknife
cano m [kanoo] pipe (for water)
canoa f [kanoh-a] canoe
canoagem f [kanwaJayng]
canoeing
cano de esgoto m [kanoo
diJgohtoo] drain
cansado [kansadoo] tired
cantar to sing
canto m [kantoo] corner
no canto [noo] in the corner
cantor m [kantohr], cantora f
singer
cão m [kowng] dog
cão de guarda [gwarda] guard
dog
capacete m [kapasayt] helmet
capaz: não seria capaz de ...
[siree-a kapaJ di] I couldn't ...
capela f [kapehla] chapel
capelista f [kapeleeshta]
haberdasher
capô m [kapoh] bonnet (of car),
(US) hood
cápsula f capsule
cara f face
caranguejo m [karangayJoo]
crab
caravana f caravan, (US) trailer
carburador m [karbooradohr]
carburettor
careca [karehka] bald
carga máxima maximum load
carnaval m carnival
caro [karoo] expensive
carpete f [karpeht] carpet
carrinho m [karreen-yoo] trolley

carrinho de bagagem [di
bagaJayng] luggage trolley
carrinho de bebé [bebeh]
pushchair; pram
carro m [karroo] car
de carro [di] by car
carroçaria f [karroosaree-a]
bodywork
carro de aluguer m [karroo
daloogehr] rented car
carro de mão [di mowng] trolley
carros de aluguer [daloogehr]
car hire, car rental
carruagem f [karrwaJayng]
carriage, coach
carruagem-cama f sleeper,
sleeping car
carruagem para não fumadores f
[nowng foomadohrish]
nonsmoking carriage
carruagem restaurante
[ristowrant] buffet car;
restaurant car
carta f letter
carta de condução [di
kondoosowng] driver's
licence
carta de embarque [daymbark]
boarding pass
carta de identidade [didentidad]
ID card
cartão m [kartowng] card; pass;
identity card; business card;
cardboard
cartão bancário [bankar-yoo]
cheque card
cartão de crédito [di krehdeetoo]
credit card
cartão de débito total [dehbeetoo

tootal] charge card

cartão de embarque [daymbark] boarding pass

cartão de garantia [di garantee-a] cheque card

cartão de telefone [di telefohn] phonecard

cartão de visitas [di vizeetash] business card

cartão Eurocheque Eurocheque card

carta por correio expresso [poor koorray-oo shprehsoo] express letter

cartas letters

carta verde [vayrd] green card (car insurance)

cartaz m [kartash] poster

carteira f [kartayra] purse; wallet

carteirista m/f [kartayreeshta] pickpocket

carteiro m postman

casa f [kaza] home; house
em casa [ayng] at home
na sua casa [soo-a] at your place

casaco m [kazakoo] jacket; coat

casaco de malha [di mal-ya] cardigan

casa de antiguidades f [kaza dantigweedadsh] antique shop

casa de banho [di ban-yoo] bathroom; toilet, rest room

casa de banho dos homens [dooz ohmayngsh] gents' toilet

casa de banho privativa [privateeva] private bathroom

casa de banho pública [pooblika] public convenience

casa de fados [di fadoosh] restaurant where traditional Portuguese fado songs are sung

casa de hóspedes [doshpidsh] guesthouse

casa de jantar [di jantar] dining room

casa de pasto [pashtoo] canteen-style eating place, usually open at lunchtime and serving a cheap three-course menu

casa de saúde [disa-ood] clinic; nursing home

casado [kazadoo] married

casal m [kazal] couple

casamento m [kazamayntoo] wedding

casar-se [kazarsi] to get married

casas de banho mpl [kazaJ di ban-yoo] toilets, rest rooms

caseiro [kazayroo] home-made

caso m [kazoo] case
em caso de in case of

castanho [kashtan-yoo] brown

castelo m [kashtehloo] castle

catarata f waterfall; cataract

catedral f [katidral] cathedral

categoria f [katigooree-a] category

católico (m) [katolikoo] Catholic

catorze [katohrz] fourteen

causa f [kowza] cause

por causa de [poor – di]
because of

cautela take care

cavaleiro m [kavalayroo]
horseman

cavalheiro m [kaval-yayroo]
gentleman

cavalheiros mpl [kaval-yayroosh]
gents' toilet, men's room

cavalo m [kavaloo] horse

cave f [kav] cellar; basement

caveira f [kavayra] skull

caverna f [kavehrna] cave

cavilha f [kaveel-ya] tent peg

c/c current account

CE f [say eh] EC

cedo [saydoo] early
mais cedo [mīsh] earlier

cego [sehgoo] blind

cem [sayng] hundred

cemitério m [simitehr-yoo]
cemetery

centígrado m [senteegradoo]
centigrade

centímetro m [senteemitroo]
centimetre

cento e ... [sayntwee] one
hundred and ...

central [sen-tral] central

central de correios f [di koorray-
oosh] main post office

centro m [sayntroo] centre

centro comercial [komayrs-yal]
shopping centre

centro da cidade [sidad] city
centre, town centre

centro de enfermagem
[dingfirmaJayng] clinic

centro de informação turística

[dinfoormasowng tooreestika]
tourist information office

centro de turismo [di
tooreeJmoo] tourist
information

cerâmicas fpl [siramikash]
ceramics

cerca f [sayrka] fence

cerimónia f [sirimohn-ya]
ceremony
de cerimónia [di] formal

certamente [sirtamaynt]
certainly
certamente que não [ki nowng]
certainly not

certeza: de certeza [di sirtayza]
definitely
de certeza que não [ki nowng]
definitely not
tem a certeza? [tayng] are you
sure?

certidão f [sirtidowng]
certificate

certo [sehrtoo] correct, right;
sure

cervejaria f [sirvayJaree-a] beer
cellar/tavern serving food

cesto m [sayshtoo] basket

cesto de compras [di komprash]
basket

céu m [seh-oo] sky

chaleira f [shalayra] kettle

chamada f [shamada] call

chamada de longa distância [di
lohnga dishtans-ya] long-
distance call

chamada internacional
[internas-yoonal] international
call

chamada interurbana [interoorbana] long-distance call

chamada local [lookal] local call

chamada paga no destinatário [noo dishtinatar-yoo] collect call, reverse charge call

chamada para despertar [dishpirtar] wake-up call

chamar [shamar] to call

chamar-se [–si] to be called como se chama? [kohmoo si shama] what's your name?

champô m [shampoh] shampoo

chão m [showng] ground; floor no chão [noo] on the floor; on the ground

chapa da matrícula f [shapa da matreekoola] licence plate

chapelaria f [shapilaree-a] hat shop

chapéu m [shapeh-oo] hat

chapéu de sol [di] beach umbrella, sunshade

charcutaria f [sharkootaree-a] delicatessen

charuto m [sharootoo] cigar

chateado [shat-yadoo] bored

chave f [shav] key

chave de fendas [di fayndash] screwdriver

chave de porcas [porkash] spanner

chave inglesa [inglayza] wrench; spanner

chaveiro m [shavayroo] keyring

chávena f [shavena] cup

chefe da estação m [shehf dishtas-owng] station master

chega [shayga] that's plenty; that's enough

chegada f [shigada] arrival

chegadas arrivals

chegar [shigar] to arrive, to get in; to reach

cheio [shay-oo] full

cheirar [shayrar] to smell

cheiro m [shayroo] smell

cheque de viagem m [shehk di v-yaJayng] travellers' cheque

chinês (m) [shinaysh] Chinese

chique [sheek] posh

chocante [shookant] shocking

choque m [shok] shock

chorar [shoorar] to cry

chover [shoovayr] to rain está a chover it's raining

chumbo m [shoomboo] lead; filling

chupa-chupa m [shoopa-shoopa] lollipop

chupeta f [shoopayta] dummy

churrascada f [shoorrashkada] barbecue

chuva f [shoova] rain

Cia. company

ciclismo m [sikleeJmoo] cycling

ciclista m/f [sikleeshta] cyclist

cidadã/cidadão de terceira idade f/m [sidadang/sidadowng di tirsayra idad] senior citizen

cidade f [sidad] town; city; town centre fora da cidade out of town

cidade antiga [anteega] old town

ciência f [s-yayns-ya] science

cigarro m [sigarroo] cigarette

cima: em cima de ... [ayng seema di] on top of ...

lá em cima up there; upstairs

cinco [seenkoo] five

cinquenta [sinkwaynta] fifty

cinto m [seentoo] belt

cinto de salvação [di salvasowng] lifebelt

cinto de segurança [sigooransa] seatbelt

cintura f [sintoora] waist

cinzeiro m [sinzayroo] ashtray

cinzento [sinzayntoo] grey

circuito turístico m [sirkoo-eetoo tooreeshtikoo] sightseeing tour

circule pela direita/esquerda keep right/left

círculo m [seerkooloo] circle

ciumento [s-yoomayntoo] jealous

claro [klaroo] pale; light; clear; of course

claro! sure!

claro que não [ki-nowng] of course not

é claro [eh] of course

classe f [klas] class

classe económica [ekoonohmika] economy class

clima m [kleema] climate

clínica f [kleenika] clinic

clínica médica clinic

clínica veterinária veterinary clinic

clube m [kloob] club

clube de golfe [di golf] golf club

clube de ténis [di tehnish] tennis club

cobertor m [koobirtohr] blanket

cobra f snake

cobrar to cash

cobrir to cover

código m [kodigoo] code

código da estrada highway code

código postal m [pooshtal] postcode, zip code

cod. postal postcode, zip code

coelho m [kwayl-yoo] rabbit

cofre m safe

coisa f [koh-iza] thing

cola f glue

colar m [koolar] necklace

colarinho m [koolareen-yoo] collar

colchão m [koolshowng] mattress

colchão de praia [di prī-a] beach mat

colecção f [koolehsowng] collection

colégio m [koolehჟ-yoo] college

colete m [koolayt] waistcoat

colete de salvação [di salvasowng] life jacket

colher f [kool-yehr] spoon

colher de chá f [di sha] teaspoon

colisão f [kooleezowng] crash

collants mpl [koolansh] tights, pantyhose

com [kong] with

comandante m [koomandant] captain

combinação f [kombinasowng] slip, underskirt

comboio m [komboy-oo] train

de comboio [di] by train
comboio rápido express train
com certeza [kong sirtayza]
certainly, of course, sure
começar [koomesar] to begin, to
start
começo m [koomaysoo] start,
beginning
comédia f [koomehd-ya] comedy
comer [koomayr] to eat
comerciante m/f [koomayrs-yant]
business person
comichão f [koomishowng] itch
comida f [koomeeda] food;
meal
comida congelada [konJilada]
frozen food
comida de bebé f [di bebeh]
baby food
comidas fpl food; meals
comissão m [koomisowng]
commission
comissário de bordo m
[koomisar-yoo di bordoo]
steward
com licença [kong lisaynsa]
excuse me
como [kohmoo] how; like;
since, as
como? what?, pardon (me)?,
sorry?
como é? [eh] what's it like?
como está? [shta] how are
you?, how do you do?
como este [kohmwaysht] like
this
como vai? [vī] how are
things?
com os melhores cumprimentos

best wishes
companheira f [kompan-yayra]
partner, girlfriend
companheiro m [kompan-yayroo]
partner, boyfriend
companhia f [kompan-yee-a]
company
companhia aérea [a-ehr-ya]
airline
compartimento m
[kompartimayntoo]
compartment
completamente [komplitamaynt]
completely
completo [komplehtoo] full
complicado [komplikadoo]
complicated
compra f [kohmpra] purchase
comprar [komprar] to buy
compras fpl [kohmprash]
shopping
ir às compras [eer ash] to go
shopping
compreender [kompr-yayndayr]
to understand
comprido [kompreedoo] long
comprimento m [komprimayntoo]
length
comprimido m [komprimeedoo]
tablet
comprimido para dormir
[doormeer] sleeping pill
comprimidos mpl tablets
computador m [kompootadohr]
computer
Comunidade Europeia EC
concerto m [konsayrtoo] concert
concessionário m [konsis-yoonar-
yoo] agent

concha f [**koh**nsha] shell

concha do mar [doo] seashell

concordar [konkoor**dar**] to agree
  concordo [kon**kor**doo] I agree

condições fpl [kondis**oy**ngsh]
  terms

condução f [kondoos**ow**ng]
  driving; transport

condução enquanto embriagado
  [aynkw**a**ntoo aymbr-yag**a**doo]
  drunken driving

condutor m [kondoot**ohr**],
  condutora f driver

conduza com cuidado drive
  carefully

conduzir [kondooz**eer**] to lead;
  to drive

cone de gelado m [kohn di
  Jil**a**doo] ice-cream cone

confecções de criança fpl
  [konfehs-**oy**ngsh di kr-y**a**nsa]
  children's wear

confecções de homem
  [d**oh**mayng] menswear

confecções de senhora [di sin-
  y**o**ra] ladies' wear

confeitaria [konfaytar**ee**-a] sweet
  shop, candy store

conferência f [konfir**ay**ns-ya]
  conference

confirmar [konfir**mar**] to confirm

confortável [konfoort**a**vil]
  comfortable

confusão f [konfooz**ow**ng]
  confusion, mix-up

congelador m [konJil**adohr**]
  freezer

congestionamento m [konJisht-
  yoonam**ay**ntoo] traffic

congestion

conhecer [kon-yis**ayr**] to know

connosco [kon**oh**shkoo] with us

consciente [konsh-sy**ay**nt]
  conscious

consertar [konsir**tar**] to fix, to
  mend

conservar afastado da luz solar
  directa store away from
  direct sunlight

conservar no frio store in a cold
  place

consigo [kons**ee**goo] with you

constipação f [konshtipas**ow**ng]
  cold

constipado: estou constipado
  [shtoh konshtip**a**doo] I have a
  cold

consulado m [konsool**a**doo]
  consulate

consulta f [kons**oo**lta]
  appointment

consultório m [konsoolt**or**-yoo]
  surgery

consultório dentário dental
  surgery

consumir dentro de ... dias to be
  consumed within ... days

conta f [**koh**nta] bill; account

conta bancária [bank**ar**-ya] bank
  account

contactar to contact

contaminado [kontamin**a**doo]
  polluted

conta-quilómetros m [konta-
  kil**oh**mitroosh] speedometer

contar to count; to tell

contente [kont**ay**nt] happy;
  glad, pleased

contigo [konteegoo] with you

conto m [kohntoo] tale, story; a thousand escudos

contra against

contraceptivo m [kontrasipteevoo] contraceptive

contra-indicações fpl contraindications

contrário [kontrar-yoo] opposite

controlo de passaportes passport control

contusão f [kontoozowng] bruise

conveniente [konvin-yaynt] convenient

convento m [konvayntoo] convent

conversação f [konversasowng] conversation

convés m [konvehsh] deck

convidada f [konvidada], convidado m [konvidadoo] guest

convidar [konvidar] to invite

convir [konveer] to suit; to be convenient

convite m [konveet] invitation

copo m [kopoo] glass; cup

cor f [kohr] colour

coração m [koorasowng] heart

corajoso [kooraJohzoo] brave

corda f rope

cordeiro m [koordayroo] lamb

cordel m [koordehl] string

cor de laranja [kohr di laranJa] orange (colour)

cor de rosa [roza] pink

corpo m [kohrpoo] body

corredor m [koorridohr] corridor

correia f [koorray-a] strap

correia da ventoinha [da ventooween-ya] fan belt

correia de relógio [di riloJ-yoo] watch strap

correio m [koorray-oo] post, mail; post office

correio aéreo [a-ehr-yoo] airmail

correio azul [azool] express mail

correio expresso [koorray-oo shprehsoo] express mail, special delivery

correios mpl [koorray-oosh] post office

Correios de Portugal S.A. National Mail Service

corrente f [koorraynt] chain, current

corrente de ar [koorraynt dar] draught

correr [koorrayr] to run

correspondente m/f [koorrishpondaynt] penfriend

corrida f [koorreeda] race

cortado [koortadoo] cut; blocked

cortar to cut

cortar e fazer brushing [ee fazayr] cut and blow-dry

corte m [kort] cut

corte de cabelo [di kabayloo] haircut

corte de energia [denirJee-a] power cut

cortiça f [koorteesa] cork (material)

cortiças fpl [koort**ee**sash] cork goods

cortina f [koort**ee**na] curtain

cortinados mpl [koortin**a**doosh] curtains

coser [kooz**ayr**] to sew

cosméticos mpl [kooJm**eh**tikoosh] cosmetics, make-up

costa f [k**o**shta] coast
na costa on the coast

costas fpl [k**o**shtash] back (of body)

costela f [koosht**eh**la] rib

cotação cambial f [kootas**ow**ng kamb-y**al**] exchange rate

cotovelo m [kootoov**ay**loo] elbow

couro m [k**oh**roo] leather

coxa f [k**oh**sha] thigh

coxia f [koosh**ee**-a] aisle

cozer [kooz**ayr**] to cook

cozinha f [kooz**ee**n-ya] kitchen

cozinhar [kozeen-y**ar**] to cook

cozinheiro m [kozeen-y**ay**roo] cook

C.P. [say pay] Portuguese Railways

crédito m [kr**eh**ditoo] credit

creme m [kraym] cream, lotion

creme amaciador [amas-yad**oh**r] conditioner

creme de barbear [di barb-y**ar**] shaving cream

creme de base [baz] foundation cream

creme de limpeza [leemp**ay**za] cleansing lotion

creme écran total [ekr**a**ng toot**al**] sunblock

creme hidratante [kraymeedrat**a**nt] moisturizer

crer [krayr] to believe

criada f [kr-y**a**da] maid

criada de quarto [di kw**a**rtoo] chambermaid

criança f [kr-y**a**nsa] child

crianças children; children crossing

cru, crua [kroo, kr**oo**-a] raw

cruzamento m [kroozam**ay**ntoo] junction, crossroads

cruzamento perigroso dangerous junction

cruzar [krooz**ar**] to cross

cruzeiro m [krooz**ay**roo] cruise

cruzeta f [krooz**ay**ta] coathanger

Cruz Vermelha Red Cross

CTT [say tay tay] National Mail Service

cuecas fpl [kw**eh**kash] underpants; pants, panties

cuecas de mulher [kw**eh**kaJ di mool-y**ehr**] pants, panties

cuidado m [kwid**a**doo] care
cuidado! look out!, be careful!, take care!

cuidado com o cão beware of the dog

cuidadoso [kwidad**oh**zoo] careful

cujo [k**oo**Joo] of which; whose

culpa f [k**oo**lpa] fault
é culpa minha/dele it's my/his fault

culpado [koolp**a**doo] guilty

cumprimento m [koomprim**ay**ntoo]

compliment
com os melhores
cumprimentos with best
wishes
cunhada f [koon-yada] sister-in-
law
cunhado m [koon-yadoo]
brother-in-law
curar [koorar] to cure
curso m [koorsoo] course
curso de línguas [di leengwash]
language course
curto [koortoo] short
curva f [koorva] turning; bend
curva perigosa dangerous bend
custar [kooshtar] to charge, to
cost
cutelaria f [kootilaree-a] cutlery
shop
c/v basement

D

d. right
da of the; from the
dá he/she/it gives; you give
damas f [damash] ladies'
toilets, ladies' room
damos [damoosh] we give
dança f [dansa] dance
dança folclórica [foolklorika] folk
dancing
dançar [dansar] to dance
dão [downg] they give; you give
daqui [dakee] from now
dar to give
dar prioridade give way
dar (uma) boleia a [(ooma)
boolay-a] to give a lift to

das [dash] of the; from the
dás you give
da senhora [sin-yora], das
senhoras [sin-yorash] your;
yours
data f date
data de validade [di validad]
expiry date
da tarde [tard] p.m.
de [di] from; of; by; in
de autocarro [dowtookarroo] by
bus
de avião [dav-yowng] by air
de carro [di karroo] by car
de manhã [di man-yang] in the
morning
debaixo de ... [dibīshoo di]
under ...
decepcionado [disips-yoonadoo]
disappointed
decepcionante [disips-yonant]
disappointing
decidir [disideer] to decide
décimo [dehsimoo] tenth
decisão f [disizowng] decision
declaração f [diklarasowng]
statement
dedo m [daydoo] finger
dedo do pé [doo peh] toe
defeito m [difaytoo] fault,
defect
deficiente [difis-yaynt]
disabled
deficientes físicos mpl disabled
degrau m [digrow] step
deitar fora [daytar] to throw
away
deitar-se [daytarsi] to lie down;
to go to bed

deixar [dayshar] to leave (behind), to let

deixar cair [ka-eer] to drop

dela [dehla] her; hers

delas [dehlash] their; theirs

dele [dayl] his

deles [daylish] their; theirs

delicioso [dilis-yohzoo] lovely, delicious

demais [dimīsh] too much

demasiado [dimaz-yadoo] too
demasiado grande too big

dê-me [daymi] give me

demora f delay

de nada my pleasure, don't mention it

dentadura postiça f [dentadoora pooshteesa] dentures

dente m [daynt] tooth

dentista m/f [denteeshta] dentist

dentro de ... [dayntroo] inside ...
dentro de ... dias [di ... dee-ash] in ... days' time
dentro de um momento [doong moomayntoo] in a minute
dentro do hotel [dwohtehl] inside the hotel

dentro de casa [di kaza] indoors

de onde? [dohnd] where from?
de onde é? [dohnd-eh] where are you from?

departamento m [dipartamayntoo] department

depende [dipaynd] it depends
depende de ... [di] it depends on ...

depois [dipoh-ish] then, after that; afterwards

depois de ... [di] after ...

depois de amanhã [daman-yang] the day after tomorrow

depósito m [dipozitoo] deposit; tank

depósito de bagagem [di bagaJayng] left luggage (office), baggage checkroom

depósitos mpl deposits

depressa [diprehsa] quickly

deprimido [diprimeedoo] depressed

dê prioridade give way, yield

de qualquer forma [di kwalkehr] anyway

derrubar [dirroobar] to knock over

desafio de futebol m [dizafee-oo di footbol] football match

desagradável [dizagradavil] unpleasant

desaparecer [dizaparisayr] to disappear

desapareceu [dizaparisay-oo] it's disappeared

desapontado [dizapontadoo] disappointed

desarranjo intestinal m [dizarranJoo intishtinal] upset stomach

descansar [dishkansar] to relax

descanso m [dishkansoo] rest

descer [dishsayr] to go down; to get off

descobrir [dishkoobreer] to find out

descolagem f [dishkoolaJayng] take-off

descolar [dishkoolar] to take off, to unglue

descontar [dishkontar] to cash

desconto m [dishkohntoo] discount

descrição f [dishkrisowng] description

desculpar-se [dishkoolparsi] to apologize

desculpas fpl [diskoolpash] apologies

desculpe [dishkoolp] I'm sorry, excuse me, pardon (me)

desde [dayɹdi] since; from

desempregado [dizaymprigadoo] unemployed

desenho m [disayn-yoo] drawing; pattern

desentupidor de cachimbo m [dizayntoopidohr di kasheemboo] pipe cleaner

desenvolver [disaynvolvayr] to develop

desfazer as malas [dishfazayr aɹ malash] to unpack

desfiladeiro m [dishfiladayroo] pass

desfolhada f [disfool-yada] party held at threshing time

desgarradas fpl [diɹgarradash] improvised popular songs cantar à desgarrada to sing impromptu in competition

desinfectante m [dizinfetant] disinfectant

desligado [diɹligadoo] off, switched off

desligar [diɹligar] to turn off; to switch off

desligue o motor switch off your engine

desmaiar [diɹmī-ar] to faint; to collapse

desmaiou [diɹmī-oh] he's/she's fainted

desmaquilhador de olhos m [dishmakil-yadohr dol-yoosh] eye make-up remover

desocupar antes das ... vacate before ...

desodorizante m [dizohdoorizant] deodorant

despacha-te! [dishpashat] hurry up!

despertador m [dishpirtadohr] alarm clock

desporto m [dishpohrtoo] sport

desportos náuticos mpl [dishpohrtoosh nowtikoosh] water sports

destinatário m addressee

destino m [dishteenoo] destination

desvio m [diɹvee-oo] detour, diversion

detergente m [deterɹaynt] soap powder, washing powder

detergente líquido [leekidoo] washing-up liquid

detergente para lavar a louça [lohsa] washing-up liquid

detestar [ditishtar] to hate

detestável [ditishtavil] obnoxious

Deus [day-oosh] God

devagar [divagar] slow; slowly

deve [dehv] you must, you have to

dever (m) [divayr] duty; to owe; to have to

devia [divee-a] you should

de vocês [di vosaysh] your; yours

devolver [divolvayr] to give back

dez [dehsh] ten

dezanove [dizanov] nineteen

dezasseis [dizasaysh] sixteen

dezassete [dizaseht] seventeen

Dezembro [dezaymbroo] December

dezoito [dizoh-itoo] eighteen

dia m [dee-a] day

diabética (f) [d-yabehtika], diabético (m) [d-yabehtikoo] diabetic

dia de anos m [dee-a danoosh] birthday

dialecto m dialect

diamante m [d-yamant] diamond

diapositivo m [d-yapooziteevoo] slide

diária cost per day

diariamente [d-yar-yamaynt] daily

diário (m) [d-yar-yo] diary; daily

diarreia f [d-yarray-a] diarrhoea

dias de semana weekdays

dias verdes cheap travel days

dicionário m [dis-yoonar-yoo] dictionary

dieta f [d-yehta] diet

diferença f [difiraynsa] difference

diferente [difiraynt] different

difícil [difeesil] difficult, hard

dificuldade f [difikooldad] difficulty

digo I say

diluir num pouco de água dissolve in a little water

Dinamarca f [dinamarka] Denmark

dinamarquês [dinamarkaysh] Danish

dinheiro m [deen-yayroo] money; cash

dirá [dira] he/she will say; you will say

dirão [dirowng] they will say; you will say

dirás [dirash] you will say

direcção f [direhsowng] direction; steering

directo [direhtoo] direct

direi [diray] I will say

direita: à direita [dirayta] on the right

à direita (de) [di] on the right (of)

vire à direita [veer] turn right

direito [diraytoo] straight; right (not left)

direitos mpl [diraytoosh] rights

livre de direitos [leevr di] duty-free

diremos [diraymoosh] we will say

disco m [deeshkoo] disco; record

discoteca f [dishkoot**eh**ka]
record shop; disco

disjuntor principal m [diJoont**ohr**
preensip**al**] mains switch

disquete f [dishk**eht**] disk,
diskette

disse [dees] I said, I have said;
he/she/it said, he/she/it has
said; you said, you have
said

dissemos [dis**ay**moosh] we said,
we have said

disseram [dis**eh**rowng] they
said, they have said; you
said, you have said

disseste [dis**eh**sht] you said,
you have said

distância f [disht**a**ns-ya] distance

distribuição f [dishtribwees**ow**ng]
delivery

distribuidor m [dishtribweed**ohr**]
distributor

dito [d**ee**too] said

DIU m [d**ee**-oo] IUD, coil

divertido [div**ee**doo] fun,
amusing, enjoyable

divertir-se [divirt**ee**rsi] to enjoy
oneself

divisas fpl foreign currency

divorciado [divoors-y**a**doo]
divorced

dizer [diz**ay**r] to say; to tell
o que quer dizer? [oo ki kehr]
what do you mean?

do of the; from the

dobro [d**oh**broo] twice as much

doce [dohs] sweet

documento m [dookoom**ay**ntoo]
document

doença f [dw**ay**nsa] disease,
illness

doente [dwaynt] ill, sick, unwell

doer [dwayr] to hurt

doido [d**oh**-idoo] crazy, mad

dois [d**oh**-ish] two

doloroso [dooloor**oh**zoo] painful

domingo [doom**ee**ngoo] Sunday

domingos e dias feriados
Sundays and holidays

Dona Mrs

dona f [d**oh**na] owner;
respectful way of addressing
a woman, precedes the first
name

donde [dohnd] where from
donde é? [dohnd**eh**] where do
you come from?

dono m [d**oh**noo] owner

do que [doo ki] than

dor f [dohr] ache, pain

dor de cabeça [di kab**ay**sa]
headache

dor de dentes [dayntsh]
toothache

dor de estômago [disht**oh**magoo]
stomachache

dor de garganta [di garg**a**nta]
sore throat

dor de ouvidos [dohv**ee**doosh]
earache

dormidas rooms to let (in a
private house)

dormir [doorm**ee**r] to sleep
a dormir asleep

dor nas costas f [dohr nash
k**o**shtash] backache

dos of the; from the

dose f [doz] portion

do senhor [doo sin-yohr] your; yours

dose para crianças f [doz kr-yan-sash] children's portion

dos senhores [doosh sin-yohrish] your; yours

dou [doh] I give

doutor m [dohtohr], doutora f [dohtora] doctor

doutro modo [dohtroo modoo] otherwise

doze [dohz] twelve

droga f [droga] drugs, narcotics

drogaria f [droogaree-a] drugstore, shop selling toiletries

dto. right

duas vezes [doo-aJ vayzish] twice

duche m [doosh] shower
com duche [kong] with shower

dunas fpl [doonash] sand dunes

duplo [dooploo] double

durante [doorant] during

duro [dooroo] hard; stale

duzentas [doozayntash], duzentos [doozayntoosh] two hundred

dúzia f [dooz-ya] dozen

E

e [ee] and

e. left

é [eh] he/she/it is; you are
é ...? is he/she/it ...?; are you ...?

écran m [ekrang] screen

edifício m [idifees-yoo] building

Edimburgo [edeenboorgoo] Edinburgh

edredão m [idridowng] duvet

efervescente [ifirvish-saynt] effervescent, sparkling

eh! hey!

eixo m [ayshoo] axle

ela [ehla] she; her; it

elas [ehlash] they; them

elástico m [ilashtikoo] elastic; elastic band

ele [ayl] he; him; it

electricidade f [eletrisidad] electricity

electricista m [eletriseeshta] electrician

eléctrico (m) [elehtrikoo] electric; tram, streetcar

electro-domésticos mpl [doomehshtikoosh] electrical appliances

ele mesmo himself

eles [aylish] they; them

elevador m [elevadohr] lift, elevator

em [ayng] in; at; on

embaixada f [aymbīshada] embassy

embaixo [aymbīshoo] down, downstairs; underneath
embaixo de ... [di] underneath ...
lá embaixo down there

embalagem económica f economy pack

embalagem familiar family pack

embaraçoso [aymbarasohzoo]
embarrassing
embora [aymbora] although
embraiagem f [aymbrī-aJayng]
clutch
em breve [ayng brev] soon
embrulhar [aymbrool-yar] to
wrap
embrulho m [aymbrool-yoo]
parcel
ementa f [emaynta] menu
ementa fixa f [feeksa] set menu
ementa turística [tooreestika]
today's menu, set menu
emergência f [emirJayns-ya]
emergency
emergências casualty,
emergencies
emocionante [emoos-yoonant]
exciting
em outro lugar [ayng ohtroo
loogar] elsewhere
em parte nenhuma [part nin-
yooma] nowhere
emperrado [aympirradoo] stuck
empoeirado [aympoo-ayradoo]
dusty
empolha f [aympohl-ya] blister
empregada f [aympregada]
waitress
empregada de balcão [di
balkowng] barmaid
empregada de mesa [mayza]
waitress
empregada de quarto [kwartoo]
chambermaid, maid
empregado (de mesa) m
[aympregadoo (di mayza)]
waiter

emprego m [aympraygoo] job
empresa f [aymprayza]
company, firm
emprestado: pedir emprestado
[pideer aymprishtadoo] to
borrow
emprestar [aymprishtar] to lend
empurrar [aympoorrar] to push
em toda a parte [tohda a part]
everywhere
em vez [ayng vaysh] instead
em vez de ... [ayng vayJ di]
instead of ...
E.N. national highway
encantador [aynkantadohr]
lovely
encaracolado [aynkarakooladoo]
curly
encerrado [aynsayrradoo] closed
encher [aynshayr] to fill up, to
fill
encomenda f [aynkoomaynda]
package; parcel
encomendas fpl parcels,
parcels counter
encontrar [aynkontrar] to find;
to meet
encravado [aynkravadoo]
jammed
endereço m [ayndiraysoo]
address
end. tel. (endereço telegráfico)
telegraphic address
enevoado [inivwadoo] foggy;
misty; cloudy
enfarte m [aynfart] heart attack
enfermaria f [aynfirmaree-a]
hospital ward
enfermeira f [aynfirmayra],

enfermeiro m [aynfirmayroo] nurse

enganado [aynganadoo] wrong

enganar-se [aynganarsi] to be wrong, to make a mistake

enganei-me [aynganaym] I've made a mistake

engarrafamento m [ayngarrafamayntoo] traffic jam

engolir [ayngooleer] to swallow

engraçado [ayngrasadoo] funny, amusing

enjoado [aynJwadoo] seasick

enorme [enorm] enormous

enquanto [aynkwantoo] while

ensinar [aynsinar] to teach

então [ayntowng] then, at that time

entrada f [ayntrada] entrance, way in; starter, appetizer; admission charge

entrada livre admission free

entrada proibida no entry

entrar [ayntrar] to go in, to enter

entre [ayntr] among; between; to come in

entre! come in!

entrega ao domicílio delivery service

entregar [ayntrigar] to deliver

entrevista [ayntriveeshta] appointment

entupido [ayntoopeedoo] blocked

envelope m [aynvilop] envelope

envelope de avião m [davyowng] airmail envelope

envergonhado [aynvirgoon-yadoo] ashamed

enviar [aynv-yar] to send

enviar posteriormente to forward

enxaqueca f [aynshakayka] migraine

época f [ehpooka] season

equipa f [ekeepa] team

equipamento m [ekipamayntoo] equipment

era [ehra] I was; he/she/it was; you were

eram [ehrowng] they were; you were

éramos [ehramoosh] we were

eras [ehrash] you were

ermida f [ermeeda] chapel

errado [erradoo] wrong

erro m [ayrroo] mistake, error

erupção f [eroopsowng] rash

ervanário m [ervanar-yoo] herbalist

és [ehsh] you are

esc. escudo (Portuguese unit of currency)

escada f [shkada] ladder; stairs

escadas fpl [shkadash] stairs

escadas rolantes [roolantsh] escalator

escala f [shkala] intermediate stop

escalar [shkalar] to climb

escocês (m) [shkoosaysh] Scottish; Scotsman

escocesa (f) [shkoosayza] Scottish; Scots woman

Escócia f [shkos-ya] Scotland

escola f [shkola] school

escola de línguas f [di leengwash] language school

escolher [shkool-yayr] to choose

esconder [shkondayr] to hide

escorregadio [shkoorrigadee-oo] slippery

escova f [shkohva] brush

escova de cabelo [di kabayloo] hairbrush

escova de dentes [dayntsh] toothbrush

escova de unhas [doon-yash] nailbrush

escrever [shkrivayr] to write

escrito por ... [shkreetoo poor] written by ...
por escrito in writing

escritório m [shkritor-yoo] office

escudo m [shkoodoo] escudo (Portuguese unit of currency)

escurecer [shkooresayr] to get dark

escuro [shkooroo] dark

escutar [shkootar] to listen (to)

esferográfica f [shfiroografika] ballpoint pen

Espanha f [shpan-ya] Spain

espanhóis: os espanhóis [shpan-oysh] the Spanish

espanhol [shpan-yol] Spanish

espantoso [shpantohzoo] amazing, astonishing

especialidade f [shpis-yalidad] speciality

especialmente [shpis-yalmaynt] especially

espectáculo m [shpitakooloo] show

espelho m [shpayl-yoo] mirror

espelho retrovisor [ritroovizohr] rearview mirror

esperar [shpirar] to expect; to hope; to wait
espero que não [shpehroo ki nowng] I hope not
espero que sim [seeng] I hope so

espere [shpehr] wait

espere pelo sinal wait for the tone

esperto [shpehrtoo] clever

espesso [shpaysoo] thick

espetáculo m [shpitakooloo] show

espigados mpl [shpigadoosh] split ends

espingarda f [shpeengarda] gun

espirrar [shpirrar] to sneeze

espirro m [shpeerroo] sneeze

esplanada f [shplanada] esplanade; pavement café

esplêndido [shplayndidoo] terrific

esposa f [shpohza] wife

espuma de barbear f [shpooma di barb-yar] shaving foam

esq. left

esquadra da polícia f [shkwarda da poolees-ya] police station

esquecer [shkisayr] to forget
esqueci-me [shkiseemi] I forget, I've forgotten

esquerda: à esquerda [shkayrda] on the left (of), to the left
vire à esquerda [veera] turn left

esquerdo [shkayrdoo] left

esqui aquático m [shkee

akwatikoo] waterskiing

esquisito [shkizeetoo] weird, odd, strange

essa [ehsa] that; that one

essas [ehsash] those

esse [ays] that

essencial [esayns-yal] essential

esses [aysish] those

esta [ehshta] this; this one

está [shta] hello (on the phone); he/she/it is; you are
ele está? [ayl] is he in?
está ... it is ...
está ...? is it ...?; hello? (on the telephone)
está bem [bayng] that's fine, all right, it's OK

estação f [shtasowng] station; season

estação alta high season

estação baixa [bīsha] low season

estação de autocarros [dowtookarroosh] bus station

estação de caminho de ferro [di kameen-yoo di fehrroo] railway station

estação de camionetas [kam-yoonaytash] bus station, coach station

estação de comboios [komboy-oosh] train station

estação de serviço [di sirveesoo] service station

estação dos autocarros [dooz owtookarroosh] bus station, coach station

estacionamento m [shtas-yoonamayntoo] car park,

parking lot

estacionamento privado [privadoo] private parking

estacionamento proibido no parking

estacionamento reservado aos hóspedes parking reserved for patrons, patrons only

estacionar [shtas-yoonar] to park

estadia f [shtadee-a] stay

estádio m [shtad-yoo] stadium

estado m [shtadoo] state

Estados Unidos (da América) mpl [shtadooz ooneedooɹ (damehrika)] United States (of America)

estafado [shtafadoo] shattered, exhausted

estalagem f [shtalaɹayng] luxury hotel

estamos [shtamoosh] we are

estância f [shtans-ya] timber yard

esta noite [ehshta noh-it] tonight

estão [shtowng] they are; you are

estar [shtar] to be

estará [shtara] he/she/it will be; you will be

estarão [shtarowng] they will be; you will be

estarás [shtarash] you will be

estar com sono [shtar kong sohnoo] to be sleepy

estar de pé [di peh] to stand

estarei [shtaray] I will be

estaremos [shtaraymoosh] we will be

estar na casa do/da [shtar na kaza doo] to stay with

estas [ehshtash] these

estás [shtash] you are

estátua f [shtatwa] statue

estava [shtava] I used to be; he/she/it used to be; you used to be

estavam [shtavam] they used to be; you used to be

estávamos [shtavamoosh] we used to be

estavas [shtavash] you used to be

este [aysht] this; this one

este m [ehsht] east

estendal m [shtendal] clothes line

estes [ayshtish] these

esteve [shtayv] he/she/it was; you were

estive [shteev] I was

estivemos [shtivaymoosh] we were

estiveram [shtivehrowng] they were; you were

estiveste [shtivehsht] you were

estômago m [shtohmagoo] stomach

estou [shtoh] I am

estou-me nas tintas [shtoh-mi nash teentash] I don't give a damn

estrada f [shtrada] road

estrada nacional [nas-yoonal] national highway

estrada principal [preensipal] main highway

estragado [shtragadoo] faulty;

out of order

estragar [shtragar] to damage

estrangeira (f), estrangeiro (m) [shtranJayroo] foreign; foreigner

estranha (f) [shtran-ya], estranho (m) [shtran-yoo] stranger; peculiar; funny; strange; odd

estreia f [shtray-a] first showing

estreito [shtraytoo] narrow

estrela f [shtrayla] star

estudante m/f [shtoodant] student

estupendo [shtoopayndoo] amazing

estúpido [shtoopidoo] stupid; thick

etiqueta f [etikayta] label

eu [ay-oo] I

E.U.A. USA

eu mesmo [ay-oo mayJmoo] myself

Europa f [ay-ooroopa] Europe

europeia (f) [ay-ooroopay-a], europeu (m) [ay-ooroopay-oo] European

exactamente! [ezatamaynt] exactly!

exacto [ezatoo] accurate, correct

exagerar [ezagirar] to exaggerate

exame m [ezam] exam, test

exausto [ezowshtoo] exhausted, tired

excelente [ish-selaynt] terrific; excellent; lovely; wonderful excepto [ish-**seh**too] except

excepto aos domingos Sundays
excepted

excesso de bagagem m [ish-
sehsoo di baga**J**ayng] excess
baggage

excursão f [shkoors**ow**ng] coach
trip; trip

excursão com guia [kong]
guided tour

excursão de um dia [doong dee-
a] day trip

excursão organizada
[organi**za**da] package holiday

excursões fpl [shkoors**oy**ngsh]
excursions

exemplo m [ez**ay**mploo]
example

por exemplo [poor] for
example

exigir [ezi**J**eer] to demand

Exmo. Sr. (Excelentíssimo
Senhor) Dear Sir

exorbitante [ezoorbit**a**nt] rip-off

experiente [shpir-y**ay**nt]
experienced

experimentar [shpirimaynt**a**r] to
try; to try on

explicar [shplik**a**r] to explain

exposição f [shpoozis**ow**ng]
exhibition

extensão f [shtens**ow**ng]
extension; extension lead

extintor m [shtint**oh**r] fire
extinguisher

extraordinário [shtra-ohrdin**a**r-
yoo] extraordinary

extremamente [shtremam**ay**nt]
extremely

F

F cold

fábrica f [**fa**brika] factory

fabricado em ... made in ...

faca f [**fa**ka] knife

fácil [**fa**sil] easy

faço [**fa**soo] I do

factor de protecção m [**fa**tohr di
prootes**ow**ng] protection
factor

factura f [fat**oo**ra] invoice

fadista m/f [fad**ee**shta] singer of
traditional Portuguese fado
songs

fado m [**fa**doo] traditional
Portuguese song, usually
sad and romantic

faiança f [fi-**a**nsa] glazed
earthenware

faixa f [**fi**sha] lane

falar to speak; to talk

fala ...? do you speak ...?

não falo inglês I don't speak
English

falido [fal**ee**do] broke;
bankrupt

falso [**fa**lsoo] fake; false

falta missing

faltar to be lacking; to be
missing

família f [fam**ee**l-ya] family

famoso [fam**oh**zoo] famous

fantástico [fant**a**shtikoo]
fantastic

fará [fa**ra**] he/she/it will do;
you will do

farão [far**ow**ng] they will do;
you will do

farás [farash] you will do

farei [faray] I will do

faremos [faraymoosh] we will do

farmácia f [farmas-ya] pharmacy, chemist's

farmácias de serviço fpl [di sirveesoo] emergency pharmacies, duty chemists

faróis máximos mpl [faroyɹ masimoosh] headlights

faróis médios dipped headlights

faróis mínimos [meenimoosh] sidelights

farol m headlight; lighthouse

farto [fartoo] fed up

fato m [fatoo] suit

fato de banho [di ban-yoo] swimming costume

fato de treino [traynoo] tracksuit

favorito [favooreetoo] favourite

favor: por favor [favohr] please

se faz favor [si fash] please

é favor fechar a porta please close the door

favor não incomodar please do not disturb

fazem-se chaves keys cut here

fazer [fazayr] to do; to make

fazer a barba to shave

fazer amor [amohr] to make love

fazer as malas [aɹ malash] to pack

fazer bicha [beesha] to queue, to stand in line

fazer brushing to blow-dry

fazer mudança [moodansa] to change (trains)

fazer o check in to check in

fazer surf to surf

fazer vela [vehla] to sail

fazer windsurf to windsurf

faz favor [fash favohr] please, excuse me

febre f [fehbr] temperature, fever

febre dos fenos [fehbr doosh faynoosh] hayfever

febril [febreel] feverish

fechado [fishadoo] shut, closed; reserved; overcast

fechado à chave [fishadwa shav] locked

fechado até ... closed until ...

fechado para balanço closed for stocktaking

fechado para férias closed for holidays

fechado para obras closed for repairs

fechadura f [fishadoora] lock

fechar [fishar] to close; to shut

fechar à chave [shav] to lock

fecho m [fayshoo] handle

fecho éclair® zip

feio [fay-oo] ugly

feira f [fayra] funfair; trade fair

feira popular fairground

feiras das vilas local village fairs

feito [faytoo] made; done

feito à mão [faytwa mowng] hand-made

feliz [fileesh] happy

feliz aniversário! [fil**ee**z anivirs**ar**-yoo] happy birthday!

Feliz Ano Novo! [**a**noo n**oh**voo] Happy New Year!

felizmente [filiJm**ay**nt] fortunately

Feliz Natal! [fil**ee**J] Merry Christmas!

feminista (f) [femin**ee**shta] feminist

feriado m [fir-y**a**doo] public holiday

férias fpl [f**ehr**-yash] holiday; vacation

de férias [di] on holiday; on vacation

férias de inverno fpl [dinv**eh**rnoo] winter holiday

férias grandes fpl [gr**a**ndsh] summer holidays

ferida f [fir**ee**da] wound

ferido [fir**ee**doo] injured

ferragens fpl [firra**J**ayngsh] ironmongery

ferramenta f [firram**ay**nta] tool

ferro m [f**eh**rroo] iron

ferro de engomar m [dayngoom**ar**] iron

festa f [f**eh**shta] party

Boas Festas! [b**oh**-ash f**eh**shtash] merry Christmas and a happy New Year

festas dos santos populares feast days of saints

Fevereiro [fivr**ay**roo] February

fez [faysh] he/she/it did, he/she/it has done; you did, you have done

fibras naturais natural fibres

ficar [fik**ar**] to remain, to stay

ficam dois [f**ee**kowng d**oh**-ish] there are two left

ficar com [kong] to keep

fígado m [f**ee**gadoo] liver

filha f [f**ee**l-ya] daughter

filho m [f**ee**l-yoo] son

filho da puta! [p**oo**ta] son-of-a-bitch!

filme m [feelm] film, movie

filme colorido m [koolo**oree**doo] colour film

filtro m [f**ee**ltroo] filter

filtros de café mpl [f**ee**ltroosh di kaf**eh**] filter papers

fim m [feeng] end

no fim de ... [noo – di] at the end of ...

fim de autoestrada end of motorway/highway

fim de estação end of season

fim de semana [di sim**a**na] weekend

finalmente [finalm**ay**nt] at last

fino [f**ee**noo] thin; fine

fio m [f**ee**-oo] lead; thread; wire

fio de fusível m [di fooz**ee**vil] fuse wire

fio dentário m [dent**ar**-yoo] dental floss

fique quieto! [feek k-y**eh**too] keep still!

fita f [f**ee**ta] tape, cassette

fita-cola f sticky tape

fita elástica f [el**a**shtika] rubber band

fita gomada [goom**a**da] Sellotape®, Scotch tape®

fita métrica [me**h**trika] tape measure

fiz [feesh] I did, I have done

fizemos [fiz**ay**moosh] we did, we have done

fizeram [fiz**eh**rowng] they did, they have done; you did, you have done

fizeste [fiz**eh**sht] you did, you have done

flertar [flirtar] to flirt

flor f [flohr] flower

floresta f [floor**eh**shta] forest

fluentemente [flwentim**ay**nt] fluently

fogão m [foog**ow**ng] cooker

fogo m [fo**h**goo] fire
  fogo! fire!

fogos de artifício mpl [fogoosh dartif**ee**s-yoo] fireworks

fogueira f [foog**ay**ra] fire, campfire

foi [fo**h**-i] it was, he/she went, he/she has left

folha f [fo**h**l-ya] leaf; sheet

folha de prata silver foil

folheto m [fool-y**ay**too] brochure; leaflet

fome [fohm] hunger
  tenho fome [t**ay**n-yoo] I'm hungry
  tens fome? [t**ay**nsh] are you hungry?

fomos [fo**h**moosh] we were, we have been; we went, we have gone

fonte f [fohnt] fountain

fora: lá fora outside
  do lado de fora [doo la**d**oo di] outside

fora de casa [di k**a**za] outdoors

foram [fo**h**rowng] they were, they have been; they went, they have gone; you were, you have been; you went, you have gone

forçados mpl [foork**a**doosh] group of men who wrestle with the bull during the bullfight

forma: em forma [ayng forma] fit

formiga f [foorm**ee**ga] ant

forno m [fo**h**rnoo] oven

forte [fort] strong; rich

fósforos mpl [fo**sh**fooroosh] matches

foste [fohsht] you were, you have been; you went, you have gone

fotocópias fpl [footook**o**p-yash] photocopies

fotografar [footoografar] to photograph

fotografia f [footoografee-a] photograph; photographic goods

fotógrafo m [foot**o**grafoo] photographer

fraco [fr**a**koo] weak

fractura f [frat**oo**ra] fracture

frágil [fra**J**il] fragile

fralda f [fr**a**lda] nappy, diaper

fraldas descartáveis fpl [dishkart**a**vaysh] disposable nappies/diapers

França f [fr**a**nsa] France

francês (m) [frans**ay**sh] French; Frenchman

francesa (f) [fransayza] French;
French woman

franquia f [frankee-a] postage

free-shop f duty-free shop

frente f [fraynt] front
em frente [ayng] in front
em frente a [fraynta] opposite;
in front of
na frente at the front

frequência f [frikwayns-ya]
frequency

frequentado [frikwayntadoo]
busy

frequente [frikwaynt] frequent

frequentemente [frikwayn-
temaynt] frequently

fresco [frayshkoo] fresh; cool

frigideira f [friJidayra] frying
pan

frigorífico m [frigooreefikoo]
fridge

frio [free-oo] cold
tenho frio [tayn-yoo] I'm cold

fritar [fritar] to fry

fronha da almofada f [frohn-ya
dalmoofada] pillow case

fronteira f [frontayra] border,
frontier

frutaria f [frootaree-a] fruit shop

fuga f [fooga] leak

fui [fwee] I went, I have gone; I
was, I have been

fumadores mpl [foomadohrish]
smokers, smoking

fumar [foomar] to smoke
fuma? [fooma] do you
smoke?
não fumo [nowng] I don't
smoke

fumo m [foomoo] smoke

funcionar [foons-yonar] to work
não funciona [nowng] out of
order

fundo (m) [foondoo] deep;
bottom

funil m [fooneel] funnel

furado [fooradoo] flat (tyre)

furgão m [foorgowng] van

furgoneta f [foorgoonayta] van

furioso [foor-yohzoo] furious

furo m [fooroo] puncture

fusível m [foozeevil] fuse

futebol m [footbol] football

futuro m [footooroo] future
no futuro [noo] in future

G

gado m [gadoo] cattle

gajo m [gaJoo] bloke

galão m [galowng] gallon

galeria de arte f [galiree-a dart]
art gallery

galeria de arte moderna
[moodehrna] modern art
gallery

Gales m [galish] Wales

galês (m) [galaysh] Welsh;
Welshman

galesa (f) [galayza] Welsh;
Welsh woman

gama f range

ganhar [gan-yar] to win; to earn

ganso m [gansoo] goose

garagem f [garaJayng] garage

garantia f [garantee-a]
guarantee

garfo m [garfoo] fork

garganta f throat

garrafa f bottle

garraiadas fpl [garrī-adash] bull-running

gás m [gash] gas

gás Cidla® m camping gas

gasóleo m [gazol-yoo] diesel

gasolina f [gazooleena] petrol, gasoline

gasolina-normal three-star petrol, regular gas

gasolina sem chumbo [sayng shoomboo] unleaded petrol

gasolina-super [sooper] four-star petrol

gás para campismo m [gash para kampeeJmoo] camping gas

gastar [gashtar] to spend

gato m [gatoo] cat

gaveta f [gavayta] drawer

G.B. [Jay bay] Great Britain

geada f [J-yada] frost

gelado (m) [Jiladoo] frozen; ice cream; ice lolly

gelataria f [Jilataree-a] ice-cream parlour

gel de duche m [Jehl di doosh] shower gel

gelo [Jayloo] ice

gel para o cabelo m [Jehl par-oo kabayloo] hair gel

gémeos mpl [Jaym-yoosh] twins

gengiva f [JenJeeva] gum

genro m [Jaynroo] son-in-law

gente f [Jaynt] people

genuíno [Jinweenoo] genuine

geral [Jeral] general

geralmente [Jeralmaynt] usually

gerente m/f [Jeraynt] manager; manageress

gesso m [Jaysoo] plaster cast

ginásio m [Jinaz-yoo] gym

gira-discos m [Jeera-deeshkoosh] record player

glutão [glootowng] greedy

G.N.R. [Jay en err] branch of the Portuguese police

golfe m [golf] golf

Golfo da Biscáia m [gohlfoo da bishkī-a] the Bay of Biscay

gordo [gohrdoo] fat

gorduroso [goordoorohzoo] greasy

gorgeta f [goorJayta] tip

gostar [gooshtar] to like

gosta de ...? [goshta di] do you like ...?

gosto [goshtoo] I like, I like it

gostoso [gooshtohzoo] tasty; pleasant; nice

gota f [gohta] drop

gotas para os olhos fpl [gohtash parooz ol-yoosh] eye drops

governo m [goovayrnoo] government

Grã-Bretanha f [gran britan-ya] Great Britain

gradualmente [gradwalmaynt] gradually

grama m gram(me)

gramática f [gramatika] grammar

grande [grand] large, big

grandes armazéns mpl [grandz armazayngsh] department store

granizo m [graneezoo] hail

gratuito [gratoo-eetoo] free (of charge)

gravador (de cassetes) m [gravadohr (di kasehtsh)] tape recorder

gravata f tie, necktie

grave [grav] nasty

grávida pregnant

graxa para sapatos f [grasha para sapatoosh] shoe polish

Grécia f [grehs-ya] Greece

grego (m) [graygoo] Greek

grelhador m [gril-yadohr] grill

gripe f [greep] flu

gritar [gritar] to shout

grosseiro [groosayroo] rude

grosso [grohsoo] pissed

grupo m [groopoo] group, party

grupo de sange [di sang] blood group

guarda m/f [gwarda] caretaker

guarda-chuva m [gwarda shoova] umbrella

Guarda Fiscal Customs police

Guarda Nacional Republicana branch of the Portuguese police

guardanapo m [gwardanapoo] napkin, serviette

guardar [gwardar] to keep

guerra f [gehrra] war

guia f [gee-a] guide, courier

guia turística f [tooreeshtika], guia turístico m [tooreeshtikoo] tour guide

guichet m [geeshay] window; ticket window

H

h is not pronounced in Portuguese

há ... [a] there is ..., there are ...

há ...? is there...?, are there ...?

há uma semana [ooma simana] a week ago

hábito m [abeetoo] custom; habit

hall m lobby

há pouco [pohkoo] recently

há vagas vacancies, rooms free

H.C. state hospital

hemorróidas fpl [emoorroydash] piles

hepatite f [epateet] hepatitis

hipermercado m [eepermerkadoo] hypermarket

história f [ishtor-ya] history; story

hoje [ohJ] today

Holanda f [olanda] Netherlands, Holland

holandês (m) [olandaysh] Dutch; Dutchman

holandesa (f) [olandayza] Dutch; Dutch woman

homem m [ohmayng] man

homens mpl [ohmayngsh] men; gents' toilet, men's room

honesto [onehshtoo] honest

hora f [ora] hour; time

hora de chegada [di shigada] time of arrival

hora de partida [part**ee**da] time
of departure

hora de ponta [p**oh**nta] rush
hour

hora local local time

horário m [or**a**r-yoo] timetable,
(US) schedule

horário das consultas [dash
kons**oo**ltash] surgery hours

horas fpl [**o**rash] hours; o'clock
às seis horas [ash sayz **o**rash]
at six o'clock
que horas são? [k-y**o**rash
sowng] what's the time?

horas de abertura fpl [**o**rash
dabirt**oo**ra] opening times

horas de visita fpl [di viz**ee**ta]
visiting hours

horrível [orr**ee**vil] awful,
dreadful, horrible

hortelã-pimenta f [ortilang
pim**ay**nta] peppermint

hospedado [oshpid**a**doo] lodged
estar hospedado em [shtar –
ayng] to be a guest at, to stay
at

hospedaria f [oshpidar**ee**-a]
guesthouse

hospedar-se [oshspid**a**rsi] to
stay

hóspede m/f [**o**shpidi] guest

hospedeira (de bordo) f
[oshpid**ay**ra (di b**o**rdoo)]
stewardess, air hostess

Hospital Civil m state hospital

hospitalidade f [oshpitalid**a**d]
hospitality

houve [ohv] there has been

húmido [**oo**meedoo] damp;

humid

humor m [oom**oh**r] mood;
humour

hydroplano m [idroopl**a**noo]
hydrofoil

I

iate m [yat] yacht

ida: bilhete de ida [bil-y**ay**t
d**ee**da] single ticket, one-
way ticket

idade f [**ee**dad] age
que idade tem? [keed**a**d tayng]
how old are you?

ideia f [id**ay**-à] idea

idiota m [id-y**o**ta] stupid

ignição f [ignis**ow**ng] ignition

igreja f [igr**ay**Ja] church

igual [igw**a**l] same

ilha f [**ee**l-ya] island

imbecil [imbes**ee**l] idiot

imediatamente [imid-yatam**ay**nt]
immediately, at once

imenso [im**ay**nsoo] immensely,
a lot

imitação f [imitas**ow**ng]
imitation

impermeável m [impirm-y**a**vil]
raincoat

impermeável de nylon m [di]
cagoule

importante [impoort**a**nt]
important

importar to matter, to be
important; to import
importa-se de ...? [imp**o**rtasi]
will you ...?
importa-se se ...? [si] do you

mind if ...?

não me importo [nowng mimportoo] I don't mind

importuno [importoonoo] annoying

impossível [impooseevil] impossible

imprescindível [impreshsindeevil] vital

impressionante [impris-yoonant] impressive

impresso m [imprehsoo] form, document

impressos mpl [imprehsoosh] printed matter

incêndio m [insaynd-yoo] fire

inchaço m [inshasoo] lump, swelling

inchado [inshadoo] swollen

incluído [inklweedoo] included

incluir [inklweer] to include

inconsciente [inkonsh-syaynt] unconscious

inconstante [inkonshtant] changeable

incrível [inkreevil] incredible

indiano (m) [ind-yanoo] Indian

indicações indications

indicador m [indikadohr] indicator

indicativo m [indikateevoo] dialling code, area code

indigestão f [indiJishtowng] indigestion

indústria f [indooshtr-ya] industry

infecção f [infehsowng] infection

infeccioso [infehs-yohzoo]

infectious

infectado [infehtadoo] septic

infelizmente [infiliJmayngt] unfortunately

inflamação f [inflamasowng] inflammation

inflamável inflammable

informação f [infoormasowng] information, piece of information

informações fpl [infoormasoyngsh] directory enquiries; information

informal [infoormal] informal

Inglaterra f [inglatehrra] England

inglês (m) [inglaysh] English; Englishman

em inglês [ayng] in English

inglesa (f) [inglayza] English; English woman

ingleses: os ingleses [inglayzish] the English

ingredientes mpl [ingrid-yayntsh] ingredients

íngreme [eengrim] steep

início m [inees-yoo] beginning

no início [noo] at the beginning

início de autoestrada start of motorway/highway

injecção f [inJehsowng] injection

inocente [inoosaynt] innocent

insecto m [insehtoo] insect

insistir [insishteer] to insist

insolação f [insoolasowng] sunstroke

insónia f [inson-ya] insomnia

Instituto do Vinho do Porto m
Port Wine Institute
inteiro [intayroo] whole
inteligente [intiliJaynt]
intelligent, clever
Intercidades fast train,
Intercity train
interdito a menores de ... anos
no admission to those under
... years of age
interessado [intrisadoo]
interested
interessante [intrisant]
interesting
internacional [internas-yoonal]
international
interpretar [interpritar] to
interpret
intérprete m/f [intehrprit]
interpreter
interruptor m [intirooptohr]
switch
interruptor de ligar/desligar m [di
ligar/diJligar] on/off switch
intervalo m [intervaloo] interval
intoxicação alimentar f
[intoksikasowng] food
poisoning
introduza a moeda na ranhura
insert coin in slot
inundação f [inoondasowng]
flood
Inverno m [invehrnoo] winter
ir [eer] to go
ir a dar um passeio [oong pasay-
oo] to go for a walk
ir a pé [peh] to walk
ir às compras [ash kohmprash]
to go shopping

ir buscar [booshkar] to get, to
fetch
ir dar um passeio [daroom
pasay-oo] to go for a walk
ir de avião [dav-yowng] to fly
ir deitar-se [daytarsi] to go to
bed
ir embora [aymbora] to go away
Irlanda f [eerlanda] Ireland
Irlanda do Norte f [eerlanda doo
nort] Northern Ireland
irlandês (m) [eerlandaysh] Irish;
Irishman
irlandesa (f) [eerlandayza] Irish;
Irishwoman
irmã f [eermang] sister
irmão m [eermowng] brother
ir nadar to go swimming
ir para casa [kaza] to go home
isqueiro m [ishkayroo] cigarette
lighter
isso [eesoo] that; that one
isso é ... [eh] that's ...
isso é ...? is that ...?
isso é canja [eesweh kanJa]
piece of cake (literally: this is
chicken soup)
isto [eeshtoo] this; this one
isto é ...? [eeshtweh] is
this ...?
Itália f [ital-ya] Italy
italiana (f) [ital-yana] Italian,
italiano (m) [ital-yanoo] Italian

J

já [Ja] ever; already
Janeiro [Janayro] January
janela f [Janehla] window

jantar (m) [Jant**a**r] evening meal, dinner; supper; to have dinner

jarda f [J**a**rda] yard

jardim m [Jard**ee**ng] garden

jardim público [p**oo**blikoo] park

jardim zoológico [zwol**o**Jikoo] zoo

jarra f [J**a**rra] vase

jarro m [J**a**rroo] jug; jar

joalharia f [Jwal-yaree-a] jewellery

joalheiro m [Jwal-y**a**yroo] jeweller

joelho m [Jw**a**yl-yoo] knee

jogar [Joog**a**r] to play

jogar fora to throw away

jogo m [J**oh**goo] game, match

jóias fpl [J**o**-yash] jewellery

jornal m [Joorn**a**l] newspaper

jovem [J**o**vayng] young

jovens mpl [Jov**a**yngsh] young people

judaico [Joodīkoo] Jewish

Julho [J**oo**l-yoo] July

Junho [J**oo**n-yoo] June

junta da culatra f [J**oo**nta da koolatra] cylinder head gasket

junto: junto da ... [J**oo**ntoo da] beside the ...

juntos [J**oo**ntoosh] together

justo [J**oo**shtoo] just, fair

L

l. square

lá over there, there

lã f [lang] wool

lábios mpl [lab-yoosh] lips

laca f hair spray

lado m [l**a**doo] side

do outro lado [doo-**oh**troo] opposite

do outro lado de ... [doo **oh**troo ladoo di] across the ...

ladra f, ladrão m [ladr**ow**ng] thief

lá fora outside

lago m [l**a**goo] lake; pond

lama f mud

lamentar [lamaynt**a**r] to regret, to be sorry

lâminas para barbear fpl [l**a**minash para barb-y**a**r] razor blades

lâmpada f light bulb

lanterna f [lant**eh**rna] torch

lápis m [lapsh] pencil

lápis para as sobrancelhas [parash sobrans**a**yl-yash] eyebrow pencil

lápis para os olhos [parooz **o**l-yoosh] eyeliner

largo (m) [l**a**rgoo] wide; square

lata f can; tin

lata de gasolina f [di gazool**ee**na] petrol can

lavabos mpl [lav**a**boosh] toilets, rest room

lavagem a seco f [lava**J**ayng a s**a**ykoo] dry-cleaning

lavagem automática [owtoom**a**tika] carwash

lavagem e mise [ee m**ee**z] shampoo and set

lava-louça f [l**a**va l**oh**sa] sink

lavandaria f [lavandar**ee**-a] laundry (place)

lavandaria automática [owtoom**a**tika] launderette

lavar to wash

lavar à mão [mowng] to handwash

lavar a roupa [r**oh**pa] to do the washing

lavar e pentear [paynt-y**a**r] wash and set

lavar na máquina machine wash

lavar-se [–si] to wash oneself

lavatório m [lavat**o**r-yoo] washhand basin

lavrador m [lavrad**oh**r] farmer

laxativo m [lashat**ee**voo] laxative

lei f [lay] law

leitaria f [laytar**ee**-a] shop selling dairy products

leite de limpeza m [layt di leemp**ay**za] skin cleanser

leitor de CDs m [layt**oh**r di say daysh] CD-player

lembrança f [laymbr**a**nsa] gift; souvenir

lembrar-se [–si] to remember

lembra-se? [l**ay**mbrasi] do you remember?

lembro-me [l**ay**mbroomi] I remember

não me lembro [n**ow**ng mi l**ay**mbroo] I don't remember

lenço m [l**ay**nsoo] handkerchief

lenço de cabeça [di kab**ay**sa] headscarf

lenço de pescoço [pishk**oh**soo] scarf (for neck)

lençol m [layns**ol**] sheet

lenços de papel mpl [l**ay**nsoosh di pap**eh**l] tissues, paper handkerchiefs, Kleenex®

lentes de contacto fpl [layntsh di kont**a**too] contact lenses

lentes gelatinosas [Jilatin**o**zash] soft lenses

lentes rígidas [r**ee**Jidash] hard lenses

lentes semi-rígidas [simir**ee**Jidash] gas permeable lenses

lento [l**ay**ntoo] slow

leque m [lehk] fan (handheld)

ler [layr] to read

lésbica f [l**eh**Jbika] lesbian

leste m [lehsht] east

no leste [noo] in the east

letra f [l**ay**tra] letter

letra de imprensa block letters

levada m country walkway along irrigation channels on Madeira

levantar-se [livant**a**rsi] to get up

levante o auscultador lift the receiver

levar to take; to carry

leve [lehv] light (not heavy)

lhe [l-yi] (to) him; (to) her; (to) you

lhes [l-yaysh] (to) them; (to) you

libra f [l**ee**bra] pound

libras esterlinas fpl [l**ee**braz ishtirl**ee**nash] pounds sterling

lição f [lis**ow**ng] lesson

licença f [lis**ay**nsa] licence; permit

com licença [kong] excuse me

licenciatura f [lisayns-yatoora] degree

liceu m [lisay-oo] secondary school, high school

ligação f [ligasowng] connection

ligação com ... connects with ...

ligadura f [ligadoora] bandage

ligar to turn on; to switch on

lima de unhas f [leema doon-yash] nailfile

limite de velocidade m [limeet di viloosidad] speed limit

limpa pára-brisas m [leempa parabreezash] windscreen wiper

limpar [leempar] to clean

limpeza a seco f [leempayza a saykoo] dry-clean; dry-cleaning

limpo [leempoo] clean

língua f [leengwa] language; tongue

linha f [leen-ya] line

liquidação sale

liquidação total clearance sale

Lisboa [liJboh-a] Lisbon

liso [leezoo] plain

lista f [leeshta] list

lista telefónica [telefohnika] phone book; telephone directory

litro m [leetroo] litre

livraria f [livraree-a] bookshop, bookstore

livre [leevr] free, vacant

livro m [leevroo] book

livro de cheques [di shehksh] cheque book

livro de expressões [dishprisoyngsh] phrasebook

livro de moradas [di mooradash] address book

livro-guia m [gee-a] guidebook

livros mpl [leevroosh] books

lixívia f [lisheev-ya] bleach

lixo m [leeshoo] rubbish, trash; litter

local de encontro m [lookal daynkohntroo] meeting place

localidade f [lookalidad] place

loção f [loosowng] lotion

loção de bronzear f [di bronz-yar] suntan lotion

loção écran total f [ekrang tootal] sunblock

loção para depois do sol f [dipoh-ish doo] aftersun cream

locomotiva f [lokoomooteeva] engine

logo [logoo] immediately, at once

logo que possível [ki pooseevil] as soon as possible

loiça f [loh-isa] crockery

loiça de barro [di barroo] pottery

loja f [loJa] shop

loja de aluguer de automóveis [daloogehr dowtoomovaysh] car hire, car rental

loja de antiguidades f [dantigweedadsh] antique shop

loja de artesanato [dartizan**a**too]
craft shop, handicrafts shop
loja de artigos fotográficos
[dart**ee**goosh fotogr**a**fikoosh]
camera shop
loja de brinquedos [di
breenk**ay**doosh] toyshop
loja de desportos [dishp**o**rtoosh]
sports shop
loja de ferragens [di firra**J**ayngsh]
hardware store
loja de fotografia [footoografee-a]
photography shop
loja de lembranças
[laymbr**a**nsash] gift shop
loja de malas [m**a**lash] handbag
shop
loja de peles [pehlsh] furrier
loja de produtos naturais
[prood**oo**toosh natoor**ī**sh]
health food shop
lomba f [l**oh**mba] crest of hill
Londres [l**o**hndrish] London
longe [lohn**J**] far
ao longe [ow] in the distance
fica longe? [f**ee**ka] is it far
away?
lotação esgotada all tickets
sold
louça: lavar a louça [l**oh**sa] to
do the washing-up
louça de barro f [di b**a**rroo]
earthenware
louça para lavar f washing-up
louco [l**oh**koo] nutter
louro [l**oh**roo] blond
lua f [l**oo**-a] moon
lua-de-mel f [l**oo**-a di mehl]
honeymoon

lugar m [loog**a**r] greengrocer's;
seat; place
lugar ao pé da janela [ow peh da
Jan**eh**la] window seat
lugar de corredor [di koorid**oh**r]
aisle seat
lugar de vegetais [di vigit**ī**sh]
greengrocer's
lugares em pé standing room
lugares reservados a cegos,
inválidos, grávidas e
acompanhantes de crianças
com menos de 4 anos seats
reserved for the blind,
disabled, expectant mothers
and those with children
under four
lume m [loom] light; fire
luvas fpl [l**oo**vash] gloves
luxo m [l**oo**shoo] luxury
de luxo [di] de luxe
luxuoso [loosh-w**oh**zoo]
luxurious
luz f [loosh] light
luz do sol f [loo**J** doo] sunshine
luzes de presença fpl [loo**J** di
priz**ay**nsa] sidelights
luzes de trânsito traffic lights
luzes de trás [l**oo**zish di trash]
rear lights
Lx Lisbon

M

M. underground, (US) subway
má bad; nasty; poor quality
macaco m [mak**a**koo] jack
maçada f [mas**a**da] bother
maçador [masad**oh**r] boring

maçaneta f [masan**ay**ta] door knob

machão m [mash**ow**ng] macho

machista [mash**ee**shta] sexist

maço m [m**a**soo] packet

madeira f [mad**ay**ra] wood

madrasta f [madr**a**shta] stepmother

madrugada f [madroog**a**da] dawn
de madrugada [di] at dawn

maduro [mad**oo**roo] ripe

mãe f [m**ay**ng] mother

magricela [magris**eh**la] skinny

magro [m**a**groo] slim; thin

Maio [m**i**-oo] May

maior [m**i**-**o**r] greater; bigger, larger
a maior parte (de) [part (di)] most (of)

maioria: a maioria dos/das ...
[m**i**-oor**ee**-a doosh/dash] most ...

mais [m**i**sh] more
mais alguma coisa? [m**i**z alg**oo**ma k**oh**-iza] anything else?
mais de ... [m**i**J di] more than ...; over ...
mais ... do que ... more ... than ...
mais um/uma [m**i**z oong/**oo**ma] an extra one
não há mais [nowng a m**i**sh] there's none left

mais longe [m**i**J lohnJ] further

mais nada no more; nothing else

mais ou menos [m**i**z oh m**ay**noosh] about,

approximately, more or less; average, so-so

mais tarde [m**i**sh tard] later, later on

mal hardly; badly

mala f bag; suitcase; handbag
fazer as malas [faz**a**yr aJ m**a**lash] to pack one's bags

mala de mão [di mowng] handbag, (US) purse

mal cozido [kooz**ee**doo] not cooked, undercooked

mal-entendido m [malayntaynd**ee**doo] misunderstanding

maluco [mal**oo**koo] barmy, nuts

mamã f [mam**a**ng] mum

mamar: dar de mamar a to breastfeed

mancha f spot

mandar to send

manga f sleeve

manhã f [man-y**a**ng] morning
às sete da manhã [ash seht] at seven a.m.
de manhã [di] in the morning
esta manhã [**eh**shta] this morning

manivela do motor f [maniv**eh**la doo mot**oh**r] crankshaft

manta f blanket

mantenha-se à direita, caminhe pela esquerda (cars) keep to the right, (pedestrians) walk on the left

mão f [mowng] hand

mapa m map

mapa da cidade m [sid**a**d] street map

mapa das estradas m [daz shtradash] road map

maquilhagem f [makil-yaJayng] make-up

máquina f [makina] machine

máquina de barbear [di barb-yar] electric shaver

máquina de escrever [dishkrivayr] typewriter

máquina de lavar [lavar] washing machine

máquina de venda [di vaynda] vending machine

máquina fotográfica [footoografika] camera

mar m sea

maravilhoso [maravil-yohzoo] wonderful

marca f make, brand name

marcação f [markasowng] appointment

marcar to dial

marca registada registered trademark

marcha f [marsha] candlelit procession

marcha atrás [marshatrash] reverse gear

Março [marsoo] March

marco de correio m [markoo di kooray-oo] letterbox, mailbox

maré f [mareh] tide

margem f [marJayng] shore

marido m [mareedoo] husband

marisqueira f [marishkayra] seafood restaurant

marque o número desejado dial the number you require

Marrocos m [marrokoosh] Morocco

martelo m [martehloo] hammer

mas [mash] but

matar to kill

maternidade f [maternidad] maternity hospital

matrícula f [matreekoola] registration number

mau [mow] bad; nasty; poor quality

maxila f [makseela] jaw

me me; to me; myself

mecânico m [mekanikoo] mechanic

média: em média [ayng mehd-ya] on average

médica f [mehdika] doctor

medicamento m [midikamayntoo] drug

médico m [mehdikoo] doctor

medida f [mideeda] size

médio [mehd-yoo] medium; medium-rare

de tamanho médio [di taman-yoo] medium-sized

Mediterrâneo m [miditirran-yoo] Mediterranean

medo m [maydoo] fear

meia dúzia f [may-a dooz-ya] half a dozen

meia hora f [ora] half an hour

meia-noite f [noh-it] midnight

meia pensão f [paynsowng] half board

meias fpl [may-ash] stockings; socks

meias collants stockings

meias de vidro [di **vee**droo] hosiery

meio m [**may**-oo] middle; half
no meio [noo] in the middle

meio bilhete m [bil-**yayt**] half fare

meio-dia m [**may**-oo **dee**-a] midday; noon
ao meio-dia [ow] at midday

mel m [mehl] honey

melhor [mil-**yor**] best; better

melhorar [mil-**yorar**] to improve

mencionar [mayns-yoonar] to mention

menina f [mineena] girl; young lady

menino m boy

menor [minor] smaller

menos [**may**noosh] less
menos de [di] under, less than
menos do que [doo ki] less than

mentir [maynteer] to lie

menu de preço fixo [di praysoo feeksoo] fixed-price menu

menu turístico [tooreeshtikoo] tourist menu

mercado m [mirkadoo] market

mercearia f [mirs-yaree-a] grocery store

merceeiro m [mirs-**yay**roo] grocery store

merda! [mehrda] shit!

mergulhar [mirgool-yar] to dive

mergulho m [mirgool-yoo] skin-diving

mês m [maysh] month

mesa f [**may**za] table

mesma [**may**Jma], mesmo [**may**Jmoo] same; myself
o/a mesmo/mesma the same

mesmo se ... [**may**Jmo si] even if ...

metade f [mitad] half

metade do preço [doo **pray**soo] half price

metro m [**meh**troo] metre; underground, (US) subway

metropolitano m underground, (US) subway

meu [**may**-oo] my; mine

meu próprio ... [propr-yoo] my own ...

meus [**may**-oosh] my; mine

mexer [mishayr] to move

microondas f [mikroo-**oh**ndash] microwave (oven)

mil [meel] thousand

milha f [**meel**-ya] mile

milhão m [mil-**yowng**] million

milímetro m [mil**ee**mitroo] millimetre

mim [**mee**ng] me

minha [**mee**n-ya], minhas [**mee**n-yash] my; mine

ministério m [minish**teh**r-yoo] ministry, government department

minúsculo [min**oo**shkooloo] tiny

minuto m [min**oo**too] minute

míope [mee-oopi] shortsighted

miradouro m scenic view, vantage point

missa m [**mee**sa] mass

misturar [mishtoorar] to mix

mobília f [moobeel-ya] furniture

mochila f [moosh**ee**la]
rucksack, backpack

moda f fashion

modas para senhoras fpl
[m**o**dash p**a**ra sin-y**o**rash]
ladies' fashions

moderno [mood**eh**rnoo] modern

moeda f [mw**eh**da] coin

moinho (m) [moo-**ee**n-yoo] mill;
dull (pain)

mola f spring (in seat); clothes
peg

mola de roupa [di r**oh**pa]
clothes peg

mola para o cabelo [p**a**roo
kab**ay**loo] hairgrip

mole [mol] soft

molhado [mool-y**a**doo] wet

momento m [moom**ay**ntoo]
moment

um momento [oong] hold on,
just a moment

montanha f [mont**a**n-ya]
mountain

montar a cavalo [kav**a**loo] to go
horse-riding

monte m [mohnt] hill

montra f [m**oh**ntra] shop
window

monumento m [moonoom**ay**ntoo]
monument

monumento nacional national
monument

morada f [moor**a**da] address

morar [moor**a**r] to live

mordedura f [moorded**oo**ra] bite

morrer [moorr**ay**r] to die

morte f [mort] death

morto [m**oh**rtoo] dead

morto de fome [di fohm]
starving

mosca f [m**oh**shka] fly

mosquito m [mooshk**ee**too]
mosquito

mosteiro m [moosht**ay**roo]
monastery

mostrar [mooshtr**a**r] to show

mota f, motocicleta f
[mootoosikl**ch**ta] motorbike

motor m [moot**oh**r] engine

motor de arranque [darr**a**nk]
starter motor

motoreta f [mootoor**ay**ta]
scooter

motorista m/f [mootoor**ee**shta]
driver; motorist

motorizada f [mootooriz**a**da]
moped

mourisco [mohr**ee**shkoo]
Moorish

mouro m [m**oh**-ooroo] Moor
os Mouros the Moors

móveis de cozinha mpl kitchen
furniture

muçulmano [moosoolm**a**noo]
Muslim

mudança f [mood**a**nsa] gear(s)

mudar [mood**a**r] to move

mudar de roupa [di r**oh**pa] to
get changed

mudar em ... change at ...

muitas vezes [mw**ee**ngta,
v**ay**zish] often

muito [mw**ee**ngtoo] a lot, lots;
plenty of; much; very
(much); quite

muito mais [mīsh] a lot more

não muito [nowng] not (very)

much; not a lot; not too much

muito tempo [**tay**mpoo] a long time

muito bem [bayng] very well

muito bem! well done!

muito obrigado [obrig**a**doo] thank you very much

muito prazer [praz**ay**r] how do you do?, nice to meet you

muito prazer em conhecê-lo [ayng koon-yis**ay**loo] very pleased to meet you

muitos mpl [m**wee**ngtoosh] many

não muitos [nowng] not many

muletas fpl [mool**ay**tash] crutches

mulher f [mool-y**eh**r] woman; wife

mulher-polícia f [pool**ee**s-ya] policewoman

multa f [m**oo**lta] fine

multa por uso indevido penalty for misuse

multidão f [mooltid**ow**ng] crowd

mundo m [m**oo**ndoo] world

muro m [m**oo**roo] wall

músculo m [m**oo**shkooloo] muscle

museu m [mooz**ay**-oo] museum

música f [m**oo**zika] music

música folclórica [foolkl**o**rika] folk music

música pop pop music

música rock rock (music)

músico m [m**oo**zikoo] musician

N

n. number

na in the; at the; on the

na casa do Américo at Américo's

na quinta-feira by Thursday

na televisão on television

nacional [nas-yoon**a**l] national

nacionalidade f [nas-yoonalid**a**d] nationality

nada nothing

mais nada [m**ī**J] nothing else

nada a declarar nothing to declare

nadador salvador f [nadad**oh**r salvad**oh**r] lifeguard

nadar to swim

nalguma parte [nalg**oo**ma part] somewhere

na moda fashionable, trendy

namorada f [namoor**a**da] girlfriend

namorado m [namoor**a**doo] boyfriend

não [nowng] no; not; didn't; don't

não aconselhável a menores de ... anos not recommended for those under ... years of age

não beber do not drink

não congelar do not freeze

não contém ... does not contain ...

não engolir do not swallow

não engomar do not iron

não exceder a dose indicada do not exceed the

dose indicated

não faz mal [faʃ mal] it doesn't matter, never mind; it's OK

não fumar no smoking

não funciona out of order

não há vagas no vacancies

não ingerir do not swallow

não me diga! [mi deega] you don't say!

não mexer do not touch

não ... nada nothing; not ... anything

não ... nenhum [nin-yoong] none; not ... any

não ... ninguém [ningayng] nobody, no-one; not anybody, not anyone

não ... nunca [noonka] never

não pendurar do not hang, dry flat

não pisar a relva please keep off the grass

não secar na máquina do not spin-dry

não sei [say] I don't know

não tem de quê [tayng di kay] don't mention it; you're welcome

não torcer do not wring

nariz m [nareesh] nose

nas [nash] in the; at the; on the

nascer [nash-sayr] to be born nasci em ... [nash-see ayng] I was born in ...

Na. Sra. (Nossa Senhora) Our Lady

natação f [natasowng] swimming

Natal m Christmas

natural [natooral] natural

natureza f [natoorayza] nature

náuseas fpl [nowz-yash] nausea

navio m [navee-o] ship de navio [di] by ship

necessário [nisisar-yoo] necessary

negativo m [nigateevoo] negative

negócio m [nigos-yoo] deal; business

nem eu [nayng ay-oo] nor do I

nem ... nem ... [nayng] neither ... nor ...

nenhum [nin-yoong], nenhuma [nin-yooma] none; no ... de maneira nenhuma! [di manayra] no way! de nenhum modo [modoo] not in the least nenhum deles [daylsh] neither of them; either of them

neo-zelandês m [neh-o zilandaysh], neo-zelandesa f [zilandayza] New Zealander

nervoso [nirvohzoo] nervous

neta f [nehta] granddaughter

neto m [nehtoo] grandson

nevar [nivar] to snow

neve f [nehv] snow

névoa f [nehvwa] mist

nevoeiro m [nivwayroo] fog

ninguém [ningayng] anybody; nobody, no-one

nível de óleo m [neevil dol-yoo] oil level

no [noo] in; in the; at the; on the no alto at the top

no fundo de at the bottom of
no hotel at the hotel
no sábado on Saturday
no. number
nódoa f [nodwa] stain
no estrangeiro [noo shtranJayroo] abroad
no fim [noo feeng] eventually
noite f [noh-it] evening; night
à noite in the evening; at night
de noite at night
esta noite [ehshta] this evening; tonight
noite de Santo António 13th June: Saint's day with music, fireworks and processions
noite de São João 24th June: Saint's day with music, fireworks and processions
noite de São Pedro 29th June: Saint's day with music, fireworks and processions
noiva (f) [noh-iva] engaged; fiancée
noivo (m) [noh-ivoo] engaged; fiancé
nojento [nooJayntoo] disgusting; filthy
nome m [nohm] name
nome de solteira [di sooltayra] maiden name
nome próprio [propr-yoo] Christian name, first name
nono [nohnoo] ninth
nora f daughter-in-law
nordeste m [noordehsht] northeast

normal [noormal] normal
noroeste m [noorwehsht] northwest
norte m [nort] north
ao norte [ow] to the north
no norte [noo] in the north
Noruega f [noorwehga] Norway
norueguês (m) [noorwegaysh], norueguesa (f) [noorwegayza] Norwegian
nos [noosh] in the; at the; on the; us; to us; ourselves
nós [nosh] we; us
No. Sr. (Nosso Senhor) Our Lord
nossa, nossas [nosash], nosso [nosoo], nossos [nosoosh] our; ours
nota f note; banknote, (US) bill
notas falsas fpl [notash falsash] forged banknotes
notícias fpl [nootees-yash] news
noutro m [nohtroo] in another; on another
noutro sítio [seet-yoo] somewhere else
nova morada f [moorada] forwarding address
Nova Zelândia [ziland-ya] New Zealand
nove [nov] nine
novecentas [novesayntash], novecentos [novesayntoosh] nine hundred
Novembro [noovaymbroo] November
noventa [noovaynta] ninety
novidades fpl [noovidadsh] news
novo [nohvoo] new
nu [noo], nua [noo-a] naked

num [noong], numa [nooma] in a
número m [noomiroo] number
número de telefone [di telefohn] phone number
número de voo [noomiroo di voh-oo] flight number
nunca [noonka] never
nuvem f [noovayng] cloud

O

o [oo] the; him; it; to it; you
objectiva f [obJeteeva] lens (of camera)
objectos de escritório mpl office supplies
objectos perdidos lost property
obliterador m [oblitiradohr] ticket-stamping machine
obra f work
obras (na estrada) fpl roadworks
obrigada, obrigado [obrigadoo] thanks, thank you
muito obrigado/obrigada [mweeengtoo] thank you very much
observar [obsirvar] to watch
obturador m [obtooradohr] shutter
óbvio [obv-yoo] obvious
Oceano Atlântico [os-yanoo atlantikoo] Atlantic Ocean
oculista m [okooleeshta] optician
óculos mpl [okooloosh] glasses; spectacles
óculos de sol [di] sunglasses

óculos protectores [prootetohrish] goggles
ocupado [okoopadoo] engaged; busy; occupied
oeste m [wesht] west
no oeste [noo] in the west
ofender [ofayndayr] to offend
ofensivo [ofaynseevoo] offensive
oferecer [ofrisayr] to get; to offer
oferta especial special offer
oh não! [nowng] oh no!
oiço [oh-isoo] I hear
oitavo [oh-itavoo] eighth
oitenta [oh-itaynta] eighty
oito [oh-itoo] eight
oitocentas [oh-itoosayntash], oitocentos [oh-itoosayntoosh] eight hundred
olá! [oola] hi!, hello!
óleo m [ol yoo] oil
óleo de bronzear [di brohnz-yar] suntan oil
oleoso [ol-yohzoo] oily
olhar para [ol-yar] to look at
olho m [ohl-yoo] eye
o maior m [mī-or] the biggest
ombro m [ohmbroo] shoulder
o melhor m [oo mil-yor] the best
o menor m [minor] the smallest
onda f [ohnda] wave
onde? [ohnd] where?
onde é? [ohndeh] where is it?
onde está? [ohnd shta] where is it?
onde fica ...? [feeka] where is ...?
onde vai? [vī] where are you going?

ontem [**oh**ntayng] yesterday
ontem à noite [n**oh**-it] last
night
ontem de manhã [di man-y**a**ng]
yesterday morning
onze [ohnz] eleven
operação f [opiras**ow**ng]
operation
operador turístico m [opirad**oh**r
toor**ee**shtikoo] tour operator
o pior the worst
oposto [op**oh**shto] opposite
optimista [otim**ee**shta]
optimistic
óptimo [**o**timoo] super
óptimo! great!, good!,
excellent!
o que [oo kay] what?
o que é isso? [oo k-yeh **ee**soo]
what's this?
ora essa! [**o**ra **eh**sa] don't be
stupid!
orelha f [or**ay**l-ya] ear
organizar [organiz**a**r] to
arrange
orgulhoso [orgool-y**oh**zoo] proud
orquestra f [ork**eh**shtra]
orchestra
os [oosh] the; them; you
o senhor [oo sin-y**oh**r], os
senhores [oosh sin-y**oh**rish]
you
osso m [**oh**soo] bone
otorrinolaringologista ear, nose
and throat specialist
ou [oh] or
ou ... ou ... either ... or ...
ouriço-do-mar m [ohr**ee**soo doo]
sea urchin

ourivesaria f [ohrivezar**ee**-a]
jeweller's
ouro m [**oh**roo] gold
ousar [ohz**a**r] to dare
Outono [oht**oh**noo] autumn,
(US) fall
no Outono [noo] in the
autumn, in the fall
outra coisa [**oh**tra k**oh**-iza]
something else
outras localidades [**oh**traɹ
lookalid**a**dsh] other places
outra vez [**oh**tra vaysh] again
outro [**oh**troo] different,
another; other
Outubro [oht**oo**broo] October
ouvir [ohv**ee**r] to hear
ovelha f [ov**ay**l-ya] sheep

P

P. square
pá f spade
pacote m [pak**o**t] carton; pack
padaria f [padar**ee**-a] bakery
padeiro m [pad**ay**roo] baker
padrasto m [padr**a**shtoo]
stepfather
padre m [padr] priest
pag. page
pagamento m [pagam**ay**ntoo]
payment
pagamento a pronto cash
payment
pagar to pay
pagar em dinheiro [ayng deen-
y**ay**roo] to pay cash
página f [p**a**ɹina] page
páginas amarelas [p**a**ɹinaz

amar**eh**lash] yellow pages

pai m [pī] father

painel m [pīn**eh**l] dashboard; panel

país m [pa-**ee**sh] country; nation; homeland

pais mpl [pīsh] parents

paisagem f [pīz**a**Jayng] scenery

País de Gales m [pa-**ee**J di g**a**lish] Wales

palácio m [pal**a**s-yoo] palace

palavra f word

palco m [p**a**lkoo] stage

pálido [p**a**lidoo] pale

panela f [pan**eh**la] pan, saucepan

panelas e tachos fpl [pan**eh**lazee t**a**shoosh] pots and pans

panfleto m [panfl**ay**too] leaflet

pano m [p**a**noo] fabric; cloth

pano de cozinha [di koozeen-ya] tea towel

pano de loiça [l**oh**-isa] dishcloth

pantufas fpl [pant**oo**fash] slippers

papá m dad

papeira f [pap**ay**ra] mumps

papéis waste paper

papel m [pap**eh**l] paper

papelaria f [papelar**ee**-a] stationer

papel de alumínio [daloom**ee**n-yoo] aluminium foil

papel de carta [di] writing paper, notepaper

papel de embrulho [daymbr**ool**-yoo] wrapping paper

papel higiénico [iJ-y**eh**nikoo]

toilet paper

par m pair

um par de ... [oong par di] a couple of ...; a pair of ...

para into; for; to; towards

para onde? [**oh**nd] where to?

para além de [paral**ay**ng di] beyond

para alugar [paraloog**a**r] for hire; to rent

parabéns! [parab**ay**ngsh] congratulations!; happy birthday!

pára-brisas m [parabr**ee**zash] windscreen

pára-choques m [parash**o**ksh] bumper

parafuso m [paraf**oo**zoo] screw

paragem f [par**a**Jayng] stopover; bus stop

paragem do autocarro f [par**a**Jayng doo owtook**a**rroo] bus stop

para levar to take away (food)

para não fumadores non-smoking

parapentismo m [parapaynt**ee**eJmoo] para-gliding

parar to stop

para todos suitable for all age groups

pare! [par] stop!

pare com isso! [kong **ee**soo] stop it!

parecer [pares**ay**r] to look like

parede f [par**ay**d] wall

páre, escute e olhe stop, look and listen

parente m/f [par**ay**nt] relative

parentes mpl [par**ay**ntsh] relatives

parque de campismo m [park di kamp**ee**Jmoo] campsite; caravan site, (US) trailer park

parque de estacionamento [shtas-yonam**ay**ntoo] car park, parking lot

parque de estacionamento subterrâneo [soobtirr**a**n-yoo] underground car park/ parking lot

parque para roulotes [rool**o**tsh] caravan site, (US) trailer park

parque recreativo [rekr-yat**ee**voo] amusement park

parte f [part] part

parte posterior [pooshteri**oh**r] back (part)

particular [partikool**a**r] private

partida f [part**ee**da] departure

partidas departures

partido (m) [part**ee**doo] broken; party (political)

partilhar [partil-y**a**r] to share

partir [part**ee**r] to break; to leave

a partir de [di] from

Páscoa f [p**a**shkwa] Easter

passadeira de peões f [pasad**ai**ra di p-yoyngsh] pedestrian crossing

passado (m) [pas**a**doo] past

no ano passado [noo **a**noo] last year

semana passada [sim**a**na] last week

passageira f [pasaJ**ay**ra], passageiro m [pasaJ**ay**roo] passenger

passagem de nível m [pasaJ**ay**ng] level crossing

passagem de peões pedestrian crossing

passagem subterrânea underpass

passaporte m [pasap**o**rt] passport

passar to pass

o que se passa? [oo ki si] what's happening?; what's wrong?

passar a ferro [a f**eh**rroo] to iron

pássaro m [p**a**saroo] bird

passatempo m [–t**ay**mpoo] hobby

passe (m) go, walk, cross now; weekly or monthly ticket

passeio m [pas**ay**-oo] pavement, sidewalk; walk

pasta f [p**a**shta] briefcase

pasta de dentes [di daynsh] toothpaste

pastelaria f [pashtilar**ee**-a] cake shop, café selling cakes

pastilha elástica f [pasht**ee**l-ya el**a**shtika] chewing gum

pastilhas de mentol fpl [pasht**ee**l-yaJ di] mints

pastilhas para a garganta throat pastilles

patinar [patin**a**r] to skid; to skate

patins de gelo mpl [pateenɪ di Jayloo] ice skates

pátio de recreio m [pat-yoo di rikray-oo] playground

patrão m [patrowng] boss

pavilhão desportivo sports pavilion

pé m [peh] foot
a pé on foot

peão m [p-yowng] pedestrian

peça de teatro f [pehsa di t-yatroo] play

peça sobresselente f [sobrisilaynt] spare part

pechincha f [pisheensha] bargain

peço [pehsoo] I ask for

pedaço m [pidasoo] piece

pedir [pideer] to ask; to order

pedir emprestado [aymprishtadoo] to borrow

pedra f [pehdra] stone, rock

pega f [pehga] handle; action of wrestling with the bull during a bullfight

pegar [pigar] to catch

peito m [paytoo] breast; bust, chest

peixaria f [paysharee-a] fishmonger's

pela [pila] through the; by the; about the

pelas [pilash] through the; by the; about the
pelas três horas by three o'clock

pele f [pehl] skin; leather; suede; fur

peleiro m [pilayroo] furrier

película aderente f [pileekoola adiraynt] clingfilm

pelo [piloo] through the; by the; about the

pelo menos [maynoosh] at least

pelos [piloosh] through the; by the; about the

pena: é uma pena [eh ooma payna] it's a pity
não vale a pena [nowng val-ya] there's no point

pensão f [paynsowng] guesthouse

pensão completa [komplehta] full board

pensar [paynsar] to think

penso m [paynsoo] dressing; Elastoplast®, Bandaid®

pensos higiénicos mpl [paynsooz iJ-yehnikoosh] sanitary napkins/towels

pente m [paynt] comb

peões mpl [p-yoyngsh] pedestrians

pequeno [pikaynoo] little, small

pequeno almoço m [almohsoo] breakfast

perceber [pirsibayr] to understand

percebi [pirsibee] I understood

percebo [pirsayboo] I understand, I see

perdão [pirdowng] sorry

perder [pirdayr] to lose; to miss

perdido [pirdeedoo] lost

perdidos e achados lost property

perfeito [pirfaytoo] perfect

perfumaria f [pirfoomaree-a] perfume shop

pergunta f [pirgoonta] question

perguntar [pirgoontar] to ask

perigo m [pireegoo] danger

perigo de desmoronamento danger of landslides

perigo de incêndio beware of starting fires

perigo de morte extreme danger

perigo, parar danger: stop

perigoso [pirigohzoo] dangerous

período m [piree-oodoo] period

período escolar [shkoolar] term

permanente f [pirmanaynt] perm

permitido [pirmiteedo] allowed

permitir to allow

perna f [pehrna] leg

(de) pernas para o ar [(di) pehrnash proo ar] upside down

persianas fpl [pirs-yanash] blinds

pertencer [pirtaynsayr] to belong

perto [pehrtoo] near

perto daqui [dakee] nearby; near here

perto de [di] next to

perturbar [pirtoorbar] to disturb

peruca f [pirooka] wig

pesadelo m [pizadayloo] nightmare

pesado [pizadoo] heavy

pesca f [pehshka] fishing

pescar [pishkar] to fish

pesca submarina f [soob-

mareena] underwater fishing

pescoço m [pishkohsoo] neck

peso m [payzoo] weight

peso líquido net weight

peso neto net weight

pessoa f [pisoh-a] person

pessoal m [pisoo-al] staff, employees

peúga f [p-yooga] sock

piada f [p-yada] joke

picada f [pikada] bite; sting

picada de insecto [dinsehtoo] insect bite

picado [pikadoo] stung

picante [pikant] hot, spicy

picar [pikar] to sting; to chop finely

picar o bilhete stamp/punch your ticket

pijama m [piJama] pyjamas

pilha f [peel-ya] battery

pílula f [peeloola] pill

pinça f [peensa] tweezers

pincel m [peensehl] paintbrush

pintado de fresco wet paint

pintar [peentar] to paint

pintura f [peentoora] picture

pior [p-yor] worse; worst

piquenique m [pikineek] picnic

pires m [peersh] saucer

piscina f [pish-seena] swimming pool

piscina coberta [koobehrta] indoor pool

piscina infantil [infanteel] children's pool

piso m [peezoo] floor, storey

piso escorregadio slippery road surface

piso irregular uneven road surface

piso superior [soopir-y**oh**r] top floor

pista f runway

pistola f [pisht**o**la] gun

plano (m) [pl**a**noo] plan; flat (adj)

planta f plant

plástico m [pl**a**shtikoo] plastic

plataforma f [plataf**o**rma] platform, (US) track

plateia f [plat**ay**-a] audience; ground floor of auditorium

platinados mpl [platin**a**doosh] points

P.M.P. (por mão própria) deliver by hand

pneu m [pn**ay**-oo] tyre

pneu sobresselente [soobrisil**ay**nt] spare tyre

pó m [paw] dust; powder

pobre [pobr] poor

pode [pod] you can; he can; she can

  pode (você) ...? [vos**ay**] can you ...?

  pode-se ...? [p**o**dsi] is it OK to ...?

  pode dar-me ...? [pod d**a**rmi] can I have a ...?; may I have ...?

poder [pood**ay**r] to be able to

pó de talco m [paw di t**a**lkoo] talcum powder

podia ...? [pood**ee**-a] could you ...?

podre [pohdr] rotten

põe [poyng] he/she/it puts; you put

põem [poh-**a**yng] they put; you put

põ; es [poyngsh] you put

polegada f [pooli**ga**da] inch

polegar m [pooli**ga**r] thumb

polícia m [pool**ee**s-ya] police; policeman

Polícia de Segurança Pública branch of the Portuguese police responsible for public order

polícia de trânsito traffic warden

Polícia Judiciária branch of the police force responsible for investigating crime

poliéster polyester

política f politics

político political

polvo m [p**oh**lvoo] octopus

pomada f [poom**a**da] ointment

pomada para calçados [kals**a**doosh] shoe polish

pomos [p**oh**moosh] we put

pónei m [p**o**nay] pony

ponho [p**oh**n-yoo] I put

pontão m [pont**ow**ng] jetty

ponte f [pohnt] bridge; crown

ponto de encontro meeting point

população f [poopoolas**ow**ng] population

por [poor] through; by

  por noite [n**oh**-it] per night

pôr [pohr] to put

por avião by airmail

porca f [p**o**rka] nut (for bolt)

porção f [poors**ow**ng] portion

porcaria f [poorkar**ee**-a] dirt; mess

por causa de ... [poor k**ow**za di] because of ...

porcelana f [poorsil**a**na] china

por cento [s**ay**ntoo] per cent

porco m [p**o**hrkoo] pig

por correio registado [poor koorr**ay**-oo riJisht**a**doo] by registered mail

pôr do sol m [pohr doo] sunset

por favor [poor fav**oh**r] please

pôr no correio [pohr noo koorr**ay**-oo] to post, to mail

porque [poork**ay**] because; why porque não? [nowng] why not?

porreiro! [poorr**ay**roo] bloody good!

porta f door; gate

porta-bagagens m [bag**a**Jayngsh] boot, (US) trunk

porta-bagagens na capota, porta-bagagens no tejadilho [noo tiJad**ee**l-yoo] roof rack

porta-bebés m [beb**eh**sh] carry-cot

porta de embarque f [daymb**a**rk] gate

portagem toll

porta-moedas m [mw**eh**dash] purse

porta nº ... gate number ...

portão m [poort**ow**ng] gate

portão de embarque [daymb**a**rk] gate (at airport)

porteiro m [poort**ay**roo] doorman, porter

porteiro da noite [n**oh**-it] night porter

Porto m [p**o**hrtoo] Oporto

porto m harbour, port

Portugal Telecom National Telecommunications Service

português (m) [poortoog**ay**sh] Portuguese; Portuguese man
em português in Portuguese
os portugueses the Portuguese

portuguesa (f) [poortoog**ay**za] Portuguese; Portuguese woman

por via aérea [poor v**ee**-a-**eh**r-ya] by airmail

posologia f dose

possível [poos**ee**vil] possible

posso [p**o**soo] I can
posso ...? may I ...?
posso ter ...? [tayr] can I have ...?

postal m [poosht**a**l] postcard

posta-restante f [p**o**shta risht**a**nt] poste restante

poste indicador m [posht indikad**oh**r] signpost

posterior: parte posterior f [pooshtir-y**oh**r] back (part)

postigos mpl [poosht**ee**goosh] shutters

posto [p**o**hshtoo] put

Posto da Polícia m [p**o**hshtoo da pool**ee**s-ya] police station

posto de enfermagem first-aid post

posto de socorros first-aid

centre

pouco [pohkoo] a little

um pouco [oong] a little bit; a drop

um pouco caro [karoo] a bit expensive

um pouco disto [deeshtoo] some of this

poucos [pohkoosh] few; a few

pouco vulgar [voolgar] unusual

pouquinho: um pouquinho [oong pohkeen-yoo] a little bit

pousada f [pohsada] state-owned hotel, often a historic building

praça f [prasa] square; market

praça de táxis [di taxish] taxi rank

praça de touros [tohroosh] bullring

pracista m [praseeshta] taxi-driver

praia f [prī-a] seafront; beach

na praia on the beach

prancha à vela f [pransha vehla] sailboard

prancha de saltos [di saltoosh] diving board

prancha de windsurf sailboard

prata f [prata] silver

prateleira f [pratilayra] shelf

praticar [pratikar] to practise

praticar jogging to go jogging

praticar windsurf to windsurf

prático [pratikoo] practical

prato m [pratoo] course, dish; plate

prazer: (muito) prazer em conhecê-lo/conhecê-la

[(mweengtoo) prazayr aing koon-yisayloo] pleased to meet you

precipício m [prisipees-yoo] cliff

precisar [prisizar] to need

preciso de ... [priseezoo di] I need ...

preço m [praysoo] price; charge

pré-comprado bought in advance

preço por dia [poor dee-a] price per day

preço por pessoa [pisoh-a] price per person

preço por semana [simana] price per week

preços reduzidos reduced prices

preencher [pri-aynshayr] to fill in

preferir [prifireer] to prefer

prefiro ... [prifeeroo] I prefer ...

prego m [prehgoo] nail (metal); roll with a thin slice of meat

preguiçoso [prigisohzoo] lazy

prendas fpl [prayndash] gifts

prender [prayndayr] to arrest

preocupação f [pri-ookoo-pasowng] worry

preocupado [pri-ookoopadoo] worried

preocupar-se com to worry about

pré-pagamento choose your food, drink etc then pay at the cash desk before being served preparar [priparar] to prepare

presente m [prizaynt] present, gift

preservativo m [prizirvateevoo] condom

presidente m/f [prizidaynt] president

pressa: estou com pressa [shtoh kong prehsa] I'm in a hurry
não há pressa [nowng a] there's no hurry

pressão f [prisowng] tyre pressure

pressão arterial [artiri-al] blood pressure

presta: não presta [nowng prehshta] it's no good

prestável [preshtavil] helpful

preto [praytoo] black
preto e branco black and white

previsão do tempo f [privizowng doo taympoo] weather forecast

prima f [preema] cousin

Primavera f [primavehra] spring

primeira: a primeira vez [primayra vaysh] the first time
primeira à esquerda [a-shkayrda] first on the left

primeira classe [klas] first class

primeira ministra f [mineeshtra] prime minister

primeiro [primayroo] first

primeiro andar m first floor, (US) second floor

primeiro ministro m [primayroo mineeshtroo] prime minister

primeiro piso first floor, (US)

second floor

primeiros socorros mpl [primayroosh sookorroosh] first aid

primo m [preemoo] cousin

princesa f [preensayza] princess

principal [preensipal] main

principalmente [preensipalmaynt] mostly

príncipe m [preensipi] prince

principiante m/f [preensip-yant] beginner

princípio: ao princípio [ow preenseep-yoo] at first

prioridade f right of way; priority

prisão f [prizowng] jail

prisão de ventre [di vayntr] constipation
com prisão de ventre [kong] constipated

privado [privadoo] private

problema m [prooblayma] problem

procissão f [proosisowng] candlelit procession held to celebrate feast days and Good Friday

procurar [prookoorar] to look for; to search

produto m [proodootoo] product

produtos alimentares [alimayntarish] foodstuffs

produtos de beleza [di belayza] beauty products

produtos de limpeza [leempayza] household cleaning materials produtos para diabéticos mpl [d-yab**eh**tikoosh] products for diabetics

professor m [proofes**ohr**], professora f [proofes**ohr**a] teacher

programa m [proogr**a**ma] program(me)

proibida a entrada a ... no admittance to ...

proibida a entrada a cães no dogs

proibida a entrada a menores de ... anos no admittance to those under ... years of age

proibida a inversão de marcha no U-turns

proibida a paragem no stopping

proibida a passagem no access

proibido [proo-ib**ee**doo] forbidden

proibido ... no ...

proibido acampar no camping

proibido a pessoas estranhas ao serviço personnel only

proibido estacionar no parking

proibido fazer lume no campfires

proibido fumar no smoking

proibido nadar no swimming

proibido pescar no fishing

proibido tirar fotografias no photographs

proibido tomar banho no bathing

proibido ultrapassar no overtaking

prometer [proomit**ay**r] to promise

prometo [proom**ay**too] I promise

pronto [pr**oh**ntoo] ready

pronto a vestir ready-to-wear

pronto-socorro m [pr**oh**ntoo sook**oh**rroo] breakdown service

pronunciar [proonoons-y**ar**] to pronounce

propósito: de propósito [di proop**o**zitoo] deliberately

própria: a sua própria [s**oo**-a propr-ya], o seu próprio [oo s**ay**-oo pr**o**pr-yoo] his/her own; its own; your own; their own

propriedade privada private property

proteger [prooti**J**a**y**r] to protect

proteger do calor e humidade store away from heat and damp

protestante (m/f) [prootisht**a**nt] Protestant

provar [proov**ar**] to try; to try on; to taste

provavelmente [proovavilm**ay**nt] probably

próxima sessão às ... horas next showing at ... o'clock

próximo [pr**o**simoo] near; next o/a ... mais próximo/próxima [mi**J**] the nearest ...

próximo de [di] next to

ps. weight

P.S.P. branch of the Portuguese police

pua f [p**oo**-a] splinter

público (m) [**poo**blikoo]
audience; public

pular [poo**lar**] to jump

pulga f [**poo**lga] flea

pulmões mpl [poolm**oy**ngsh]
lungs

pulseira f [pools**ayr**a] bracelet;
watchstrap

pulso m [**poo**lsoo] wrist

pura lã pure wool

pura lã virgem pure new wool

puxar [poosh**ar**] pull; to pull

puxar (a alavanca) em caso de
emergência pull (lever) in
case of emergency

puxe pull

Q

quais? [kwīsh] which ones?

qual? [kwal] which?

qual deles? [daylsh] which
one?

qualidade f [kwalid**ad**] quality

qualquer [kwalk**ehr**] any

qualquer coisa [k**oh**-iza]
anything

qualquer medicamento deve
estar fora do alcance das
crianças keep all medicines
out of the reach of
children

quando? [kw**a**ndoo] when?

quantia f [kwant**ee**-a] amount

quanto? [kw**a**ntoo] how much?

quanto custa? [k**oo**shta] how
much does it cost?

quanto é? [kwantw**eh**] how
much is it?

quantos? [kw**a**ntoosh] how
many?

quarenta [kwar**ay**nta] forty

quarentena f [kwarayntay**na]
quarantine

quarta-feira f [kwarta f**ayr**a]
Wednesday

quarta parte f [part] quarter

quarto (m) [kw**ar**too] bedroom;
room; quarter; fourth

quarto andar fourth floor, (US)
fifth floor

quarto com duas camas [kong
d**oo**-ash k**a**mash] twin room

quarto de banho das senhoras
[di b**a**n-yoo dash sin-y**or**ash]
ladies' toilets, ladies' room

quarto de casal [di kaz**a**l]
double room

quarto de hotel [doht**eh**l] hotel
room

quarto duplo [d**oo**ploo] double
room

quarto individual [individw**a**l]
single room

quarto para duas pessoas [d**oo**-
ash pis**oh**-ash] double room

quarto para uma pessoa [**oo**ma]
single room

quase [kwaz] almost; nearly

quase nunca [n**oo**nka] hardly
ever

quatro [kw**a**troo] four

quatrocentas [kwatros**ay**ntash],
quatrocentos [kwatros**ay**ntoosh]
four hundred

que that; than

o que é isso? [oo k-yeh **ee**soo]
what's that?

o que é que está a acontecer
[oo k-yeh kishta akontisayr]
what's happening?

o que se passa? [oo ki si]
what's the matter?

que bom! [ki bong] that's nice!

quê? [kay] what?

quebrar [kibrar] to break

quebre em caso de emergência
break in case of emergency

que chatice! [ki shatees] oh no!,
blast!

queda f [kehda] fall

queda de pedras falling stones

queda de rochas falling rocks

que deseja? [ki disayJa] how
can I help you?

que disparate! [dishparat]
rubbish!, nonsense!

que droga! [droga] blast!

queimado [kaymado] burnt

queimado de sol [di] sunburnt

queimadura f [kaymadoora]
burn

queimadura de sol f sunburn

queimar [kaymar] to burn

queixas complaints

queixo m [kayshoo] chin

quem? [kayng] who?

de quem? [di] whose?

de quem é isto? [eh eeshtoo]
whose is this?

quem é? [kayngeh] who is it?

quem fala? who's calling?

quente [kaynt] warm; hot

que pena! [ki payna] what a
shame!

quer ...? [kehr] would you
like ...?, do you want...?

querer [kirayr] to want

queria [kiree-a] I want; I'd
like

queria ...? could I have ...?

quero [kehroo] I want

não quero I don't want (to)

não quero nada I don't want
anything

quieto [k-yehtoo] still

quilo m [keeloo] kilo

quilometragem ilimitada
[kilomitraJayng ilimitada]
unlimited mileage

quilómetro m [kilomitroo]
kilometre

quinhentas [keen-yayntash],
quinhentos [keen-yayntoosh]
five hundred

quinta f [keenta] farm

quinta-feira f [keenta fayra]
Thursday

quintas: está nas suas sete
quintas he's/she's in his/her
element

quinto [keentoo] fifth

quinze [keenz] fifteen

quinzena f [keenzayna]
fortnight

quiosque m [k-yoshk] kiosk

quiosque de jornais [di Joornish]
newspaper kiosk

R

R. street

rabo m tail; backside, behind

radiador m [rad-yadohr] radiator

Radiodifusão Portuguesa
Portuguese Radio

radiografia f [rad-yoografee-a] X-ray

Radiotelevisão Portuguesa Portuguese Television

rainha f [ra-een-ya] queen

raio m [rī-oo] ray, beam; spoke

raios me partam! [ra-yoosh mi partowng] damn!

raios o partam! [rah-yooz oo] damn you!

raio X m [ra-yoo sheesh] X-ray

rapariga f [rapareega] girl

rapaz m [rapash] boy

Rápido m [rapidoo] express (train)

rápido fast, quick

raqueta f [rakehta] racket

raqueta de ténis tennis racket

raro [raroo] rare, uncommon

ratazana f [ratazana] rat

rato m [ratoo] mouse

razão f [razowng] reason
tinhas razão [teen-yaJ razowng] you were right

razoável [razwavil] reasonable

r/c ground floor, (US) first floor

R.D.P. Portuguese Radio

realmente [r-yalmaynt] really

reaver [r-yavayr] to get back

rebentado [ribentadoo] burst

reboque m [ribok] trailer (for carrying tent etc)

rebuçado m [riboosadoo] sweet, candy

recado m [rikadoo] message
deixar um recado [dayshar oong] to leave a message

receber [risibayr] to receive

receita f [risayta] recipe; prescription

recepção f [risehsowng] reception

recepcionista m/f [risehs-yooneeshta] receptionist

recibo m [riseeboo] receipt

reclamação f [riklamasowng] complaint

reclamação de bagagens [di bagaJayngsh] baggage claim

reclamações complaints

reclamar [riklamar] to complain

recomendar [rikoomayndar] to recommend

reconhecer [rikoon-yisayr] to recognize

rede f [rayd] net; hammock

redondo [ridohndoo] round

reembolsar [ri-aymboolsar] to refund

reembolso m [ri-aymbohlsoo] refund

refeição f [rifaysowng] meal

reformada (f) [rifoormada] pensioner; retired

reformada de terceira idade f [di tirsayra idad] old-age pensioner

reformado (m) [rifoormadoo] pensioner; retired

reformado de terceira idade m old-age pensioner

refugo m [rifoogoo] rubbish

reg. registered

região f [riJ-yowng] region; area
da região local

Regional local train, usually

stopping at most stations

registado [riJishtadoo]
registered

por correio registado [poor
koorray-oo] by registered
mail

registos registered mail

reg.to. regulation

regulamento m regulation

rei m [ray] king

Reino Unido m [raynooneedoo]
United Kingdom

relâmpago m [rilampagoo]
lightning

religião f [riliJ-yowng] religion

relógio m [riloJ-yoo] clock;
watch, wristwatch

relógio de pulso [di poolsoo]
watch, wristwatch

relojoaria f [rilooJwaree-a]
watchmaker's shop

relva f [rehlva] grass

relvado m [relvadoo] lawn

rem. sender

remar to row

remédio m [rimehd-yoo]
medicine

remetente m/f sender

renda f [raynda] lace

reparar [riparar] to fix; to
repair

repele-insectos m [ripehl
insehtoosh] insect repellent

repele-mosquitos m [moosh-
keetoosh] mosquito repellent

repelente de insectos eléctrico m
[ripilaynt dinsehtoosh
elehtrikoo] electric mosquito
killer

repetir [ripiteer] to repeat

repousar [ripohzar] to rest

repouso m [ripohzoo] rest

representante m/f [riprizayntant]
agent

repugnante [ripoognant]
revolting

rés de chão m [rehJ doo showng]
ground floor, (US) first floor

reserva f [rizehrva] reservation

reserva de lugares [di loogarish]
seat reservation

reservado [rizirvadoo] reserved

reservar [rizirvar] to book; to
reserve

reservas reservations

residencial m [rizidayns-yal] bed
and breakfast hotel

respirar [rishpirar] to breathe

responder [rishpondayr] to
answer

responsável [rishponsavil]
responsible

resposta f [rishposhta] answer

ressaca f [risaka] hangover

restaurante m [rishtowrant]
restaurant

resto m [rehshtoo] rest,
remainder

retalho m [rital-yoo] oddment

retirado [ritiradoo] secluded

retrato m [ritratoo] portrait

retretes fpl [ritrehtsh] toilets,
rest rooms

retrosaria f [ritroozaree-a]
haberdasher

reumatismo m rheumatism

reunião f [r-yoon-yowng]
meeting

revelação de filmes f [rivilasowng di feelmsh] film processing

revisor m [rivizohr] ticket inspector

revista f [riveeshta] magazine

ribeiro m [ribayroo] stream

rico [reekoo] rich

ridículo [rideekooloo] ridiculous

rímel m [reemil] mascara

rinque de patinagem m [reenk di patinaJayng] ice rink

rins mpl [reengsh] kidneys

rio m [ree-oo] river

rir [reer] to laugh

R.N. National bus/coach service

rocha f [rosha] rock

rochedo m [rooshaydoo] cliff

roda f [roda] wheel

rodada f [roodada] round

Rodoviária Nacional National bus/coach service

rolha f [rohl-ya] cork

romance m [roomans] novel

roncar [ronkar] to snore

rosa f [roza] rose

rótulo m [rotooloo] label

rotunda f [rotoonda] roundabout

roubado [rohbadoo] robbed

roubar [rohbar] to steal

roubo m [rohboo] burglary; theft; rip-off

roulotte f [roolot] caravan, (US) trailer

roupa f [rohpa] clothes

roupa de cama [di kama] bed linen

roupa de homens [dohmayngsh] menswear

roupa de senhoras [sin-yorash] ladies' wear

roupa interior [intir-yohr] underwear

roupão m [rohpowng] dressing gown

roupa para lavar laundry, washing

roxo [rohshoo] purple

R.T.P. Portuguese Television

rua f [roo-a] road; street

rua! get out of here!

rua principal [preensipal] main road

rua secundária [sikoondar-ya] side street

rua sem saída cul-de-sac, dead end

rubéola f [roobeh-ola] German measles

ruínas fpl [rweenash] ruins

ruivo [roo-ivoo] red-headed

S

S ladies' toilets, ladies' room

S. saint

S/ without

sábado [sabadoo] Saturday

saber [sabayr] to know; to be able to

sabia [sabee-a] I knew
    não sabia [nowng] I didn't know

sabonete m [saboonayt] soap

sabor m [sabohr] taste; flavour

saboroso [saboorohzoo] tasty, delicious

sacana! bastard!

saca-rolhas m [sakarrohl-yash] corkscrew

saco m [sakoo] bag

saco de compras [di kohmprash] shopping bag

saco de dormir [doormeer] sleeping bag

saco (de) plástico [plashtikoo] plastic bag

sacos de lixo mpl [sakoosh] bin liners

saia f [sī-ya] skirt

saia! get out!

saída f [sa-eeda] departure; exit

saída de emergência [demirJayns-ya] fire escape, emergency exit

saio [sī-oo] I get off; I go out; I leave

sair [sa-eer] to get off, to get out; to go out; to leave

sais de banho mpl [sīJ di ban-yoo] bath salts

saiu [sa-ee-oo] he/she is out; he/she has gone out

sala f lounge

sala de chá tea room

sala de convívio [di konveev-yoo] lounge

sala de embarque [daymbark] departure lounge

sala de espera [dishpehra] lounge, departure lounge

sala de estar [dishtar] living room

sala de jantar [di Jantar] dining room

salão de beleza m [salowng di belayza] beauty salon

salão de cabeleireiro [di kabilayrayroo] hairdressing salon

saldos mpl [saldoosh] sale

salgado [salgadoo] savoury; salty

salto m [saltoo] heel (of shoe)

sandálias fpl [sandal-yash] sandals

sangrar to bleed

sangue m [sang] blood

santinho! [santeen-yoo] bless you!

são [sowng] healthy; they are; you are

sapataria f [sapataree-a] shoe shop

sapateira f [sapatayra] crab

sapateiro m [sapatayroo] shoe repairer's

sapatos mpl [sapatoosh] shoe

sapatos de treino [di traynoo] trainers

sarampo m [sarampoo] measles

sardinhada f [sardin-yada] party where grilled sardines are eaten

S.A.R.L. (Sociedade Anónima de Responsabilidade Limitada) limited company

satisfeito [satisfaytoo] satisfied, full

saudável [sowdavil] healthy

saúde f [sa-ood] health
saúde! cheers!

à sua saúde! [soo-a] your
health!

se [si] if; yourself; himself;
herself; themselves;
yourselves; itself; oneself

secador de cabelo m [sikadohr
di kabayloo] hairdryer

secador de roupa [di rohpa]
spin-dryer

secar [sikar] to dry

secar com secador (de mão)
[kong sikadohr (di mowng)] to
blow-dry

secção f [sehksowng]
department

secção de crianças [di kry-
ansash] children's
department

secção de perdidos e achados
[di pirdeedooz ee-ashadoosh]
lost property office

seco [saykoo] dry

secreto [sikrehtoo] secret

século m [sehkooloo] century

seda f [sayda] silk

sede: ter sede [tayr sayd] to be
thirsty

se faz favor [si fash favohr]
please; excuse me

seguida: em seguida [ayng
sigeeda] straight away

seguinte [sigeengt] following;
next

dia seguinte m the day after

seguir [sigeer] to follow

seguir pela direita [pila dirayta]
keep to your right

seguir pela esquerda
[pilashkayrda] keep to your

left

segunda classe [sigoonda klas]
second class

segunda-feira f [sigoonda fayra]
Monday

segunda mão: em segunda mão
[sigoonda mowng] second-
hand

segundo (m) [sigoondoo]
second

segundo andar m second floor,
(US) third floor

segurar [sigoorar] to hold

seguro (m) [sigooroo]
insurance; safe; sure

seguro de viagem [di v-yaJayng]
travel insurance

sei [say] I know

seis [saysh] six

seiscentas [sayshsayntash],
seiscentos [sayshsayntoosh] six
hundred

sela f [sehla] saddle

selo m [sayloo] stamp

selvagem [silvaJayng] wild

sem [sayng] without

semáforos mpl [simafooroosh]
traffic lights

semana f [simana] week

na próxima semana [prosima]
next week

Semana Santa Easter

sem chumbo [sayng shoomboo]
leadfree, unleaded

sem conservantes does not
contain preservatives

sem corantes does not contain
artificial colouring

sem corantes nem conservantes

does not contain artificial
colouring or preservatives
semelhante [simil-yant] similar
sem pensão no meals served
sempre [saympr] always
sempre em frente [saymprayng
fraynt] straight ahead
sem preservativos does not
contain preservatives
senha f [sayn-ya] ticket; receipt
Senhor [sin-yohr] Mr
senhor (m) sir; gentleman; you
Senhora [sin-yora] Mrs
senhora madam; lady; you
senhoras ladies' toilet, ladies'
room
sensato [saynsatoo] sensible
sensível [saynseevil] sensitive
sentar-se [sayntarsi] to sit, to sit
down
como se sente? [kohmoo si
saynt] how are you feeling?
sente-se [sayntsi] sit down
sentido proibido no entry
sentido único one way
sentimento m [sayntimayntoo]
feeling
sentir [saynteer] to feel
separadamente [siparadamaynt]
separately
separado [siparadoo] separate;
separated
ser [sayr] to be
será [sira] he/she/it will be;
you will be
serão [sirowng] they will be;
you will be
serás [sirash] you will be
serei [siray] I will be

seremos [siraymoosh] we will
be
sério [sehr-yoo] serious
serve-se ... das ... horas às ...
horas ... served from ...
o'clock until ... o'clock
serviço m [sirveesoo] service
serviço automático direct
dialling
serviço de quartos [di kwartoosh]
room service
serviço de urgências [doorJayns-
yash] casualty department
serviço expresso express
service
serviço incluído service
included
serviço internacional
international service
serviço permanente 24-hour
service
servir [sirveer] to serve
sessenta [sesaynta] sixty
sete [seht] seven
setecentas [setesayntash],
setecentos [setesayntoosh]
seven hundred
Setembro [sitaymbroo]
September
setenta [setaynta] seventy
setentrional [setayntr-yoonal]
northern
sétimo [sehtimoo] seventh
seu [say-oo], seus [say-oosh]
his; her; hers; its; your;
yours; their; theirs
sexo m [sehxoo] sex
sexta-feira f [sayshta fayra]
Friday

Sexta-Feira Santa Good Friday

sexto [**say**shtoo] sixth

S.f.f. please

si [see] you

SIDA f [**see**da] AIDS

siga-me [**see**gami] follow me

significar [signifik**ar**] to mean

silêncio m [sil**ay**ns-yoo] silence

silencioso [silayns-y**oh**zoo] quiet

sim [seeng] yes; it is

sim? really?

simpático [simp**a**tikoo] friendly

simples [**see**mplish] simple,
easy

sinagoga f [sinag**o**ga]
synagogue

sinal m sign; signal; roadsign

sinal de alarme [dal**arm**]
emergency alarm

sincero [sins**eh**roo] sincere

sino m [**see**noo] bell

sintético [sint**eh**tikoo] synthetic

sinto-me [**see**ntoomi] I feel

sinto-me bem [bayng] I'm OK,
I'm fine

só [saw] alone; just; only

só um momento [oong
moom**ay**ntoo] just a minute

sobrancelha f [soobrans**ay**l-ya]
eyebrow

sobre [**soh**br] about,
concerning; on

sobretudo m [soobrit**oo**doo]
overcoat

sobrinha f [soobr**een**-ya] niece

sobrinho m [soobr**een**-yoo]
nephew

sóbrio [**so**br-yoo] sober

sociedade f [soos-yayd**a**d]

society; company

socorro! [sook**oh**rroo] help!

sofá m [soo**fa**] sofa; couch

sofisticado [soofishtik**a**doo]
upmarket

sogra f mother-in-law

sogro m [**soh**groo] father-in-law

sogros mpl [**so**groosh] in-laws

soirée evening performance

sol m sun

ao sol [ow] in the sun

está (a fazer) sol [shta (a
faz**ay**r)] it's sunny

solteiro (m) [soolt**ay**roo] single;
bachelor

solto [**soh**ltoo] loose

solução de limpeza f
[sooloos**ow**ng di leemp**ay**za]
cleaning solution

solução para as lentes de
contacto [**para**ʒ layntsh di
kont**a**ktoo] soaking solution

soluços mpl [sool**oo**soosh]
hiccups

sombra f [**soh**mbra] shade;
shadow

à sombra in the shade

sombra para os olhos [**para**ooz ol-
yoosh] eye shadow

somente [som**ay**nt] only; just

somos [**soh**moosh] we are

sonho m [**soh**n-yoo] dream

sonífero m [soon**ee**firoo]
sleeping pill

sono m [**soh**noo] sleep

estou com sono [shtoh kong]
I'm sleepy

sopé: no sopé do ... [noo soop**eh**
doo] at the bottom of ...

só pode vender-se mediante receita médica available only on prescription

sorrir [soorreer] to smile

sorriso m [soorreezoo] smile

sorte f [sort] luck

sou [soh] I am

sou de ... [di] I am from ...

soutien m [soot-yang] bra

sozinha [sozeen ya], sozinho [sozeen-yoo] by myself

Sr. Mr

Sra. Mrs

Sto. saint

sua [soo-a] his; her; hers; its; your; yours; their; theirs

suar [soo-ar] to sweat

suas [soo-ash] his; her; hers; its; your; yours; their; theirs

suave [swav] delicate; mild

subir [soobeer] to go up

subitamente [soobitamaynt] suddenly

sucesso m [soosehsoo] success

sudeste m [soodehsht] southeast

sudoeste m [soodwehsht] southwest

Suécia f [swehs-ya] Sweden

sueca (f) [swehka], sueco (m) [swehkoo] Swedish; Swede

suficiente [soofis-yaynt] enough

suficientemente [soofis-yayntimaynt] enough

Suíça f [sweesa] Switzerland

suíça (f) [sweesa], suíço (m) [sweesoo] Swiss

sujidade f [sooJidad] dirt

sujo [sooJoo] dirty

sul m [sool] south

no sul [noo] in the south

sul-africana (f) [soolafrikana], sul-africano (m) [soolafrikanoo] South African

supermercado m [soopermerkadoo] supermarket

suplemento m [sooplimayntoo] supplement, extra charge

supositório m [soopoozitor-yoo] suppository

surdo [soordoo] deaf

surpreendente [soorpr-yayndaynt] surprising

surpresa f [soorprayza] surprise

T

tabacaria f [tabakaree-a] tobacconist; tobacco store; tobacco goods; newsagent

tabaco m [tabakoo] tobacco

taberna m [tabehrna] pub

tabuleiro m [taboolayroo] tray

talheres mpl [tal-yehrish] cutlery

talho m [tal-yoo] butcher's shop

talvez [talvaysh] maybe, perhaps

talvez não [nowng] perhaps not

tamanho m [taman-yoo] size

também [tambayng] also, too, as well

eu também [ay-oo] so am I; so do I; me too

tampa f cap, lid

tampa do ralo f [doo **ra**loo] plug (in sink)

tampões mpl [tamp**oy**ngsh] tampons

tanto [**ta**ntoo] so much

tanto faz [fash] it's all the same to me

tão [towng] so

tão ... como ... as ... as ...

tão ... quanto [kw**a**ntoo] as ... as

tão ... quanto possível [poos**ee**vil] as ... as possible

tapete m [tap**ay**t] carpet

tarde f [tard] afternoon; late

à tarde in the afternoon

esta tarde [**eh**shta] this afternoon

três da tarde 3 p.m.

tarifa f [tar**ee**fa] charges

tasca f [**ta**shka] small tavern serving food

taxa de serviço f [**ta**sha di sirv**ee**soo] service charge

te [ti] you; to you; yourself

teatro m [t-**ya**troo] theatre

tecido m [tis**ee**doo] cloth, material

tecto m [**teh**too] ceiling

tejadilho m [tiJad**ee**l-yoo] car roof

tel. telephone

teleférico m [telef**eh**rikoo] cable car

telefonar [telefoon**ar**] to call, to phone

telefone m [telef**oh**n] telephone

telefone de cartão [di kart**ow**ng] cardphone

telefone público [p**oo**blikoo] payphone

Telefones de Lisboa e Porto S.A. telephone company for Lisbon and Oporto

telefonista m/f [telefoon**ee**shta] operator

telemóvel m [telem**o**vil] mobile phone

televisão f [televiz**ow**ng] television

telhado m [til-y**a**doo] roof

tem [tayng] he/she/it has; you have

tem ...? have you got any ...?, do you have ...?

ele/ela tem de ... he/she must ...

têm [**tay**-ayng] they have; you have

temos [**tay**moosh] we have

temos que ... [ki] we've got to ..., we must ...

temperatura f [taympirat**oo**ra] temperature

tempestade f [taympisht**ad**] storm

tempo m [**tay**mpoo] time; weather

a tempo on time

por quanto tempo? [poor kw**a**ntoo] for how long?

tenda (de campismo) f [**tay**nda (di kamp**ee**Jmoo)] tent

tenho [**tay**n-yoo] I have; I am; I have to

não tenho [nowng] I don't have any

tenho de/que ... [di/ki] I

must ...
tenho muita pena [mweengta payna] I'm sorry
ténis m [tehnish] tennis
ténis de mesa [di mayza] table tennis
tens [taynsh] you have
tensão f [taynsowng] voltage
tensão arterial alta [artir-yal] high blood pressure
tentar [tayntar] to try
tépido [tehpidoo] lukewarm
ter [tayr] to have; to hold; to be; to contain; to have to
ter que to have to
terça-feira [tayrsa fayra] Tuesday
ter calor [tayr kalohr] to be warm
terceiro [tirsayroo] third
terceiro andar m third floor, (US) fourth floor
ter de fazer [tayr di fazayr] to have to do
termas fpl [tehrmash] spa
terminado [tirminadoo] over; finished; it's over
terminal m [tirminal] terminus
terminar [tirminar] to finish
termo m [tayrmoo] vacuum flask
termómetro m [tirmohmitroo] thermometer
terra f [tehrra] earth
terraço m [tirrasoo] terrace
terrível [tirreevil] terrible
ter uma fuga [tayr ooma fooga] to leak
tesoura f [tizohra] scissors

testa f [tehshta] forehead
testemunha m/f [tishtimoon-ya] witness
teu [tay-oo], teus [tay-oosh] your; yours
teve [tayv] he/she/it had; you had
têxteis textiles
ti you
tia f [tee-a] aunt
tigela f [tiJehla] dish, bowl
tijolo m [tiJohloo] brick
tímido [teemidoo] shy
tinha [teen-ya] I used to have; he/she/it used to have; you used to have
tinham [teen-yowng] they used to have; you used to have
tínhamos [teen-yamoosh] we used to have
tinhas [teen-yash] you used to have
tinta f [teenta] paint; tint
tinturaria f [teentooraree-a] dry-cleaner
tio m [tee-oo] uncle
típico [teepikoo] typical
tipo m [teepoo] sort, type, kind
tiragem f [tiraJayng] collection; edition; circulation
tirar to remove
tive [teev] I had
tivemos [tivaymoosh] we had
tiveram [tivehrowng] they had; you had
tiveste [tivehsht] you had
TLP telephone company for Lisbon and Oporto
toalha f [twal-ya] towel

toalha de banho [di ban-yoo] bath towel

toalha de cara [kara] flannel

toalha de mesa [mayza] tablecloth

toalhas higiénicas fpl [twal-yaz iJ-yehnikash] sanitary towels

tocar [tookar] to touch

toda a gente [tohda a Jaynt] everyone

todas [tohdash] all; all of them
todas as vezes [aJ vayzish] every time

todo [tohdoo] all; all of it
todo o dia/o dia todo [oo dee-a] all day

todos [tohdoosh] all; all of them
todos os dias [tohdooz-ooJ dee-ash] every day, daily

toilette m [twaleht] toilet, rest room

tolo [tohloo] silly

tomada f [toomada] socket; plug; power point

tomada para a máquina de barbear [makina di barb-yar] shaving point

tomar [toomar] to take
o que vai tomar? [oo ki vī] what'll you have?

tomar antes de se deitar to be taken before going to bed

tomar a seguir às refeições to be taken after meals

tomar banho [ban-yoo] to have a bath

tomar banho de sol to sunbathe

tomar conta de [kohnta] to look after, to take care of

tomar em jejum take on an empty stomach

tomar ... vezes ao dia to be taken ... times a day

tome lá [tohm] there you are

tónico m [tonikoo] toner

tonturas: sinto tonturas [seentoo tontoorash] I feel dizzy

topo: no topo de ... [tohpoo di] at the top of ...

toque (a campainha) ring (the bell)

torcer [toorsayr] to sprain; to twist

tornar-se [toornarsi] to become

torneira f [toornayra] tap, faucet

tornozelo m [toornoozayloo] ankle

torre f [tohrr] tower

tosse f [tos] cough

tossir [tooseer] to cough

tostão coin worth one tenth of an escudo

totalmente [tootalmaynt] altogether

touca de banho f [tohka di ban-yoo] bathing cap

tourada f [tohrada] bullfight

toureiro m [tohrayroo] bullfighter

touro m [tohroo] bull

tóxico [toksikoo] toxic, poisonous

trabalhar [trabal-yar] to work

trabalho m [trabal-yoo] work

tradição f [tradisowng] tradition

tradicional [tradis-yoonal] traditional

tradução f [tradoosowng] translation

tradutor m [tradootohr], tradutora f [tradootohra] translator

traduzir [tradoozeer] to translate

tragédia f [traɹehd-ya] disaster

trajecto m [traɹehtoo] route

trancar [trankar] to lock

tranquilo [trankweeloo] peaceful

transferência f [transfirayns-ya] transfer

trânsito m [tranzitoo] traffic

trânsito condicionado traffic congestion

trânsito fechado road blocked

trânsito nos dois sentidos two way traffic

trânsito proibido no thoroughfare, no entry

transmissão f [tranɹmisowng] transmission

traseiro (m) [trazayroo] bottom (of person); back

traumatismo m [trowmateeɹmoo] concussion

travão m [travowng] brake

travão de mão [di mowng] handbrake

travar to brake

travel-cheque m [shehk] travellers' cheque

travessa f [travehsa] tray

travessia f [travisee-a] crossing

trazer [trazayr] to bring

trazer de volta [di] to bring back

três [traysh] three

trespassa-se premises for sale

treze [trayz] thirteen

trezentas [trizayntash], trezentos [trizayntoosh] three hundred

tribunal m [triboonal] court

tricotar [trikootar] to knit

trinta [treenta] thirty

tripulação f [tripoolasowng] crew

triste [treesht] sad

trocar [trookar] to change (verb: money)

troco m [trohkoo] change (money)

trombose f [tromboz] thrombosis

trombose cerebral [siribral] stroke

trovão m [troovowng] thunder

trovoada f [troovwada] thunder

tu [too] you

tua [too-a], tuas [too-ash] your; yours

tubo de escape m [tooboo dishkap] exhaust pipe

tudo [toodoo] everything
é tudo [eh] that's all

tudo bem! [bayng] no problem!
tudo bem? how are you?

tudo incluído all-inclusive

túnel m [toonil] tunnel

turismo m [tooreeɹmoo] tourist information office

turista m/f [tooreeshta] tourist

U

UE [oo eh] EU
úlcera f [oolsira] ulcer
último m [ooltimoo] last, latest
ultrapassar [ooltrapasar] to
  overtake
um [oong], uma [ooma] a, an;
  one
umas [oomash] some
uma vez [ooma vaysh] once
unha f [oon-ya] fingernail
União Europeia f [ooni-owng ay-
  ooroopay-a] European Union
unicamente para adultos for
  adults only
universidade f [oonivirsidad]
  university
uns [oonsh] some
urgência f [oorJayns-ya]
  casualty, emergencies
urgente [oorJaynt] urgent
usar [oozar] to use
uso m [oozoo] use
uso externo for external use
  only
usual [oozwal] usual
utensílios de cozinha mpl
  [ootaynseel-yoosh di koozeen-
  ya] cooking utensils
útil [ootil] useful

V

vá à fava! go away!
vaca f cow
vacina f [vaseena] vaccine
vacinação f [vasinasowng]
  vaccination

vagão m [vagowng] carriage (on
  train)
vagão restaurante [rishtowrant]
  dining car
vai he/she/it goes; you go
vais [vīsh] you go
vale m [val] valley
vale postal internacional
  international money order
validação de bilhetes punch
  your ticket here
válido [validoo] valid
válido até ... valid until ...
valioso [val-yohzoo] valuable
valor m [valohr] value
válvula f [valvoola] valve
vamos [vamoosh] we go
  vamos! let's go!
vão [vowng] they go; you go
vá para o caralho! [oo karal-yoo]
  fuck off!
vá para o diabo! [d-yaboo] go to
  hell!
vá para o inferno! [infehrno] go
  to hell!
varanda f balcony
varicela f [varisehla]
  chickenpox
vários [var-yoosh] several
vá-se embora! [vasi aymbora] go
  away!
vassoura f [vasohra] broom
vazio [vazee-oo] empty
vedação f [vidasowng] fence
vedado ao trânsito no
  thoroughfare
vegetariana (f) [viJitar-yana],
  vegetariano (m) [viJitar-yanoo]
  vegetarian

veículo m [vi-**ee**kooloo] vehicle

veículos longos long vehicles

veículos pesados heavy vehicles

veio [**vay**-oo] he/she/it came, he/she/it has come; you came, you have come

vela f [**veh**la] sparkplug; sail; candle

velejar [viliʝar] to sail; sailing

velho [**veh**l-yoo] old

velocidade f [viloosid**a**d] speed

velocidade máxima ... km/h maximum speed ... km/h

velocímetro m [viloos**ee**mitroo] speedometer

vem [vayng] he/she/it comes; you come

vêm they come; you come

venda f [**vay**nda] sale

à venda [**vay**nda] for sale

vendedor de jornais [di ʝorn**ī**sh] newsagent, news vendor

vendem-se [**vay**ndaynsi] for sale

vender [vaynd**ayr**] to sell

vende-se [**vay**ndi-si] for sale

veneno m [vin**ay**noo] poison

venenoso [vinin**oh**zoo] poisonous

venho [**vay**n-yoo] I come

vens [vaynsh] you come

vento m [**vay**ntoo] wind

ventoinha f [vayntw**ee**n-ya] fan (electrical)

ver [vayr] to look; to have a look; to see

Verão m [vir**ow**ng] summer

verdade: de verdade? [di virdad] really?

verdadeiro [virdad**ay**roo] real; true

verde [vayrd] green

vergas fpl [**vay**rgash] wicker goods

verificar [virifik**a**r] to check

vermelho [virm**ay**l-yoo] red

verniz de unhas m [virneeʝ doon-yash] nail varnish

vespa f [**vay**shpa] wasp

Véspera de Natal f [**veh**shpira di] Christmas Eve

véspera do dia de Ano Novo [**veh**shpira doo d**ee**-a d**a**noo n**oh**voo] New Year's Eve

vestiário m [visht-y**a**r-yoo] cloakroom

vestido m [visht**ee**doo] dress

vestir [visht**ee**r] to dress

vestir-se [visht**ee**rsi] to get dressed

veterinário m [vitirin**a**r-yoo] vet

vez f [vaysh] time

a próxima vez [pr**o**sima] next time

a última vez [**oo**ltima] last time

esta vez [**eh**shta] this time

via (f) [**vee**-a] via; lane

via aérea: por via aérea by airmail

viagem f [v-y**a**ʝayng] journey

viagem de negócios [di nigos-yoosh] business trip

via intravenosa intravenously

viajar [v-yaʝar] to travel

via oral to be taken orally

via rápida dual carriageway

via rectal per rectum

via superfície surface mail

vida f [**vee**da] life

videogravador m [veed-yoogravad**ohr**] video recorder

vidraria f [vidra**ree**-a] glazier's

vidro m [**vee**droo] glass

viela f [v-**yeh**la] lane

viemos [v-y**ay**moosh] we came, we have come

vieram [v-y**eh**rowng] they came, they have come; you came, you have come

vieste [v-y**eh**sht] you came, you have come

vim [veeng] I came, I have come

vimos [**vee**moosh] we come; we saw

vindima f [vind**ee**ma] grape harvest

vindo [**vee**ndoo] come

vinha f [**vee**n-ya] vineyard

vinte [veent] twenty

vinte e um [v**ee**nti-oong] twenty-one

viola f [v-**yo**la] traditional Portuguese guitar

violação f [v-yoolas**ow**ng] rape

vir [veer] to come

virar [veer**ar**] to turn; to turn off

vir de carro [veer di k**ar**roo] to drive

vire à esquerda/direita [veer-ya shk**ay**rda/dir**ay**ta] turn left/right

vírgula f [**veer**goola] comma; decimal point

visita f [viz**ee**ta] visit

visita guiada [viz**ee**ta gee-**a**da] tour

visitar [vizit**ar**] to visit

visor m [viz**ohr**] viewfinder

vista f [**vee**shta] view

visto (m) [**vee**shtoo] visa; seen

visto que [**vee**shtoo ki] since

viu [vee-oo] you have seen

viúva f [v-**yoo**va] widow

viúvo m [v-**yoo**voo] widower

vivenda f [viv**ay**nda] villa

viver [viv**ayr**] to live

vivo [**vee**voo] bright; alive

vizinha f [viz**ee**n-ya], vizinho m [viz**ee**n-yoo] neighbour

voar [v-**war**] to fly

você [vos**ay**] you

você primeiro [prim**ay**roo] after you

vocês [vos**ay**sh] you

volante m [vool**ant**] steering wheel

com volante à direita [kong] right-hand drive

volta: por volta de ... [poor] about ..., approximately ...

voltar to go back, to get back, to come back, to return

voltar a telefonar [v**o**ltwa telefoon**ar**] to ring back

volto já [v**o**ltoo Ja] back in a minute

vomitar [voomit**ar**] to be sick, to vomit

voo m [v**oh**-oo] flight

voo de ligação [di ligas**ow**ng] connecting flight

voo directo [dir**eh**too] direct flight

voo **doméstico** [doome**eh**shtikoo]
  domestic flight
voo **fretado** [frit**a**doo] charter
  flight
voo **regular** [rigool**ar**] scheduled
  flight
vou [voh] I go
voz f [vosh] voice
vulgar [vool**ga**r] ordinary

X

xadrez m [shadr**ay**sh] chess
xarope m [shar**o**p] cough
  medicine; cordial

Z

zangado [zang**a**doo] angry; mad
zona azul f [zohnaz**oo**l] parking
  permit zone
zona de banhos swimming
  area under the surveillance
  of lifeguards
zona interdita no thoroughfare
zona para peões pedestrian
  precinct
zona perigrosa danger zone

Menu Reader:

Food

ESSENTIAL TERMS

bread o pão [**pow**ng]
butter a manteiga [mant**ay**ga]
cup a chávena [sh**a**vena]
dessert a sobremesa [sobrim**ay**za]
fish o peixe [p**ay**-ish]
fork o garfo [**ga**rfoo]
glass o copo [k**o**poo]
knife a f**a**ca
main course o prato principal [pr**a**too prinsip**a**l]
meat a carne [karn]
menu a ementa [em**ay**nta]
pepper a pimenta [pim**ay**nta]
plate o prato [pr**a**too]
salad a sal**a**da
salt o sal
set menu a ementa fixa [em**ay**nta f**ee**ksa], a ementa turística
  [toor**ee**shtika]
soup a sopa [s**oh**pa]
spoon a colher [kool-y**eh**r]
starter a entrada [ayntr**a**da]
table a mesa [m**ay**za]

another ..., please outro/outra ..., por favor [**oh**troo – poor fav**oh**r]
excuse me! (to call waiter/waitress) se faz favor! [si fash]
could I have the bill, please? pode-me dar a conta, por favor?
  [p**o**d-mi – poor fav**oh**r]

abóbora [aboboora] pumpkin

acepipes [asipeepish] hors
d'œuvres

açorda de alho [asohrda dal-yoo]
thick soup of bread and
garlic

açorda de mariscos [di
mareeshkoosh] thick soup of
bread and shellfish

açorda de miolos [m-yoloosh]
thick soup of bread and
brains

açúcar [asookar] sugar

agriões [agr-yoyngsh]
watercress

aipo [ipoo] celery

alcachofra [alkashohfra]
artichoke

alface [alfas] lettuce

alheira [al-yayra] garlic sausage

alho [al-yoo] garlic

alho francês [fransaysh] leek

à lista [leeshta] à la carte

almoço [almohsoo] lunch

almóndegas [almohndigash]
meatballs

alperces [alpehrsish] apricots

amêijoas [amayJwash] clams

amêijoas à Bulhão Pato
[amayJwaza bool-yowng patoo]
clams cooked with fresh
coriander, garlic and olive
oil

amêijoas na cataplana
[amayJwash] clams, ham,
sausages, onions, parsley,
chillies and olive oil
cooked slowly in a covered
pan

ameixa [amaysha] plum

ameixas de Elvas [dehlvash]
dried plums from Elvas

ameixas secas [saykas] prunes

amêndoas [amayndwash]
almonds

amendoins [amayndweensh]
peanuts

à moda de ... [di] ...-style

amoras [amorash] blackberries

ananás [ananash] pineapple

anchovas [anshohvash]
anchovies

anho à moda do Minho [an-yoo
a moda doo meen-yoo] roast
lamb served with rice

aniz [aneesh] aniseed

anona [anohna] custard apple

ao natural [ow natooral] plain

ao ponto [pohntoo] medium-
rare

arroz [arrohsh] rice

arroz árabe [arrohz arab] fried
rice with nuts and dried
fruit

arroz à valenciana [valayns-yana]
rice with chicken, pork and
seafood

arroz branco [arrohJ brankoo]
plain rice

arroz de cabidela [di kabidehla]
rice cooked in birds' blood

arroz de frango [frangoo] rice
with chicken

arroz de funcho [foonshoo] rice
with fennel

arroz de mariscos [mareesh-
koosh] a soupy dish of rice
with mixed seafood

arroz de pato [pa**too**] rice with duck

arroz de polvo [po**h**lvoo] rice with octopus

arroz doce [dohs] sweet rice dessert

asa [**a**za] wing

assado [as**a**doo] roasted

atum [at**oo**ng] tuna

atum assado [as**a**doo] baked tuna

avelãs [avil**a**ngsh] hazelnuts

aves [**a**vish] poultry

azeitão [azayt**ow**ng] full fat soft goat's cheese

azeite [az**ay**t] olive oil

azeitonas [azayt**oh**nash] olives

azeitonas com pimentos [kong pim**ay**ntoosh] olives stuffed with pimentos

azeitonas recheadas [rish-y**a**dash] stuffed olives

bacalhau [bakal-y**ow**] dried salted cod

bacalhau à Brás [brash] dried cod with egg and potatoes

bacalhau à Gomes de Sá [g**oh**msh di] dried cod fried with onions, boiled eggs, potatoes and black olives

bacalhau assado [as**a**doo] roast dried cod

bacalhau à Zé do Pipo [zeh doo p**ee**poo] dried cod with egg sauce

bacalhau com natas [kong n**a**tash] dried cod with cream

bacalhau dourado [dohr**a**doo] dried cod baked in the oven

bacalhau grelhado [gril-y**a**doo] grilled dried cod

bacalhau na brasa [br**a**za] barbecued dried cod

bacalhau na cataplana dried cod, onion, tomato, ham, coriander, prawns and cockles cooked slowly in a covered pan

banana flambée [flamb**ay**] flambéed banana

batata assada [batatas**a**da] baked potato

batata murro [m**oo**roo] small baked potato

batata palha [pal-ya] French fries

batatas [bat**a**tash] potatoes

batatas cozidas [kooz**ee**dash] boiled potatoes

batatas fritas [fr**ee**tash] chips, French fries

batatas salteadas [salt-y**a**dash] sautéed potatoes

baunilha [bown**ee**l-ya] vanilla

bavaroise [bavarw**a**z] dessert made from egg whites and cream

bem passado [bayng pas**a**doo] well-done

berbigão [birbeeg**ow**ng] shellfish similar to mussels

berinjela [bireen**J**ehla] aubergine, eggplant

besugos [biz**oo**goosh] sea bream

beterraba [biter**a**ba] beetroot

bifanas [beef**a**nash] pork slice

in a bread roll
bife [beef] steak
bife à cortador [koortadohr] thick tender steak
bife à portuguesa [poortoogayza] steak with mustard sauce and a fried egg
bife de alcatra [dalkatra] rump steak
bife de atum [datoong] tuna steak
bife de javali [di Javalee] wild boar steak
bife de pojadouro [pooJadohroo] type of beefsteak
bife de vaca [vaka] steak
bife de vaca com ovo a cavalo [kong ohvoo a kavaloo] steak with an egg on top
bife grelhado [gril-yadoo] grilled steak
bife tártaro [tartaroo] steak tartare
bifes de cebolada [beefsh di sihoolada] thin slices of steak with onions
bifinhos de porco [beefeen-yooJ di pohrkoo] small slices of pork
bifinhos na brasa [braza] small slices of barbecued beef
bolacha [boolasha] biscuit, cookie
bola de carne [di karn] meatball
bolo [bohloo] cake
bolo de anjo [danJoo] angel cake
bolo de chocolate [shookoolat] chocolate cake

bolo de nozes [nozish] walnut cake
bolo inglês [inglaysh] sponge cake with dried fruit
bolo Rei [ray] ring-shaped cake (eaten at Christmas)
bolos e bolachas [bohlooz ee boolashash] cakes and biscuits/cookies
bomba de creme [bohmba di kraym] cream puff
borrego [boorraygoo] lamb
brioche [br-yosh] slightly sweet round bun
broa [broh-a] maize/corn bread or rye bread
broas [broh-ash] small maize/corn cakes (eaten at Christmas)

cabeça de pescada cozida [kabaysa di pishkada koozeeda] boiled head of hake
cabreiro [kabrayroo] goat's cheese
cabrito [kabreetoo] kid
cabrito assado [asadoo] roast kid
caça [kasa] game
cachola frita [kashola freeta] fried pig's heart and liver
cachorro [kashohrroo] hot dog
caldeirada [kaldayrada] fish stew
caldo [kaldoo] broth
caldo de aves [davish] poultry soup
caldo de carne [di karn] meat soup
caldo verde [vayrd] cabbage soup

camarões [kamaroyngsh] prawns

canela [kanehla] cinammon

canja de galinha [kanJa di galeen-ya] chicken soup

caracóis [karakoysh] snails

caranguejo [karangayJoo] crab

carapau [karapow] mackerel

carapaus de escabeche [karapowJ dishkabehsh] marinated mackerel

carapaus fritos [karapowsh freetoosh] fried mackerel

caril [kareel] curry

carne [karn] meat

carne à jardineira [Jardinayra] meat and vegetable stew

carne de cabrito [di kabreetoo] kid

carne de porco [di pohrkoo] pork

carne de porco com amêijoas [kong amayJwash] pork with clams

carne de vaca [vaka] beef

carne de vaca assada roast beef

carne de vaca guisada [geezada] stewed meat

carne estufada [shtoofada] stewed meat

carneiro [karnayroo] mutton

carneiro assado [asadoo] roast mutton

carne picada [pikada] minced meat

carnes [karnish] meats

carnes frias [free-ash] selection of cold meats

caseiro [kazayroo] home-made

castanhas [kashtan-yash] chestnuts

cebola [sibohla] onion

cenoura [sinohra] carrot

cerejas [sirayJash] cherries

chanfana de porco [shanfana di pohrkoo] pork casserole

chantilly [shantilee] whipped cream

charlottes [sharlotsh] biscuits/cookies with fruit and cream

cherne [shehrn] sea bream

chocos [shohkoosh] cuttlefish

chouriço [shooreesoo] spiced sausage

choux [shoo] cake made with choux pastry

churros [shoorrosh] long thin fritters

civet de lebre [seevay di lehbr] jugged hare

cocktail de camarão [koktehl di kamarowng] prawn cocktail

codorniz [koodoorneesh] quail

codonizes fritas [koodoorneezish freetash] fried quail

coelho [kwayl-yoo] rabbit

coelho à caçadora [kasadohra] rabbit casserole with rice

coelho de escabeche [dishkabehsh] marinated rabbit

coelho de fricassé [frikasay] rabbit fricassee

coelho frito [freetoo] fried rabbit

coêntros [kwayntroosh] coriander

cogumelos [kogoom**eh**loosh] mushrooms

cogumelos com alho [kong **al**-yoo] mushrooms with garlic

comida congelada [koom**ee**da konJil**a**da] frozen food

comidas [koom**ee**dash] meals

compota stewed fruit

compota de laranja [di lar**a**nJa] marmalade

conquilhas [konk**ee**l-yash] baby clams

consomme [konsoom**ay**] consommé, clear meat soup

coração [kooras**ow**ng] heart

corações de alcachofra [kooras**oy**ngsh dalkash**oh**fra] artichoke hearts

corvina [koorv**ee**na] large saltwater fish

costela [koosht**eh**la] rib

costeleta [kooshtil**ay**ta] chop

costeletas de carneiro [kooshtil**ay**taJ di karn**ay**roo] lamb chops

costeletas de porco [di p**oh**rkoo] pork chops

costeletas fritas [fr**ee**tash] fried chops

costeletas grelhadas [gril-y**a**dash] grilled chops

courgettes com creme no forno [koorJ**eh**tsh kong kraym noo f**oh**rnoo] baked courgettes/zucchini served with cream

courgettes fritas [fr**ee**tash] fried courgettes/zucchini

couve [kohv] cabbage

couve branca com vinagre [kong vin**a**gr] white cabbage with vinegar

couve-flor [kohv flohr] cauliflower

couve-flor com molho branco no forno [kong m**oh**l-yoo br**a**nkoo noo f**oh**rnoo] cauliflower in white sauce

couve-flor com natas [n**a**tash] cauliflower with cream

couve roxa [r**oh**sha] red cabbage

couvert cover charge

couves de bruxelas [kohvsh di broosh**eh**lash] Brussels sprouts

couves de bruxelas com natas [kong n**a**tash] Brussels sprouts with cream

couves de bruxelas salteadas [salt-y**a**dash] sautéed Brussels sprouts

couves guisadas com salsichas [geez**a**dash kong sals**ee**shash] stewed cabbage with sausage

cozido [kooz**ee**doo] boiled; stewed; poached; cooked (either in a sauce or with olive oil); stew

cozido à portuguesa [poortoog**ay**za] stew made from chicken, sausage, rice, potatoes and vegetables

creme de cogumelos [kraym di kogoom**eh**loosh] cream of mushroom soup

creme de mariscos
[mareeshkoosh] cream of
shellfish soup

crepe de camarão [krehp di
kamarowng] prawn crepe

crepe de carne [karn] meat
crepe

crepe de cogumelos
[kogoomehloosh] mushroom
crepe

crepe de espinafres
[dishpinafrish] spinach
crepe

crepe de legumes [ligoomish]
vegetable crepe

crepe de pescada [pishkada]
hake crepe

crepes [krehpish] crepes,
pancakes

cru/crua [kroo/kroo-a] raw

damasco [damashkoo] apricot

dobrada [doobrada] tripe with
chickpeas

doce [dohs] jam; any sweet
dish or dessert

doce de amêndoas
[damayndwash] almond
dessert

doce de ovos [dovoosh] type of
egg custard

doces regionais regional
desserts

dose [doz] portion

dose para crianças [kr-yansash]
children's portion

dourada [dohrada] dory
(saltwater fish); browned,
golden brown

dourado [dohradoo] browned,
golden brown

éclair de café [ayklehr dih kafeh]
coffee éclair

éclair de chantilly [shantilee]
whipped cream éclair

éclair de chocolate [shookoolat]
chocolate éclair

eirozes [ayrozish] eels

ementa [emaynta] menu

ementa fixa [feeksa] set menu

ementa turística [tooreeshtika]
set menu

empada pie

empadão de carne
[aympadowng di karn] large
meat pie

empadão de peixe [paysh] large
fish pie

encharcada [aynsharkada]
dessert made from almonds
and eggs

enguias [ayngee-ash] eels

enguias fritas [freetash] fried
eels

ensopado de ... [aynsoopadoo di]
... stew

ensopado de borrego
[boorraygoo] lamb stew

ensopado de enguias [dayngee-
ash] eel stew

entradas [ayntradash] starters,
appetizers

entrecosto [ayntrikohshtoo]
entrecôte

entrecosto com amêijoas [kong
amayjwash] entrecôte with
clams

entrecosto frito [freetoo] fried
entrecôte

ervas [ehrvash] herbs

ervilhas [irveel-yash] peas

ervilhas de manteiga [di
mantayga] peas in butter

ervilhas reboçadas [riboosadash]
peas in butter with bacon

escalope ao Madeira [shkalop ow
madayra] escalope in
Madeira wine

escalope de carneiro [di
karnayroo] mutton escalope

escalope de porco [pohrkoo]
pork escalope

escalope panado [panadoo]
breaded escalope

espadarte [shpadart] scabbard
fish

espaguete à bolonhesa
[shpageht a booloon-yayza]
spaghetti bolognese

espargos [shpargoosh]
asparagus

esparregado [shparrigadoo] stew
made from chopped green
vegetables

especiaria [shpis-yaree-a] spice

espetada de leitão [shpitada di
laytowng] sucking pig kebab

espetada de rins [reensh] kidney
kebab

espetada de vitela [vitehla] veal
kebab

espetada mista [meeshta]
mixed kebab

espinafre [shpinafr] spinach

espinafres gratinados
[shpinafrish gratinadoosh]

spinach with cheese sauce
browned under the grill

espinafres salteados [salt-
yadoosh] spinach sautéed in
butter

estragão [shtragowng] tarragon

estufado [shtoofadoo] stewed

faisão [fizowng] pheasant

farinha [fareen-ya] flour

farófias [farof-yash] cream puff
with filling made from egg
whites, sugar and cinammon

farturas [fartoorash] long thin
fritters

fatia [fatee-a] slice

fatias recheadas [fatee-ash rish-
yadash] slices of bread with
fried minced meat

favas [favash] broad beans

febras de porco [faybraJ di
pohrkoo] thin slices of pork

feijão [fayJowng] beans

feijoada [fayJwada] bean and
meat stew

feijões [fayJoyngsh] beans

feijões verdes [vayrdish] French
beans

fiambre [f-yambr] ham

fiambre caramelizado
[karamileezadoo] glazed ham

fígado [feegadoo] liver

figos [feegoosh] figs

figos moscatel [mooshkatehl]
moscatel figs

figos secos [saykoosh] dried
figs

filete [feeleht] fillet

filete de bife com foie gras [di

beef kong fwa gra] beef fillet
with foie gras

filhozes [feel-yozish] sugary
buns

folhado de carne [fool-yadoo di
karn] meat in pastry

folhado de salsicha [salseesha]
sausage roll

fondue de carne [fondoo di karn]
meat fondue

fondue de chocolate [shookoolat]
chocolate fondue

fondue de queijo [kayjoo]
cheese fondue

framboesa [frambwayza]
raspberry

frango [frangoo] chicken

frango assado [frangwasadoo]
roast chicken

frango na púcara [pookara]
chicken casserole with Port
and almonds

frango no churrasco [noo
shoorrashkoo] barbecued
chicken

frango no espeto [nooshpaytoo]
spit-roasted chicken

frito [freetoo] fried

frito de ... [di] fritter (usually filled
with fruit)

fruta [froota] fruit

fruta da época [ehpooka]
seasonal fruit

fumado [foomadoo] smoked

funcho [foonshoo] fennel

galantine de carne [galanteen di
karn] cold meat roll

galantine de coelho [di kwayl-

yoo] cold rabbit roll

galantine de galinha [galeen-ya]
cold chicken roll

galantine de vegetais [vijitīsh]
cold vegetable roll

galinha [galeen-ya] chicken

galinha de África [dafreeka]
guinea fowl

galinha de fricassé [di frikasay]
chicken fricassée

gambas [gambash] prawns

gambas grelhadas [gril-yadash]
grilled prawns

ganso [gansoo] goose

garoupa [garohpa] fish similar
to bream

gaspacho [gaspashoo] chilled
vegetable soup

gelado [Jiladoo] ice cream

gelado de baunilha [di bowneel-
ya] vanilla ice cream

gelado de frutas [frootash] fruit
ice cream

geleia [Jilay-a] preserve

gengibre [JaynJeebr] ginger

gordura [goordoora] fat

grão [growng] chickpeas

grelhado [gril-yadoo] grilled

groselhas [groozehl-yash]
redcurrants

guisado [geezadoo] stewed

hamburguer com batatas fritas
[amboorgir kong batatash
freetash] hamburger and
chips/French fries

hamburguer com ovo [ohvoo]
hamburger with an egg

hamburguer no pão [noo powng]

hamburger in a roll

hortaliças [ortaleesash] green
vegetables

hortelã [ortilang] mint

iogurte [yoogoort] yoghurt

iscas fritas com batatas
[eeshkash freetash kong
batatash] dish of fried liver
and boiled potatoes

jantar [Jantar] evening meal,
dinner; supper

jardineira [Jardinayra] mixed
vegetables

lagosta [lagohshta] lobster

lagosta à Americana [amirikana]
lobster with tomato and
onions

lagosta thermidor [tirmeedohr]
lobster thermidor

lagostim [lagooshteeng]
saltwater crayfish

lampreia [lampray-a] lamprey

lampreia à moda do Minho [doo
meen-yoo] marinated
lamprey and rice, both
cooked in the juices and
blood of the lamprey

lampreia de ovos [dovoosh]
dessert made from eggs and
sugar in the shape of a
lamprey

lanche [lansh] afternoon tea

laranja [laranJa] orange

lasanha [lasan-ya] lasagne

legumes [ligoomish] vegetables

leitão assado [laytowng asadoo]
roast sucking pig

leitão da Bairrada [da bĩrrada]
sucking pig from Bairrada

leite [layt] milk

leite creme [kraym] light
custard flavoured with
cinammon

limão [limowng] lemon

língua [leengwa] tongue

língua de porco [di pohrkoo]
pig's tongue

língua de vaca [vaka] ox tongue

linguado [lingwadoo] sole

linguado à meunière [moon-
yehr] sole dipped in flour
and fried in butter

linguado frito [freetoo] fried
sole

linguado grelhado [gril-yadoo]
grilled sole

linguado no forno [noo fohrnoo]
baked sole

lista de preços [leeshta di
praysoosh] price list

lombo [lohmboo] loin

lombo de porco [di pohrkoo]
loin of pork

lombo de vaca [vaka] sirloin

louro [lohroo] bay leaf

lulas [loolash] squid

lulas com natas [kong natash]
stewed squid with cream

lulas fritas [freetash] fried squid

lulas guisadas [geezadash]
stewed squid

lulas recheadas [rish-yadash]
stuffed squid

maçã [masang] apple

maçã assada baked apple

macedónia de frutas [masidon-ya
di frootash] fruit cocktail

maionese [mī-oonehz]
mayonnaise

maionese de alho [dal-yoo]
garlic mayonnaise

mal passado [pasadoo] rare

manjericão [manJirikowng] basil

manteiga [mantayga] butter

manteiga de anchova
[danshohva] anchovy butter

manteiga queimada [kaymada]
butter sauce for fish

margarina [margareena]
margarine

marinada marinade

mariscos [mareeshkoosh]
shellfish

marmelada [marmilada] quince
jam

marmelos [marmehloosh]
quinces

marmelos assados [marmehlooz
asadoosh] roast quinces

massa pasta

massa de fartos [di fartoosh]
choux pastry

meia desfeita [may-a dishfayta]
boiled dried cod, potatoes,
chickpeas and olive oil

meia dose [doz] half portion

mel [mehl] honey

melancia [milansee-a]
watermelon

melão [milowng] melon

melão com presunto [kong
prizoontoo] melon with ham

meloa com vinho do Porto/
Madeira [miloh-a kong veen-

yoo doo pohrtoo/madayra]
small melon with Port or
Madeira wine poured over it

melocotão [milookootowng]
peach

merenda [miraynda] tea; snack

merengue [mirang] meringue

mexilhões [mishil-yoyngsh]
mussels

migas à Alentejana [meegaz a
alayntiJana] thick bread soup

mil folhas [meel fohl-yash]
millefeuille, custard slice,
(US) napoleon

miolos [m-yoloosh] brains

miolos com ovos [kong ovoosh]
brains with eggs

míscaros [meeshkaroosh]
mushrooms

moleja [moolayJa] soup made
from pig's blood

molho [mohl-yoo] sauce

molho à Espanhola [shpan-yola]
spicy onion and garlic sauce

molho ao Madeira [ow madayra]
Madeira wine sauce

molho bearnaise [bayrnehz]
béarnaise sauce

molho béchamel [bayshamehl]
béchamel sauce, white
sauce

molho branco [brankoo] white
sauce

molho holandês [olandaysh]
hollandaise sauce

molho mornay cheese sauce

molho mousseline [moosileen]
hollandaise sauce with
cream

molho tártaro [tartaroo] tartare sauce

molho veloutée [vilootay] white sauce made from cream and egg yolks

morangos [moorangoosh] strawberries

morangos com chantilly [kong shantilee] strawberries and whipped cream

morcela [moorsehla] black pudding, blood sausage

mostarda [mooshtarda] mustard

mousse de chocolate [moos di shookoolat] chocolate mousse

mousse de fiambre [f-yambr] ham mousse

mousse de leite condensado [layt kondaynsadoo] mousse made from condensed milk

na brasa [braza] charcoal-grilled

napolitanas [napoolitanash] long flat biscuits/cookies

natas [natash] cream

natas batidas [bateedash] whipped cream

nectarina [nektareena] nectarine

nêsperas [nayshpirash] loquats (yellow fruit similar to a plum)

no churrasco [noo shoorrashkoo] barbecued

no espeto [nooshpaytoo] spit-roasted

no forno [fohrno] baked

nozes [nozish] walnuts

noz moscada [noJ mooshkada] nutmeg

óleo [ol-yoo] oil

omeleta [omilayta] omelette

omeleta com ervas [kong ehrvash] vegetable omelette

omeleta de cogumelos [di kogoomehloosh] mushroom omelette

omeleta de fiambre [f-yambr] ham omelette

omeleta de queijo [kayJoo] cheese omelette

omelete [omilayt] omelette

orelha de porco de vinaigrette [orayl-ya di pohrkoo di vinagreht] pig's ear in vinaigrette dressing

ostras [ohshtrash] oysters

ovo [ohvoo] egg

ovo com maionese [kong mī-oonehz] egg mayonnaise

ovo cozido [koozeedoo] hard-boiled egg

ovo em geleia [ayng Jilay-a] egg in aspic

ovo escalfado [shkalfadoo] poached egg

ovo estrelado [shtriladoo] fried egg

ovo quente [kaynt] soft-boiled egg

ovos mexidos [misheedoosh] scrambled eggs

ovos mexidos com tomate [kong toomat] scrambled eggs with tomato

ovos verdes [vayrdish] eggs stuffed with a mixture of

egg yolks, mayonnaise and
parsley

palha de ovos [pal-ya dovoosh]
egg pastries

panqueca [pankehka] pancake

pão [powng] bread

pão branco [brankoo] white
bread

pão de centeio [di sayntay-oo]
rye bread

pão de ló de Alfazeirão [law
dalfazay-rowng] sponge cake

pão de ló de Ovar [dohvar]
sponge cake

pão de milho [meel-yoo] bread
made from maize flour, corn
bread

pão integral [intigral]
wholemeal bread

pão torrado [toorradoo] toasted
bread

pargo [pargoo] sea bream

pargo assado [pargwasadoo]
roast bream

pargo cozido [koozeedoo] bream
cooked in a sauce or with
olive oil

parrilhada [pareel-yada] grilled
fish

passas [pasash] raisins

pastéis [pashteh-ish] pastries

pastéis de bacalhau [di bakal-
yow] dried cod fishcakes

pastéis de carne [karn] puff-
pastry patties filled with
meat

pastéis de Chaves [shavish] thin
dainty puff-pastry patties

filled with meat

pastéis de nata custard tarts

pastéis de Tentúgal [tayntoogal]
filo-pastry patties with an
egg yolk and sugar filling,
sprinkled with sugar

pastel [pashtehl] cake; pie

pastelinhos de bacalhau
[pashtileen-yoosh di bakal-yow]
fishcakes made from dried
cod

pataniscas [pataneeshkash]
dried cod fritters

pataniscas de miolos [di m
yoloosh] brain fritters

paté de aves [patay davish] pâté
made from chicken, duck or
goose liver

paté de coelho [di kwayl-yoo]
rabbit pâté

paté de fígado [feegadoo] liver
pâté

paté de galinha [galeen-ya]
chicken pâté

paté de lebre [lehbr] hare pâté

pato [patoo] duck

pato assado [asadoo] roast
duck

pato com laranja [kong laranJa]
duck à l'orange

peixe [paysh] fish

peixe espada [shpada]
swordfish

peixe espada de escabeche
[dishkabehsh] marinated
swordfish

peixinhos da horta [paysheen-
yoosh da orta] French bean
fritters

pepino [pipeenoo] cucumber

pequeno almoço [pikaynoo almohsoo] breakfast

pequeno almoço continental [kontinayntal] continental breakfast

pêra [payra] pear

pêra abacate [abakat] avocado

pêra bela helena [behlaylayna] pear in chocolate sauce

percebes [pirsehbish] shellfish similar to barnacles

perdiz [pirdeesh] partridge

perdizes de escabeche [pirdeeziJ dishkabehsh] marinated partridge

perdizes fritas [pirdeezish freetash] fried partridge

perdizes na púcara [pirdeeziJ na pookara] partridge casserole

perna [pehrna] leg

perna de carneiro assada [di karnayroo] roast leg of lamb

perna de carneiro entremeada [ayntrim-yada] stuffed leg of lamb

perninhas de rã [pirneen-yash di rang] frogs' legs

peru [piroo] turkey

peru assado [asadoo] roast turkey

peru de fricassé [di frikasay] turkey fricassée

peru recheado [rish-yadoo] stuffed turkey

pescada [pishkada] hake

pescada cozida [koozeeda] hake cooked in a sauce or with olive oil

pescadinhas de rabo na boca [pishkadeen-yash di raboo na bohka] fried whiting served with their tails in their mouths

pêssego [paysigoo] peach

pêssego careca [karehka] nectarine

petiscos [piteeshkoosh] savouries

picante [pikant] hot, spicy

pimenta [pimaynta] pepper

pimenta preta [prayta] black pepper

pimentos [pimayntoosh] peppers, capsicums

piperate [peepirat] pepper stew

piri-piri [peeree-peeree] seasoning made from chillies and olive oil

polvo [pohlvoo] octopus

porção [poorsowng] portion

porco [pohrkoo] pork

porco à alentejana [alayntijana] pork cooked with clams

prato [pratoo] dish; course

prato do dia [doo dee-a] today's special

prato especial da casa [shpis-yal da kaza] speciality of the house

prato principal [prinsipal] main course

prego [prehgoo] thin slice of steak in a bread roll

prego no fiambre [noo f-yambr] steak sandwich with sliced ham

prego no pão [noo powng] steak sandwich

prego no prato [pratoo] steak, usually served with a fried egg

presunto [prizoontoo] ham

pudim de ovos [poodeeng dovoosh] egg pudding

pudim flan [flang] crème caramel

pudim molotov [molotof] crème caramel with egg whites

puré de batata [pooray di] mashed potatoes

puré de castanhas [kashtan-yash] chestnut purée

p.v. (preço variado) [praysoo varyadoo] price varies

queijadas de Sintra [kayJadaJ di seentra] small tarts with a filling made from milk, eggs, sugar and vanilla

queijo [kayJoo] cheese

queijo curado [kooradoo] dried matured hard white cheese

queijo da Ilha [eel-ya] strong cheese from the Azores flavoured with pepper

queijo da Serra [sehrra] goat's cheese from Serra da Estrela

queijo de cabra [di] goat's cheese

queijo de ovelha [dovayl-ya] sheep's cheese

queijo de Palmela [palmehla] small white mild dried cheese

queijo de Serpa [sehrpa] small strong dried goat's cheese

queijo fresco [frayshkoo] medium-firm mild cheese

queijos [kayJoosh] cheeses

rabanadas [rabanadash] bread dipped in beaten egg and fried, then sprinkled with sugar and cinammon

raia [ri*-a] skate

refeição [rifaysowng] meal

refeição ligeira [liJayra] snack, light meal

remoulade [rimoolad] dressing with mustard and herbs

requeijão [rikayJowng] curd cheese

rillete [ree-eht] potted pork meat

rins [reensh] kidneys

rins ao Madeira [reenz ow madayra] kidneys cooked in Madeira wine

rissóis [riso-ysh] deep-fried meat patties

rissol [risol] deep-fried meat patty

rissol de camarão [di kamarowng] prawn rissole

robalo [roobaloo] rock bass

rojões [rooJoyngsh] cubes of pork

rolo de carne [rohloo di karn] meat loaf

rosmaninho [rooJmaneen-yoo] rosemary

sabayon [saba-yohng] dessert made from egg yolks and

white wine
sal salt
salada salad
salada de agriões [dagr-yoyngsh]
watercress salad
salada de alface [dalfas] green
salad
salada de atum [datoong] tuna
salad
salada de chicória [di shikor-ya]
chicory salad
salada de frutas [frootash] fruit
salad
salada de lagosta [lagohshta]
lobster salad
salada de ovas [dovash] fish roe
salad
salada de tomate [di toomat]
tomato salad
salada mista [meeshta] mixed
salad
salada russa [roosà] Russian
salad, salad of diced
vegetables in mayonnaise
salgado [salgadoo] savoury,
salty
salmão [salmowng] salmon
salmão fumado [foomadoo]
smoked salmon
salmonete [salmoonayt] red
mullet
salmonetes grelhados
[salmoonaytsh gril-yadoosh]
grilled red mullet
salsa parsley
salsicha [salseesha] sausage
salsichas de cocktail [salseeshaJ
di koktehl] cocktail sausages
salsichas de peru [piroo] turkey

sausages
salsichas de porco [pohrkoo]
pork sausages
salteado [salt-yadoo] sautéed
sandes [sandish] sandwich
sandes de fiambre [di f-yambr]
ham sandwich
sandes de lombo [lohmboo]
steak sandwich
sandes de paio [pī-oo] sausage
sandwich
sandes de presunto [prizoontoo]
ham sandwich
sandes de queijo [kayJoo]
cheese sandwich
sandes mista [meeshta] mixed
sandwich, usually ham and
cheese
santola spider crab
santola gratinada [gratinada]
spider crab with cheese
sauce browned under the
grill
sapateira [sapatayra] spider
crab
sarda mackerel
sardinha [sardeen-ya] sardine
sardinhas assadas [sardeen-yaz
asadash] roast sardines
selecção de queijos [silehsowng
di kayJoosh] selection of
cheeses
sobremesas [sobrimayzash]
desserts
solha [sohl-ya] flounder
solha assada no forno [noo
fohrnoo] baked flounder
solha frita [freeta] fried
flounder

solha recheada [rish-yada]
stuffed flounder

sonho [sohn-yoo] type of
doughnut

sopa [sohpa] soup

sopa à alentejana [alayntiJana]
bread soup with a poached
egg on top

sopa de agriões [dagr-yoyngsh]
watercress soup

sopa de alho francês [dal-yoo
fransaysh] leek soup

sopa de camarão [kamarowng]
prawn soup

sopa de caranguejo
[karangayJoo] crab soup

sopa de cebola gratinada
[sibohla] French onion soup
with melted cheese on top

sopa de cogumelos
[kogoomehloosh] mushroom
soup

sopa de espargos [dishpargoosh]
asparagus soup

sopa de feijão verde [fayJowng
vayrd] green bean soup

sopa de grão [growng]
chickpea soup

sopa de lagosta [lagohshta]
lobster soup

sopa de legumes [ligoomish]
vegetable soup

sopa de mariscos
[mareeshkoosh] shellfish soup

sopa de ostras [dohshtrash]
oyster soup

sopa de panela [di panehla]
egg-based dessert

sopa de pão e coentros [powng

ee kwayntroosh] bread and
coriander soup

sopa de pedra [pehdra] thick
vegetable soup

sopa de peixe [paysh] fish soup

sopa de rabo de boi [raboo di
boy] oxtail soup

sopa de tartaruga [tartarooga]
turtle soup

sopa do dia [doo dee-a] soup of
the day

sopa dourada [dohrada] egg-
based dessert

sopa e cozido [sohpī koozeedoo]
meat stew

sopa juliana [sohpa Jool-yana]
vegetable soup

sopas [sohpash] soups

soufflé de camarão [sooflay di
kamarowng] prawn soufflé

soufflé de chocolate [shookoolat]
chocolate soufflé

soufflé de cogumelos
[kogoomehloosh] mushroom
soufflé

soufflé de espinafres
[dishpinafrish] spinach soufflé

soufflé de peixe [paysh] fish
soufflé

soufflé de queijo [kayJoo]
cheese soufflé

soufflé gelado [Jiladoo] ice-
cream soufflé

tarte de amêndoas [tart
damayndwash] almond tart

tarte de cogumelos [di
kogoomehloosh] mushroom
quiche

tarte de limão [lim**ow**ng] lemon tart

tarte de maçã [mas**a**ng] apple tart

taxa de serviço [t**a**sha di sirv**ee**soo] service charge

tempero da salada [taymp**a**yroo da sal**a**da] salad dressing

tomar [toom**a**r] fresh soft goat's cheese

tomate [toom**a**t] tomato

tomates recheados [toom**a**tish rish-y**a**doosh] stuffed tomatoes

tomilho [toom**ee**l-yoo] thyme

toranja [toor**a**nʒa] grapefruit

torrada [toorr**a**da] toast

torresmos [toorr**a**yʒmoosh] small fried rashers of bacon

torta tart

torta de maçã [mas**a**ng] apple pie

torta de nozes [di n**o**zish] walnut tart

tortilha [toort**ee**l-ya] Spanish-style omelette with potato

tosta [t**o**shta] toasted sandwich

tosta mista [m**ee**shta] toasted ham and cheese sandwich

toucinho do céu [toos**ee**n-yoo doo s**eh**-oo] kind of dessert made from eggs, sugar and almonds

tripas [tr**ee**pash] tripe

tripas à moda do Porto [tr**ee**paza m**o**da doo p**oh**rtoo] tripe with beans and vegetables

trufas de chocolate [tr**oo**faʒ di shookool**a**t] chocolate truffles

truta [tr**oo**ta] trout

truta assada no forno [noo f**oh**rnoo] baked trout

truta cozida [kooz**ee**da] trout cooked in a sauce or with olive oil

truta frita [fr**ee**ta] fried trout

uvas [**oo**vash] grapes

uvas brancas [**oo**vaʒ br**a**nkash] green grapes

uvas moscatel [mooshkat**eh**l] muscatel grapes

uvas pretas [**oo**vaʒ pr**ay**tash] black grapes

veado assado [v-y**a**doo as**a**doo] roast venison

vieiras recheadas [v-y**a**yrash rish-y**a**dash] scallops filled with seafood

vinagre [vin**a**gr] vinegar

vinagre de estragão [dishtrag**ow**ng] tarragon vinegar

vitela [vit**eh**la] veal

Menu Reader:

Drink

ESSENTIAL TERMS

beer a cerveja [sirvay Ja]
bottle a garrafa
brandy o brandy
coffee o café [kafeh]
cup a chávena [shavena]
  a cup of ... uma chávena de ... [ooma shavena di]
fruit juice o sumo de fruta [soomoo di froota]
gin o gin [Jeeng]
  gin and tonic um gin-tónico [oong Jeeng tonikoo]
glass o copo [kopoo]
  a glass of ... um copo de ... [oong kopoo di]
Madeira o (vinho da) Madeira [(veen-yoo da) madayra]
milk o leite [layt]
mineral water a água mineral [agwa]
port o vinho do Porto [veen-yoo doo pohrtoo]
red wine o vinho tinto [teentoo]
rosé rosé [roozay]
soda (water) a soda
soft drink a bebida não alcoólica [bibeeda nowng alko-oleeka]
sugar o açúcar [asookar]
tea o chá [sha]
tonic (water) a água tónica [agwa]
vodka o vodka
water a água [agwa]
whisky o whisky [weeshkee]
white wine o vinho branco [veen-yoo brankoo]
wine o vinho [veen-yoo]
wine list a lista dos vinhos [leeshta dooJ veen-yoosh]

another ..., please outro/outra ..., por favor [ohtroo – poor favohr]

açúcar [asookar] sugar

água mineral [agwa mineral]
mineral water

aguardente [agwardaynt] clear
spirit/brandy (literally:
'firewater'), distilled from
wine or grape skins

aguardente de figo [feegoo] fig
brandy

aguardente de pêra [di payra]
brandy with a pear or pears
in the bottle

aguardentes bagaceiras
[agwardayntish bagasayrash]
clear spirit/brandy distilled
from grape skins

aguardentes velhas [vehl-yash]
matured brandies

aguardentes velhas ou
preparadas [vehl-yaz oh
preparadash] brandies
matured in oak

álçool [alko-ol] alcohol

amêndoa amarga [amayndwa
amarga] bitter almond
liqueur

aperitivo [apiriteevoo] aperitif

bagaço [bagasoo] clear spirit/
brandy (literally:
'firewater'), distilled from
grape skins

Bairrada [bīrrada] region
producing fruity red wines

batido de leite [bateedoo di layt]
milkshake

bebida [bibeeda] drink

bica [beeka] small black
espresso-type coffee

branco [brankoo] white

bruto [brootoo] extra-dry

Bual [boo-al] medium-sweet
Madeira wine

Bucelas® [boosehlash] crisp
dry white wine from the
Estremadura area

cacau [kakow] cocoa

café [kafeh] small black
espresso-type coffee

café com leite [kong layt] white
coffee, coffee with milk

café com pingo [peengoo]
espresso with brandy

café duplo [dooploo] two
espressos in the same cup

café glacé [glasay] iced coffee

café instantâneo [inshtantan-yoo]
instant coffee

caneca [kanehka] half-litre

capilé [kapileh] drink made
from water, sugar and syrup

carapinhada de café [karapeen-
yada di kafeh] coffee drink
with crushed ice

carapinhada de chocolate
[shookoolat] chocolate drink
with crushed ice

carapinhada de groselha
[groozehl-ya] redcurrant
drink with crushed ice

carapinhada de morango
[moorangoo] strawberry drink
with crushed ice

carioca [kar-yoka] small weak
black coffee

cerveja [sirvayJa] beer

cerveja branca [branka] lager

cerveja de pressão [di pris**ow**ng] draught beer

cerveja preta [pr**ay**ta] bitter, dark beer

chá [sha] tea

chá com leite [kong layt] tea with milk

chá com limão [lim**ow**ng] lemon tea

chá com mel [mehl] tea with honey

chá de limão [di lim**ow**ng] infusion of hot water with a lemon rind

chá de lucialima [loos-yal**ee**ma] herb tea

chá de mentol mint tea

chá de tília [t**ee**l-ya] linden blossom tea

champanhe [shamp**an**-yi] champagne

chocolate glacé [shookool**at** glas**ay**] iced chocoláte

chocolate quente [k**ay**nt] hot chocolate

cidra [s**ee**dra] cider

cimbalino [simbal**ee**noo] small espresso

clarete [klar**ayt**] claret

Colares [kool**a**rish] table wine from the Colares region

com gás [kong gash] carbonated

com gelo [J**ay**loo] with ice, on the rocks

conhaque [koon-y**ak**] cognac, brandy

Constantino® [konshtant**ee**noo] Portuguese brandy

cubo de gelo [k**oo**boo di J**ay**loo] ice cube

Dão® [downg] red table wine from the Dão region

descafeinado [dishkafayn**a**doo] decaffeinated

doce [dohs] sweet (usually very sweet)

espumante [shpoom**ant**] sparkling

espumantes naturais [shpoom**ant**ish natoor**ee**sh] sparkling wine made by the champagne method

expresso [shpr**eh**soo] espresso

figo [f**ee**goo] fig brandy

galão [gal**ow**ng] large weak milky coffee, served in a tall glass

garoto [gar**oh**too] small coffee with milk

garrafa bottle

garrafeira [garraf**ay**ra] aged red wine set aside by the producer in years of exceptional quality

gasoso [gaz**oh**zoo] fizzy

gelo [J**ay**loo] ice

ginja [J**ee**nJa], ginjinha [JeenJ**ee**n-ya] brandy with sugar and cherries added

imperial [eempir-y**al**] regular glass size for drinking beer (about ¼ litre)

italiana [ital-y**a**na] half a very strong espresso

jarro [Jarroo] jug

Lagoa® [lagoh-a] table wine from the Algarve

leite [layt] milk

licor [likohr] liqueur; sweet flavoured spirit

Licor Beirão® [bayrowng] cognac with herbs

licor de medronho [di midrohn-yoo] berry liqueur

licor de ovo [dohvoo] advocaat

licor de pêras [di payrash] pear liqueur

licor de whisky [weeshkee] whisky liqueur

limonada [limoonada] fresh lemon juice with water and sugar

lista de preços [leeshta di praysoosh] price list

lista dos vinhos [dooJ veenyoosh] wine list

Macieira® [masi-ayra] Portuguese brandy

Madeira [madayra] wine-producing region; sweet and dry fortified wines

maduro [madooroo] mature

Malvasia [malvasee-a] Malmsey wine, a sweet heavy Madeira wine

Mateus Rosé® [matay-oosh roozay] sweet rosé wine

mazagrin [mazagrang] iced coffee with lemon

meia de leite [may-a di layt] large white coffee

meia garrafa half-bottle

meio seco [may-oo saykoo] medium-dry (usually fairly sweet)

morena [moorayna] mixture of lager and bitter

moscatel [mooshkatehl] muscatel wine

não alcoólico [nowng alko-oleekoo] non-alcoholic

pingo [peengoo] small coffee with milk

ponche [pohnsh] punch

pré-pagamento pay in advance

região demarcada wine-producing region subject to official controls

Reguengos [rigayngoosh] table wine from Alentejo

reserva [rizehrva] aged wine set aside by the producer in years of exceptional quality

Sagres® [sagrish] popular brand of lager

Sagres Europa® [sagriz ay-ooropa] brand of lager

Sagres Preta® [prayta] dark beer resembling British brown ale

saquinhos de chá [sakeen-yooJ di sha] teabags

seco [saykoo] dry

selo de garantia seal of guarantee

sem gás [sayng gash] still

sem gelo [Jayloo] without ice

Sercial [sirsee-al] the driest variety of Madeira wine

sirva gelado served chilled

sirva-se à temperatura ambiente serve at room temperature

sirva-se fresco serve cool

sumo de laranja [soomoo di laranJa] orange juice

sumo de lima [leema] lime juice

sumo de limão [limowng] lemon juice

sumo de maçã [masang] apple juice

sumo de tomate [toomat] tomato juice

Sumol® [soomol] fizzy fruit juice

Super Bock® brand of lager

tarifas de consumo price list

Tavel® [tavehl] rosé wine

tinto [teentoo] red

Tri Naranjus® [treenaranJoosh] brand name for a range of fruit drinks

Valpaças® [valpasash] table wine from Trás-os-Montes

velha [vehl-ya] old, mature

velhíssima [vehl-yeesima] very old (spirits)

Verdelho [virdayl-yoo] a medium-dry Madeira wine

vermute [vermoot] vermouth

vinho [veen-yoo] wine

vinho branco [brankoo] white wine

vinho da casa [kaza] house wine

vinho da Madeira [madayra] Madeira wine

vinho de aperitivo [dapiriteevoo] aperitif

vinho de mesa [di mayza] table wine

vinho de Xerêz [shiraysh] sherry

vinho do Porto [doo pohrtoo] port

vinho espumante [shpoomant] sparkling wine

vinho moscatel [mooshkatehl] muscatel wine

vinho rosé [roozay] rosé wine

vinho tinto [teentoo] red wine

vinho verde [vayrd] young, slightly sparkling white, red, or rosé wine produced in the Minho

whisky de malte [weeshkee di malt] malt whisky

xarope [sharop] cordial, concentrated juice

xarope de groselha [di groozehl-ya] redcurrant cordial

xarope de morango [moorangoo] strawberry cordial